Food Grain Godown and Warehouse Management

CONTENT VIBES
PUBLISHERS • PRINTERS • AGGREGATORS

About the Author

Dr. Arun Kumar is a proficient researcher and author in the field of Agronomy. In his 23 years of academic experience, Dr. Arun Kumar has served in various capacities as Assistant Professor, Junior Agronomist (1998-2005) and Associate Professor (2005 – 2011). Dr. Arun Kumar has also served as the Director Planning at Bihar Agricultural University, Sabour during which he developed the Road Map of the university and headed the PME Cell and Institutional Quality Assurance Cell (IQAC) of the university. He has also served as the Dean (Agriculture), DRI cum Dean (PGS), Comptroller and Director of Research at Bihar Agricultural University, Sabour. During 2021-22, Dr. Arun Kumar has also served as the Vice Chancellor of Bihar Agricultural University. During his tenure as Vice Chancellor, the Bihar Agricultural University and all its constituent colleges were accredited by ICAR and three new colleges were established under the BAU, Sabour. Dr. Kumar has also guided a number of Master's and PhD students and has a number of publications to his credit including 37 Research Papers, 32 Edited/Authored Books, 19 Popular Articles and many more. Dr. Arun Kumar has handled various projects including nine consultancy projects of BAMETI, Patna. He has also chaired/co-chaired technical sessions of various national and international seminars, symposia and conferences. He has also led the state-level committee for the preparation of the agricultural road map of the Bihar State. Considering his outstanding contributions to the field of agriculture, Dr Arun Kumar has been awarded an award for excellent contribution in agriculture sector by his Excellency, the Governor of Bihar. He has done justice to all positions which were previously held by him with such admirable grace and calmness that he is an inspiration to all and Swami Keshwanand Rajasthan Agricultural University, Bikaner is strongly committed to steady development under his able leadership.

Food Grain Godown and Warehouse Management

Arun Kumar
Vice-Chancellor
Swami Keshwanand Rajasthan Agricultural University
Bikaner, Rajasthan, India

CONTENT VIBES
PUBLISHERS • PRINTERS • AGGREGATORS

PUBLISHERS • PRINTERS • AGGREGATORS

1168, Sector 13, Urban Estate
Karnal-132 001, Haryana
Tel: 91-84470 75807, 18440 41168
Email: contentvibesppa@gmail.com
www.contentvibes.in

Print ISBN: 978-93-67557-56-3

ebooks ISBN: 9789367559-03-1

Preface

The management of food grain godowns and warehouses plays a crucial role in ensuring the safe storage and preservation of grains, which are essential to food security and economic stability. In a country like India, where agriculture forms the backbone of the economy, effective grain storage is pivotal to maintaining supply chain integrity, reducing post-harvest losses, and ensuring that food grains remain fit for consumption. This book aims to provide a comprehensive guide to the various aspects of food grain godown and warehouse management, focusing on the best practices, modern techniques, and regulatory frameworks that govern the storage of food grains.

From the initial receipt of grains to their final distribution, warehouse management covers a broad spectrum of activities. Proper storage conditions, such as controlling temperature, humidity, and pest management, are essential to prevent spoilage, contamination, and loss of nutritional value. In addition, understanding the importance of inventory management, grading, and quality control is critical for maintaining the value and quality of the stored grains.

The book also addresses the technological advancements in warehouse operations, including automated systems and digital tools that streamline inventory tracking, improve safety, and enhance operational efficiency. The content of this book is designed to cater to both novice and experienced professionals in the field, offering practical insights, case studies, and actionable recommendations. It emphasizes the need for strategic planning and timely intervention to manage food grains effectively, ensuring that they remain in optimal condition for extended periods. The objective is not only to maintain the quality and safety of the grains but also to contribute to sustainable practices that benefit farmers, distributors, and consumers alike.

The book Food Grain Godown and Warehouse Management is an indispensable component of the agricultural sector, and this book serves as a valuable resource for anyone involved in the storage and handling of food grains.

Author

Contents

1

Grain Storage

Food is a vital requirement for all living beings, as it provides the essential nutrients necessary for growth, development, and recovery. Humans depend on both plants and animals for nourishment, which we acquire through agricultural practices and animal farming. With the increasing global demand for food, crop yields have risen, which has led to a greater reliance on warehouses for grain storage. However, merely increasing food production is insufficient to combat hunger and malnutrition, as food security also heavily depends on ensuring that food is accessible to everyone. Crops, however, are exposed to various threats, such as pests, weeds, and diseases, which can drastically reduce yields if not managed adequately.

A significant issue is storage losses, which are driven by both biological elements (such as fungi, insects, and rodents) and environmental factors (such as unsuitable storage conditions or extreme temperatures). These losses result in various negative consequences, including:

- Reduced food quality
- Lower seed germination rates
- Loss of weight in crops
- Discolored produce

These problems can impede the marketing of harvested crops, leading to unsold goods and considerable losses for farmers and distributors.

To reduce these losses, it's crucial to adopt proper measures like efficient treatments and continuous monitoring of storage conditions. Grains should be stored in environments that prevent deterioration. This can be achieved by ensuring thorough cleaning before storage, drying grains thoroughly (both under the sun and in the shade), and taking steps to control pests, including fumigation.

CONVERSANT WITH TECHNICAL TERMS OF GRAIN STORAGE

STORAGE OF GRAIN

Storage serves as both a temporary and recurring phase during the movement of agricultural products from the producer to the processor, and then from the processor to the consumer. Food grains are stored until they transition from producers to processors, and then their processed products are stored before reaching consumers. The practice of storing grain and its products has been a long-standing one. For centuries, humans have prioritized food storage as a means of securing supplies to alleviate hunger in the future. Over time, experience has taught that dry grains can be stored for extended periods and safeguarded from various deteriorative agents, such as pests, molds, and fungi.

The storage and quality control of grains take place in three key locations: on the farm, at collection points serving multiple farms, and at terminal points where the grain is processed or moved in larger quantities. Costs arise from loading and unloading at each storage stage, transportation between storage locations, and the storage itself. Further expenses are incurred during grain conditioning, including cleaning, drying, and quality control.

Improper handling of grains after harvest leads to losses of about 7%, significantly impacting the rural economy, especially since 70% of total food grain production is stored at the farm level. Farmers often store grains for personal use, as seed or food, with the quantities varying between 22% and 71% of total production.

Figure : 1.1 Grain storage

Traditional storage methods, such as using jute bags or basic structures, are insufficient for preserving grain quality or preventing wastage. These methods do not provide long-term storage options. Therefore, adopting scientific storage methods and controlling insect infestations in grains are essential. Safe storage practices are crucial to minimize losses due to pests, diseases, and rodents, ensuring that agricultural products remain in good condition for an extended period.

CLASSIFICATION OF STORAGE TYPES

Storage types can be classified based on several factors, including:

- Duration of storage
- Scale or size of storage
- Principle of storage

Duration of Storage

Storage systems are categorized based on the length of time the goods are stored as follows:

- Short term storage
- Medium term storage
- Long term storage

Short Term Storage

- Products in short-term storage typically have a shelf life of no more than six months.
- Perishable goods such as eggs, meat, fish, and dairy products are naturally stored for short periods.
- Without controlled storage systems, highly perishable crops experience significant quality degradation during this storage phase.

Medium Term Storage

- Medium-term storage allows products to maintain their quality without significant deterioration for up to 12 months.
- After 18 months, the quality of these stored products may not be assured.

Long Term Storage

- Long-term storage ensures the preservation of product quality for more than 5 years.
- Germ banks and certain storage systems are capable of maintaining the viability and essential properties of stored materials for several decades.

Scale or Size of Storage

Storage systems can be categorized based on the scale or capacity of storage into the following types:

- Small-scale Storage
- Medium-scale storage
- Large-scale storage

Small Scale Storage

- Small-scale storage systems have a capacity of up to 1 ton, and typically do not exceed that limit.
- These systems are primarily used at the domestic and small-scale farming levels.
- They are commonly found among peasant farmers with limited landholdings.

Medium Scale Storage

- Medium-scale storage systems can hold up to a hundred tons of products.
- Most of these systems have a capacity between 2 and 50 tons, with few exceeding 50 tons.
- Some are utilized in breweries for the temporary storage of spent grains.

Large Scale Storage

- Large-scale storage can hold materials in the range of hundreds to thousands of tons.
- It is used for either temporary or permanent storage of large quantities of various products.
- Although, it has a high initial cost, it ultimately lowers the overall unit production cost.

Principle of Storage

Storage systems can be classified in terms of principle of operation. These are as follows:

- Physical storage
- Chemical storage
- Biological storage

Physical Storage

- Physical storage relies on physical principles to maintain the quality of stored products.
- The storage environment, including moisture, temperature, and humidity, is typically controlled to slow down deterioration or prevent it, such as in cold storage or controlled environments.

Chemical Storage

- Chemical storage uses chemicals to prevent or slow down deterioration.
- Chemicals like wax, methyl bromide, or phosphine tablets are used to prevent insect infestation in stored produce.
- Some chemicals are toxic and require careful monitoring during use.

Biological Storage

- Biological storage uses biological agents, particularly microorganisms, to prevent or slow deterioration and extend the shelf life of stored products.
- This is an excellent application of biotechnology in agriculture.

Need of Storage

- Meeting the needs of a growing human population.
- Price fluctuations, market demand changes, shortages, and famines.
- Agricultural products must be stored to meet seasonal and yearly demand.
- Off-season requirements, such as potatoes, onions, fruits, etc.
- Storage is needed during bumper crops of specific commodities.
- Provision for large-scale processing and piling.
- Protection of original varieties from extinction (Germ Bank).
- Preservation of nutritional value.

WHO IS RESPONSIBLE FOR STORAGE?

Farmers

For small farmers, the primary purpose of storing grains is to secure household food supplies. Farm storage also serves as a form of savings, to meet future cash needs through sales, barter, or gift-giving.

Grains are stored for use as seeds or for household activities like beer brewing or cooking. In cases of significant price fluctuations between seasons, small farmers may store grains for speculative profit, essentially "playing the market."

TRADER STORAGE IN INDIA

In India's grain storage ecosystem, trader storage is essential because it connects farmers, wholesalers, and consumers. Grain is stored by traders, such as commission agents and private merchants, to control changes in supply and demand and maintain market stability. Meeting seasonal demands and preserving price consistency depend on this storage technique.

Godowns, warehouses, and traditional storage buildings like covered sheds or pucca godowns are commonly used by traders in India. Additionally, some traders rent space in Food Corporation of India (FCI) godowns or use storage facilities licensed by the government. Grain quality is being improved and losses from moisture and pests are being decreased with the introduction of contemporary storage solutions like silos and hermetic storage.

Notwithstanding its significance, trader storage has a number of difficulties, such as poor infrastructure, post-harvest losses, and unstable prices. Financial limitations and high-interest loans for storage investments are other issues that traders frequently face.

The goal of government programs like negotiable warehouse receipts and expanded private sector involvement is to improve credit accessibility and storage efficiency. Improving trader storage through improved infrastructure, digital monitoring, and financing access will be crucial to guaranteeing food security and minimizing grain waste as India transitions to a more structured agricultural supply chain.

GOVERNMENT STORAGE

As mentioned earlier, governments may engage in storage to stabilize prices and ensure farmers' revenues. A key factor in this is their concern for national food security, which is crucial for political stability. Governments use storage to balance national supply and demand over time, aiming to reduce the risk of politically damaging shortages. In doing so, they seek to complement, and in some cases replace, market mechanisms, based on the belief that the market alone can only achieve balance with unacceptable levels of supply and price fluctuations.

Plane of Rupture

The plane of rupture refers to the surface along which a wedge of material, bounded by one wall face, the free surface, and the rupture plane, would begin to slide if the wall moved.

Angle of Repose

When a granular material is dropped through a circular opening onto a flat horizontal surface, it forms an inverted cone shape. The angle between the horizontal surface and the slope of the pile is known as the natural angle of repose. This angle indicates the material's flow ability. Cohesive materials generally have a higher angle of repose compared to non-cohesive ones. The natural angle of repose is approximately equal to the product's maximum internal friction angle.

Classification of Silos

- **Shallow Bins:** A bin where the plane of rupture reaches the grain surface before hitting the opposite side. A squat silo is an example of a shallow bin.
- **Deep Bins:** A bin where the plane of rupture reaches the opposite side before emerging from the grain. Vertical silos, which can be circular, hexagonal, or rectangular, are examples of deep bins.

IMPORTANCE AND NEED FOR STORAGE

In India, annual storage losses are estimated at 14 million tons, amounting to Rs. 7,000 crores, with insect damage alone accounting for approximately Rs. 1,300 crores. The significant financial losses caused by insects and pests are not only due to consumption but also contamination. Around 600 insect species have been linked to stored grain products, with nearly 100 species of pests causing economic damage.

According to the World Bank Report (1999), post-harvest losses in India total 12 to 16 million metric tons of food grains annually, a quantity that could feed one-third of India's poor. Among these post-harvest losses, pests alone contribute to 2.0 to 4.2 percent, followed by rats at 2.5 percent, birds at 0.85 percent, and moisture at

0.68 percent. Preventing storage losses is crucial for enhancing economic growth, which calls for the need to store grains for several reasons:

- To feed the growing population,
- To address sudden price fluctuations and high market demand,
- During natural disasters such as shortages, droughts, or famines,
- To meet seasonal and yearly agricultural demands,
- To handle off-season requirements,
- When there is a need to store for specific commodity production,
- For large-scale processing needs,
- To preserve original varieties (Germ Bank),
- To maintain nutritional quality.

STRUCTURES FOR STOROGE

Grain is typically stored either in bags or in bulk, with a combined system of bag-and-bulk storage also used in some regions. In villages, bulk storage is more common than bag storage, which is considered a practical method for government godowns and trade.

To meet the growing demand for food grains from the increasing population, it is essential to minimize food loss during and after harvest. Food grains are stored for different periods to ensure a consistent and balanced public distribution throughout the year.

Post-harvest losses in India are estimated to be around 10 percent, with storage losses accounting for approximately 6.58 percent. However, with advancements in agricultural technology, farmers can now store grains for longer periods with minimal loss.

FOR BEST STORAGE PERFORMANCE

- The produce must be carefully cleaned and graded.
- It should be dried to a safe storage moisture level of 10-12% for food grains and 7-9% for oilseeds (on a wet basis) to ensure safe storage for 6-12 months.
- Storage structures must be properly repaired, cleaned, and disinfected.
- The structures should be strong enough to support the grain's weight and prevent contact with external humid air.
- Storage structures should be located in the coolest part of the house or farm.

An ideal storage facility should satisfy the following requirements:

- It should offer maximum protection against ground moisture, rain, insect pests, moulds, rodents, birds, fire, etc.
- It should provide adequate facilities for inspection, disinfection, loading, unloading, cleaning, and reconditioning.

- It should safeguard the grain from excessive moisture and temperatures that promote insect and mould growth.
- It should be cost-effective and appropriate for the specific situation.

TYPES OF GRAIN STORAGE STRUCTURES

The following four types of storage structures are used for grain storage:

1. Traditional storage structures
2. Improved storage structures
3. Modern storage structures
4. Farm silos

STORAGE STRUCTURES USED BY FARMERS

Farmers use the following storage methods:

- Gunny bags of various capacities (35, 50, 75, and 100 kg), with or without plastic lining.
- Mud bins with capacities ranging from 100 to 1000 kg.
- Baked earthen containers with capacities between 5 and 100 kg.
- Heaps stored on flat floors in the corners of houses (100-1500 quintals).
- Bamboo structures.
- Wooden bins.
- Underground storage structures.

CONVENTIONAL GRAIN STORAGE STRUCTURES

Table 1.1 : Conventional structure of storage

Structures	Make	Items	Capacity	Remarks
1. Bamboo Structures	Split bamboo woven in the form of a cylinder with wide base and narrow mouth.	Paddy, wheat and sorghum	500 kg	Life 4-5 years. Weight loss due to insect attack is 5 % in paddy and 15 % in sorghum.
2. Mud and earthen structures	Clay, straw and cow dung- 3:3:1. Earthen structures are made, sun dried and then burnt in fire.	Paddy, wheat, sorghum, oil seeds and pulses	5 to 10 q	Life 8-10 years. During rainy season develop cracks and moisture absorption followed by insect and mould infestation.

Structures	Make	Items	Capacity	Remarks
3. Wooden structures	Local wood is painted black. At the top, 30 cm x 20 cm inlet and at the bottom 30 cm x15 cm outlet is provided	Paddy	10 q	15-20 years. Neither airtight nor moisture proof.
4. Brick structures	Rectangular, structures built as part of the house, with brick in cement or lime mortar having a wall thickness of 40 –50 cm. At the top 50 x 50 cm inlet and at bottom 15 x15 cm outlet is provided.	Paddy, sorghum and wheat	25-30 q	25-30 years. High initial cost, not insect and moisture proof.
5. Underground structures	Circular pits typically range from 100 to 400 cm in depth, with diameters of 50 to 100 cm at the neck and 250 to 300 cm at the bottom. An opening at the top allows for filling and emptying. Before filling, the sides and bottom are packed with straw and husk. After the pit is filled, it is covered with straw and stones, followed by a final layer of mud.	Cereals	100–200 q	While it protects against insects, the loss of seed viability and handling difficulties have rendered it outdated.
6. Miscellaneous plant materials a. Paddy straw b. Stem of vitex and pigeon pea stalks c. Bottle gourd shells	a. Paddy straw is wound in the form of rope to varying diameter b. Stems wound like a bin and both sides are plastered with mud and cow dung c. empty shells are used.	Paddy, other cereals and pulses Paddy and Other cereals Pulses, gourd seeds	30–100.q 1-2. q 2-5 kg	Not insect and rat proof Temporary Only small quantity of seed lots.

Structures	Make	Items	Capacity	Remarks
7. Metal corrugated G.I. sheets	Sheets, each about 3 m high, are held vertically along one edge, with the edges of the other sheets overlapping and bolted together. This forms a circle with a diameter of 2-4 m using several such sheets. The top is covered with plain M.S. or G.I. sheets.	Various types of grains	Vary	Temporary
8. Hessian cloth bags				
9. Gunny bags				

TRADITIONAL STORAGE STRUCTURES

In these types of storage structures, grain is typically stored in bulk, with capacities ranging from 1 to 50 tonnes. Grain is stored in both bulk and bag forms in various rural and urban regions of India, using one of the following storage structures:

- Morai-type storage structures
- Bukhari-type storage structures
- Kothar-type storage structures
- Mud Kothi-type storage structures
- Muda-type storage structures
- Kanaj-type storage structures
- Kuthla-type storage structures
- Metal/Steel bin-type storage structures
- Bag-type storage structures

IMPROVED GRAIN STORAGE STRUCTURES

Improved storage structures are designed for the storage of food grains, incorporating enhancements over traditional storage methods. These structures offer higher storage capacities and are suitable for long-term storage of food grains compared to traditional ones. The capacities of these storage structures generally range from 1.5 to 150 tonnes. Grain is stored in bulk, in bags, or in a combination of both in various rural and urban regions of India.

Pusa Bin

The Pusa bin, similar to other traditional storage structures made of mud, is enhanced with a plastic film on all the inner surfaces to make it moisture-proof.

Brick and Cement Bin

These storage structures are very sturdy, with minimal impact from seasonal changes.

Bunker Storage

These types of storage structures are used for long-term storage and to accommodate larger volumes of grain.

'CAP' Storage Structures

The term 'CAP' refers to the cover and plinth, with the plinth at the bottom and the cover at the top. This type of open storage is considered transit storage and is used for the short-term storage of food grains in bags.

MODERN GRAIN STORAGE STRUCTURES

In India, larger volumes of food grains are stored in bulk in 'silos' and conventional godowns (sheds) designed for bagged storage. The walls of godowns are made of brick or stone masonry, with sloped roofs covered in asbestos or Corrugated Galvanized Iron (CGI) sheets supported by steel trusses. Silos are made from steel or reinforced concrete, with clusters of adjoining silos found in modern large-capacity processing plants. Modern permanent storage systems should be chosen for the safe storage of grains and other products, prioritizing quality over cost. The following types of modern storage structures are used:

Silo Type of Storage Structures

Silos/bins are categorized into two types based on the relative dimensions of the container: (1) Deep bins and (2) Shallow bins.

Deep Bins

Vertical silos belong to this category of storage structures. There are two types of vertical silos as follows:

- flat-bottom vertical silo, and
- hopper-bottom vertical silo.

Shallow Bins

Squat silos fall under the category of shallow bins. They have a wall height-to-diameter ratio of 0.5 or less. Squat silos can compete with sheds for providing low-cost, high-quality storage.

Shed

Typically, horizontal sheds are used for low-cost, large-volume storage. The Central Warehousing Corporation has also built very large sheds for storing grains and other products.

Farm Silos

A farm silo is a structure used to store and protect animal fodder, preserving it in optimal conditions for farm animals. The fodder is cut and packed into an airtight silo to allow partial fermentation, resulting in silage. There are two types of farm silos as follows:

1. Tower silos, and
2. Horizontal silos.

Tower Silos

- Cylindrical in shape and made of masonry, wood, or metal.
- The construction cost is significantly higher compared to horizontal types.
- Loading animal fodder is challenging.
- A mechanical loader or large-capacity blower is necessary.
- This type of storage structure is not recommended for use under Indian conditions.

Horizontal Silos

In horizontal silos, pit type, bunker type, and trench or stake type storage structures are used for storing animal fodder:

- Both surface and underground storage structures are commonly used on dairy farms as temporary and permanent storage solutions for silage.
- The spoilage of silage and dry matter losses in these silos range from 20 to 30 percent.

Pit Silos

- A permanent pit silo is a circular deep well, lined around the sides and sealed at the bottom to prevent water from entering.
- It is constructed in areas where the soil is deep and the water table is very low.
- Made from bricks, stones, or concrete, with cement or lime used as a binding material.
- A wall thickness of 22.5 cm is sufficient for depths up to 15 meters.
- The entire surface in contact with the silage should be plastered to ensure it is smooth, airtight, and waterproof.
- A simple roof is placed over the silo to protect the silage from sun and rain.
- The most economical roofs are corrugated metal sheet domes or half-pitch roofs with ample overhang on all sides, providing more space for filling.

- Stairs may be constructed along the silo's wall for easy removal of silage.
- The typical diameter of a silo is limited to 6 meters, with its depth being 2 to 3 times the diameter.
- When the silo is opened to remove silage, no one should enter until the gases have dissipated.

Trench Silos

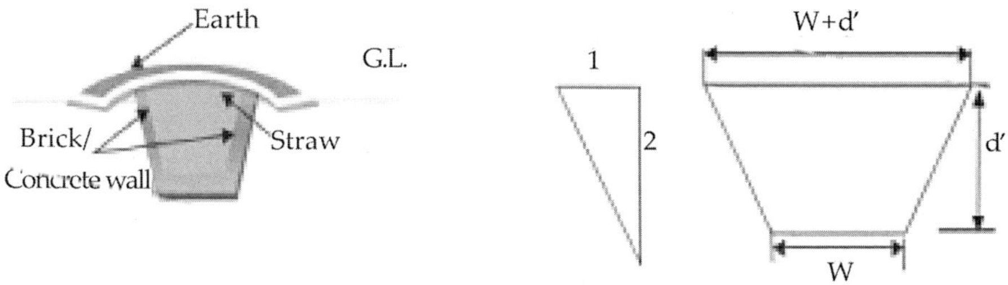

Figure: 1.2 Cross-section of trench silo showing wall lining

- An unlined trench silo is easy to build and does not require investment in materials such as bricks, cement, and sand.
- Unlined silos tend to have higher spoilage, and their side walls are prone to collapsing due to heavy rain. The bottom can also become muddy, making lined trench silos a more popular choice.
- The walls of trench silos can be lined with bricks, concrete, or cement plaster reinforced with wire mesh.
- If possible, the silo should be roofed.
- Drains should be constructed around the trench to redirect surface water.
- To facilitate drainage, it is preferable to locate the trench silo on sloping ground.
- The silo's capacity depends on the herd size and the number of days the silage is fed throughout the year.
- It is generally more economical to construct a single, larger trench silo.
- The sidewalls of the trench silo typically have a 33 percent slope.

STACKING

- Food grains must be stored and preserved according to scientific methods in godowns until they are distributed to consumers.
- Bags containing food grains should not simply be dumped inside the godown, as this does not allow for proper storage.
- Proper stacking ensures easy access to all parts of the godown for inspection and aids in effective disinfestation. Typically, three stacking methods are used: 1. Simple, 2. Cross, and 3. Block method.

Steps necessary for good storage practice in respect of all food grains are as follows:

- Stored product pests can be managed either through behavioral methods (such as traps like probe traps, light traps, pitfall traps, etc.) or by using various preventive and curative measures, both chemical and non-chemical.
- Once a facility is in place, several steps must be taken to ensure the safe storage of grains. These steps include:

Before Storage of Grain

- Inspecting for rainwater leaks and ensuring adequate drainage facilities.
- Maintaining cleanliness of the facility and surrounding environment.
- Assessing the facility's storage capacity.
- Conducting pesticidal treatments.
- Ensuring security and firefighting arrangements.
- Performing repairs on available equipment.

After Receipt of Grain

- Inspecting for variety and quality soundness.
- Carefully checking for infestation, if any, and determining the type and extent of the infestation
- Examining whether the grain has excess moisture, has been heated during previous storage, or has a musty or rancid odor
- Segregating and salvaging any wet or damaged grain using available facilities
- Verifying the weight of the received grain

During Storage

- Maintaining cleanliness.
- Ensuring proper aeration where needed.
- Checking for leaks after rainfall.
- Conducting inspections for insects, rats, and mites every two weeks.
- Monitoring for any signs of deterioration.
- Carrying out pesticidal treatments based on observations.
- Ensuring proper disposal when necessary.
- Arranging for segregation, salvage, and processing in cases of damage caused by water leakage or other factors.

GRAIN PROTECTANTS

Chemicals that can be directly applied to grains include formulations with residual toxic or repellent properties, or both. These chemicals are applied to the grain to prevent damage from stored product pests. For example, clay minerals (such as red earth and Kaolin) were used before 1950, but now their use is limited to seeds and grains intended for animal feed. These grain protectants can be applied as spray or dust on uninfested grain.

Advantages Over Fumigants

- Used as a preventive treatment
- Effective when grains are stored in loose containers where fumigation is not feasible
- Less hazardous than fumigants
- Does not negatively impact germination
- One application at harvest time is enough for the entire year

Example

- **Pyrethrum Synergized with PBO:** The safest of the available grain protectants, approved for use. It is available in powder form with 1% PBO + 0.8% pyrethrum, or as 0.83 lb synergist + 0.6% pyrethrum. It can also be applied as a spray at 3-5 gallons per 1,000 bushels, using 0.6 lb synergist + 0.066 lb pyrethrum.
- **Premium Grade Malathion:** The foul odor is removed, and it can be directly applied to grain as a 1% D or as a spray (57 EC). Other chemicals used include: Carbaryl, Dichlorvos, Fenitrothion, Malathion, PBO, and Pyrethroids (such as Deltamethrin and Fenvalerate).

THE ROLE OF TECHNOLOGY IN GRAIN STORAGE

Technology plays a crucial role in grain storage, enhancing both quality and shelf life. Modern equipment, such as automated temperature and moisture sensors, ensures that grain is stored under optimal conditions. These systems can send alerts if any conditions deviate from the ideal range, enabling quick corrective actions.

Additionally, automated systems monitor grain quality by tracking factors like moisture levels, grain size, and the presence of contaminants. Regarding pest control, innovations such as non-toxic pheromone traps and ultrasonic repellents provide effective and eco-friendly solutions. These advancements not only maintain the quality of stored grain but also make storage management more efficient.

CHOOSING THE RIGHT STORAGE FACILITY

When it comes to storing grain, selecting the appropriate storage facility is essential. Different types of facilities cater to various needs, capacities, and storage durations. Below is an overview of the most common grain storage facilities and their benefits:

- **Silos**: A staple in the agricultural world, silos are a traditional choice for grain storage. Their cylindrical shape maximizes space efficiency, and their design allows for easy unloading of grain from the bottom. Silos are particularly ideal for long-term storage since they can be equipped with temperature and moisture control systems. Regular inspections for structural integrity and ensuring the silo is clean and dry before filling are essential best practices.

- **Grain Bins:** Often mistaken for silos, grain bins are typically shorter and wider. They are best suited for on-farm storage, allowing farmers to keep their produce close to the harvesting site for easy access. Grain bins are perfect for short to medium-term storage.
- **Warehouses:** These large structures are designed for bulk grain storage. Warehouses are commonly used when large quantities of grain need to be stored in one location, especially in trading hubs or near transportation routes. They offer flexibility for handling various types of grain and protect the contents from external elements.
- **Ground Storage:** A traditional method, ground storage involves storing grain in piles on the ground, usually covered with tarpaulin. While cost-effective and suitable for short-term needs, it exposes grains to pests, moisture, and other external factors. It's important to select a dry location with a moisture-proof base to minimize risks.

Each storage facility comes with its own set of advantages and challenges. The key is to align the specific grain storage requirements with the most suitable facility.

MEASUREMENT OF GRAIN TEMPERATURE

Food loss during storage is significantly influenced by the temperatures in warehouses and granaries. Elevated temperatures can lead to sweating in the grains, promoting the growth of fungus and mold, which can render the grains toxic.

Maintaining proper temperature through aeration is a viable solution. This natural airflow helps lower the temperature in the storage area, preventing sweating. To safeguard stored food grains, it is essential to regulate the temperature. Ensuring that grains are cooled before storage is crucial for maintaining both their quality and quantity.

CONTROL OF GRAIN TEMPERATURE

Grain temperatures should be controlled by moving air through the grain mass. Whether storing wet grain for a short period or dry grain for longer durations, airflow is essential to keep the grain cool and prevent mold growth. Properly aerated grain can typically be stored much longer than grain without airflow.

Variations in grain temperatures create convection currents, which can lead to moisture accumulation at the top of the container. Problems caused by this moisture buildup or migration often become noticeable in the spring when outside temperatures begin to rise.

The Role of Moisture in Grain Interact

Several factors affect the safety of stored grains, with moisture being a key element. Conditions of warmth and moisture promote the growth of various biotic factors such as molds, fungi, pests, and insects. Water damages grains by causing discoloration and lowering their quality. To ensure grains are stored at the proper moisture level, regular inspections are necessary. Along with electronic moisture meters, there are now a variety of electronic devices available for accurate moisture measurement.

HOW TEMPERATURE AND MOISTURE WORK?

Grain is an excellent insulator and retains temperature well when undisturbed. However, if warm grain is placed into storage and left undisturbed, convection currents can form, leading to hot spots and moisture condensation. The greater the temperature difference between the grain and the outside environment, the stronger the convection currents. The stronger the convection, the more pronounced the heating and condensation effects on the grain. This is especially noticeable when stored grain is not leveled, causing the grain bulk to form a peak.

The cycle of convection currents in bin-stored grain occurs when the ambient air outside the bin is cold and the grain inside is warm.

In the bin:

- The surface of the grain bulk forms a peak.
- The grain at the surface and just below it has high moisture content.
- Warm grain is located in the center of the grain bulk.

The convection currents operate as follows:

- Cold air flows down from the surface of the grain, along the interior bin wall, surrounding the warm grain.
- At the bottom of the grain bulk, cold air is drawn toward the center by an upward flow of warmer air, creating a convection current.
- As the cold air moves toward the center of the grain, it warms up and rises to the surface where moist grain is located.
- The warm air cools as it reaches the surface, condenses, and the cycle repeats itself.

MONITORING OF TEMPERATURE

Check the temperature of the bin every two weeks. Temperature can be measured using permanently installed temperature-sensing cables or by probing the grain with an electronic sensor device.

If temperature-measuring devices are unavailable:

- Assess the general temperature by inserting a metal rod into the grain at the top of the pile, near the center. The rod should penetrate at least one meter into the grain.
- Leave the rod in place for about 30 minutes.
- Afterward, remove the rod and test it for warmth at different points along its length using the palm of your hand. Any section of the rod that feels warm indicates heating and potential grain spoilage.

Damages During the Storage

If grains are not stored properly or neglected, they can incur various damages that negatively impact both the farmer and the country. These damages can be categorized as direct or indirect:

- **Direct Damages:** These damages are caused by pests, insects, and similar factors. They consume the grains from the inside, making them hollow, which reduces the weight, causes discoloration, and leads to a foul odor. All of these are considered direct damages.
- **Indirect Damage:** This refers to the harm caused by consuming infected grains. Eating such grains can lead to food poisoning and various worm infections in humans.

WAYS TO MONITOR GRAIN TEMPERATURES

High temperatures can rapidly accelerate the deterioration of grain, making it crucial to monitor the temperature to ensure consistency throughout the storage and maintain grain quality.

By monitoring grain temperatures, store managers can make timely decisions about when and where to use crop ventilation fans and keep detailed records for crop assurance purposes. When used alongside a Martin Lishman automatic fan controller, this system enhances storage efficiency and can lead to substantial energy cost savings.

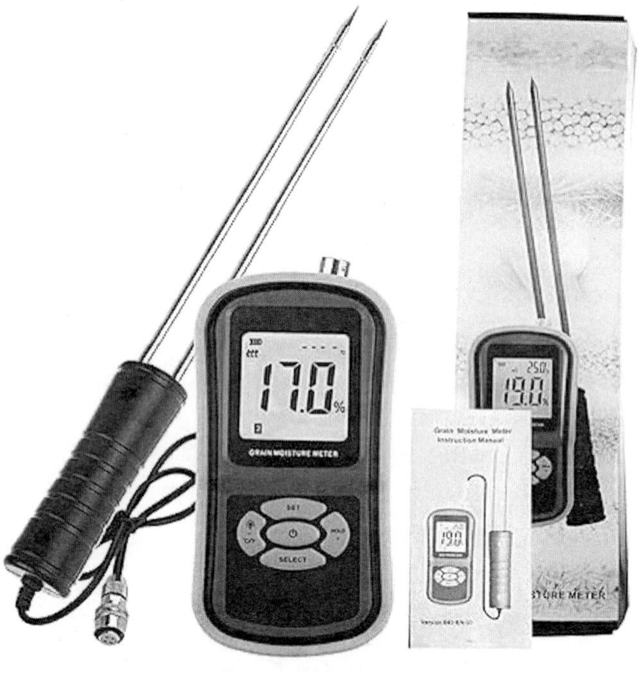

Figure: 1.3 Tools to monitor grain tempreatures

Grain Drying Options

- **Field Drying:** Field drying involves leaving the grain in the field until it reaches the desired moisture content. Weather conditions and potential harvest losses should be considered before choosing field drying. If harvesting must begin before the grain is fully dry, it must be dried to a safe moisture level for long-term storage before it can be stored safely.
- **In-bin Drying:** This method involves drying a batch of grain in a bin using natural air or low temperatures, which can take more than 24 hours and may extend to several weeks. Once the grain is dried to a safe moisture level for long-term storage, it can either remain in the bin or be transferred to another storage container, structure, or facility.
- **Independent Drying:** Batch and continuous dryer systems are used for rapid grain drying. In batch drying, a specific amount of grain is dried at a time based on the dryer's capacity. Continuous drying, on the other hand, involves a steady flow of grain through the dryer until it is fully dried.
- **Dryeration and Combination Drying:** In dryeration and combination drying systems, the drying process is paused before the grain is fully dry. In a dryeration system, the grain is held for several hours before being cooled. In combination drying, grain is partially dried at a high temperature and then transferred—either still hot or cooled—to a low-temperature bin to finish the drying process.

Grain Storage Options

- **Nonaerated Storage:** Nonaerated storage refers to any grain storage method that does not involve moving air through the grain. Types of nonaerated storage include bag storage, nonaerated piles, nonaerated flat storages, and bins without fans. These options are typically covered and have a moisture barrier underneath to reduce moisture entering the grain mass.
- **Aerated Storage:** Aerated grain storage involves circulating air through the grain. Examples of aerated systems include bins equipped with aeration fans and flat storages, such as buildings or piles, that include aeration systems. The maximum airflow in these systems is usually below 0.5 cubic feet per minute (cfm) per bushel, though it can vary throughout the grain mass.
- **Dryer-capable Storage:** Bins with fan capacities that provide airflow of at least 1.0 cfm per bushel are designed for both drying and storing grain.
- **Uncovered Piles:** Grain can be stored outdoors in piles that are not covered.

STORAGE DURATION AND MANAGEMENT ISSUES

- **All Grain:** Any grain to be stored for a month or longer must be dried to the safe, long-term moisture content. The allowable storage time depends on how long grain can be stored at a moisture content higher than the safe long-term level.

- **Nonaerated Storage:** Grain must be dried before being placed in nonaerated storage, as this type of storage lacks an aeration system to manage grain that has developed hot spots or begun to spoil. If grain begins to deteriorate in nonaerated storage, it must be moved to aerated or dryer-capable storage, used, or sold.
- **Aerated or Dryer-capable Storage:** These are the most versatile options for long-term storage, allowing for the maintenance of grain quality. If grain in such storage begins to deteriorate, the aeration or drying system can be activated to recover the grain.
- **Uncovered Piles:** Grain can be stored outdoors in uncovered piles for short periods, provided the weather is cool and dry. If the weather is unfavorable, significant losses may occur.

These grain drying and storage options should be evaluated based on both technical feasibility and economic benefits as part of the process of taking grain from the field to market.

STORAGE RELATIVE HUMIDITY

Relative Humidity (RH) is the most common measure of humidity, indicating how close the air is to being saturated — in other words, the amount of water vapor present in the air compared to the maximum amount it could hold at that temperature. Warmer air can hold more water vapor due to increased energy. When the RH reaches 100%, the air is fully saturated.

Air contains water vapor, which plays a vital role in weather phenomena. The moisture in the atmosphere comes from water bodies through evaporation and from plants through transpiration. This creates a continuous exchange of water between the atmosphere, continents, and oceans through processes like transpiration, evaporation, precipitation, and condensation.

During high temperatures, air with high RH can be very uncomfortable as it affects the body's cooling mechanism. Saturated air makes it harder for sweat to evaporate from the skin, reducing the body's ability to cool down effectively. In low temperatures, air with high RH can make us feel colder because the higher moisture content near the skin causes the cold temperature to be conducted more efficiently through the water, making us feel cooler.

Relative humidity (RH) is also crucial in determining the safe storage conditions for grain. The ideal RH for grain storage varies depending on the type of grain and the storage temperature.

EFFECT OF RELATIVE HUMIDITY

The moisture content of both the air and the stored produce can vary. The moisture that the air absorbs in the form of water vapor is called absolute humidity and is measured in g/m² of air.

However, the air cannot absorb an unlimited amount of moisture. There is a maximum amount that the atmosphere can hold at any given temperature. When the air contains this maximum amount, it is referred to as saturation, and the saturation moisture content is reached. At this point, the relative humidity is 100%.

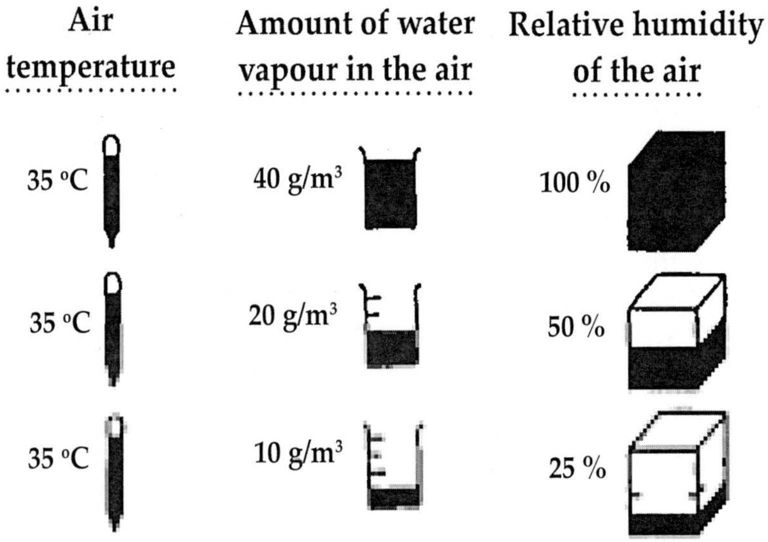

Figure: 1.4 Presentation of relative humidity

If the absolute humidity is only half of the saturation moisture content, the relative humidity will be 50%. If it is a quarter of it, the relative humidity will be 25%, and so on. Relative humidity, therefore, indicates the degree of saturation of the air with vapor, expressed as a percentage. Hygrometers measure and display relative humidity in percentage terms.

As previously mentioned, the saturation moisture content of the air is dependent on temperature. This means that the higher the atmospheric temperature, the more moisture the air can hold. Consequently, saturation occurs with different amounts of water vapor at various temperatures.

The absolute moisture content of the air can change, such as after rainfall. More moisture becomes available for the air to absorb, leading to an increase in relative humidity.

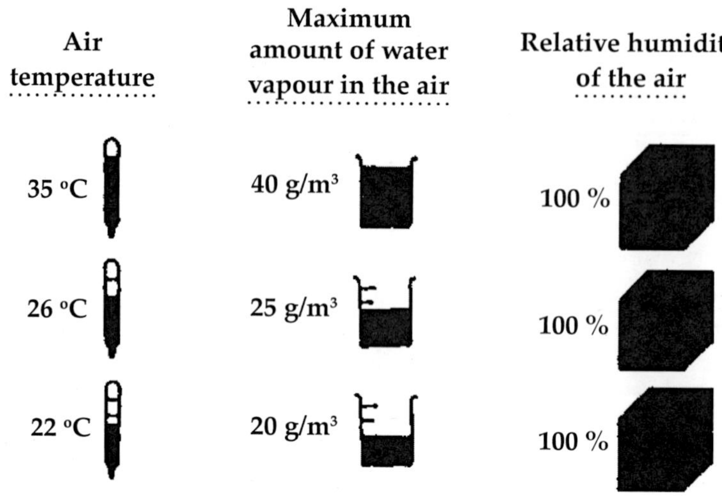

Figure: 1.5 Absolute moisture content of the air

On sunny days, the absolute humidity typically remains relatively constant. However, what happens if the temperature fluctuates? When the air warms up, its capacity to absorb moisture increases, meaning the saturation moisture content rises. If the amount of moisture in the air stays the same, the degree of saturation will decrease, causing the relative humidity to drop.

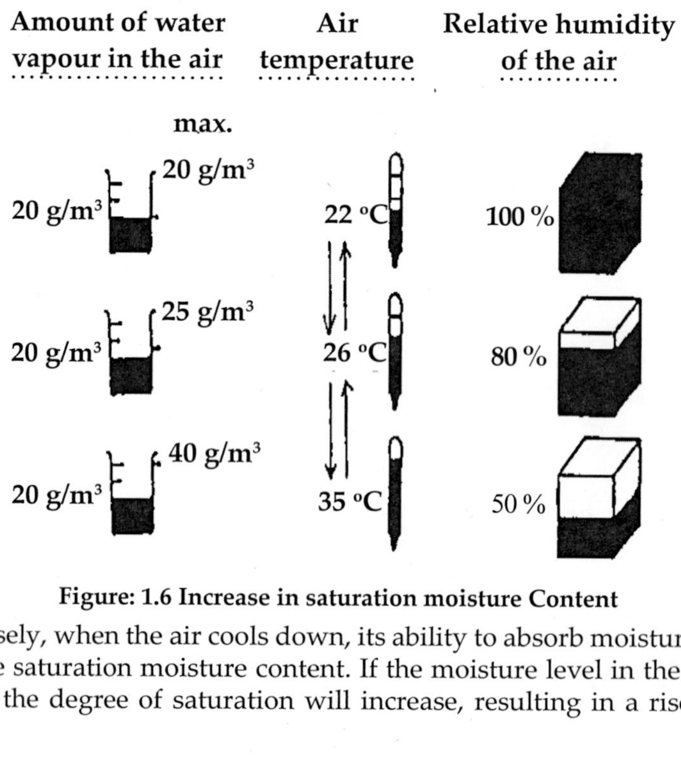

Figure: 1.6 Increase in saturation moisture Content

Conversely, when the air cools down, its ability to absorb moisture decreases, lowering the saturation moisture content. If the moisture level in the air remains unchanged, the degree of saturation will increase, resulting in a rise in relative humidity.

This indicates that, on days without rain, the relative humidity is highest in the early morning and lowest just after midday, when temperatures peak. It then rises again in the evening as the air cools.

CONDENSATION IN STORAGE

If the air cools down significantly, relative humidity may reach 100%, which is the saturation point (dew point). This indicates that the air now contains more moisture than it can hold at this lower temperature, leading to condensation. The excess water vapor appears as liquid water on cooler surfaces.

Condensation in storage typically occurs when there are significant temperature differences between the inside and outside of the storage facility. A common example is when the outside walls of the storage building become either warmer or cooler due to temperature fluctuations between day and night. These temperature imbalances cause the air inside the storage to circulate.

When the outside walls are warmed by sunlight, the air near these walls inside the store also heats up. This temperature increase reduces the relative humidity, allowing the air to absorb more moisture from the stored produce. However, if this air then comes into contact with colder surfaces, it will cool, and as its temperature drops, the relative humidity will increase, possibly surpassing the saturation point. This results in condensation. The same process occurs if the outside temperature is lower than the temperature inside the storage.

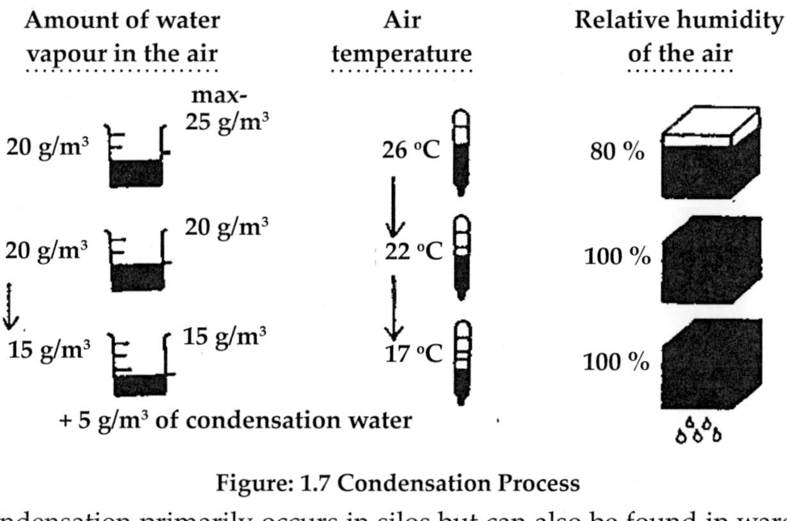

Figure: 1.7 Condensation Process

Condensation primarily occurs in silos but can also be found in warehouses, especially near the walls and roof, where it drips down onto the stored produce. It can sometimes also develop under the tarpaulins of stacked commodities. This often results in mold growth and, in some cases, even causes the stored produce to begin germinating.

Condensation can also occur in areas of the stored produce with high insect infestation. The respiratory activity of the insects raises both the temperature and humidity, creating "hot spots." If the temperature in one of these "hot spots" exceeds 40°C, it becomes too warm for the insects, causing them to move to cooler areas. As a result, the "hot spot" spreads.

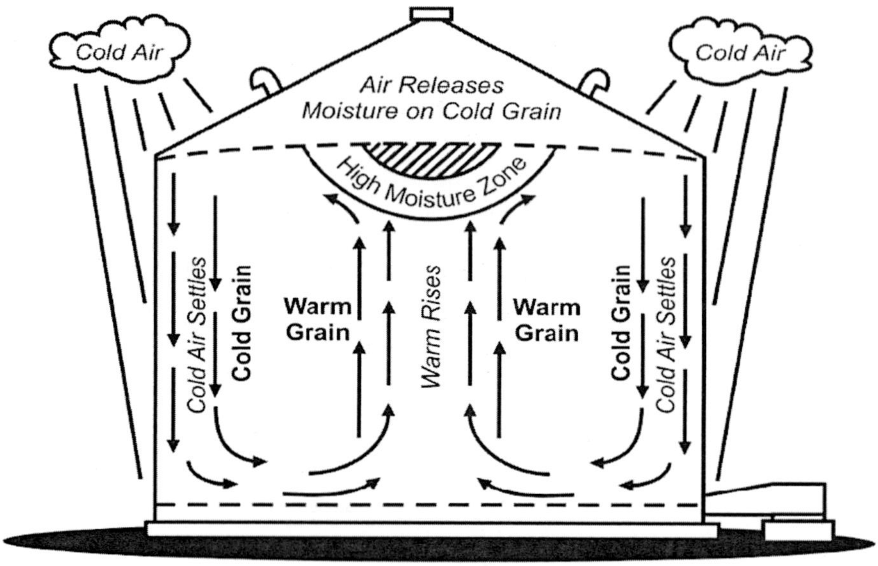

Figure: 1.8 Storing Grain Safety

THE STORED PRODUCE'S RELATIVE HUMIDITY AND MOISTURE CONTENT

The moisture content of the stored produce and the relative humidity of the surrounding air in the storage space work to achieve a state of equilibrium. Depending on the relative humidity, the stored produce either releases moisture into the air (drying) or absorbs moisture from the air (moistening) until equilibrium is reached.

Controlled ventilation of the storage facility, by aerating it when the relative humidity is low and sealing it when the relative humidity is high, facilitates further drying of the produce during storage.

SAFE LEVEL OF MOISTURE IN PRODUCE STORED FOR LONG-TERM STORAGE

When stored produce is moist, there is a risk of fungi and mold development. Fungi begin to grow when the relative humidity exceeds 65-70%. Therefore, the safe moisture content for long-term storage of foodstuffs is one that maintains an equilibrium at a relative humidity of 65-70%.

In many sources, water activity (a_w) is used in this context. Water activity refers to the equivalent equilibrium relative humidity expressed as a decimal. For example, a water activity of 0.70 corresponds to an equilibrium relative humidity of 70%.

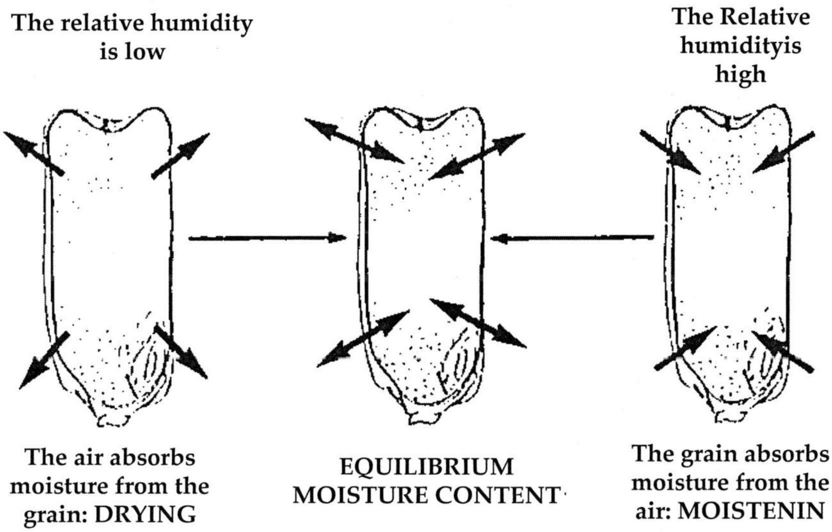

Figure: 1.9 Level of moisture in produce stored

The safe moisture content values vary depending on the chemical composition of the different types of stored produce. For instance, seeds with a high lipid content (such as fats and oils) will have a significantly lower equilibrium moisture content compared to cereals, which are primarily made up of starch.

IMPACT OF CLIMATIC CONDITIONS ON THE DEVELOPMENT OF PESTS AND MICRO-ORGANISMS

Pests and microorganisms, like all living organisms, rely on specific climatic conditions for survival. Certain temperature and humidity ranges typically make life impossible, particularly in extremely cold, hot, or dry environments. While some pests are highly adaptable to varying climates, others are limited by strict environmental constraints.

Table 1.2 : The effect of climate on development of grain

Produce	Safe moisture content	Produce	Safe moisture content
Maize	13%	Cowpeas, beans	15%
Wheat	13%	Groundnuts	7%
Millet	13%	Cocoa	7%
Sorghum	13%	Copra	7%
Paddy	14%	Palm kernels	5%
Rice	13%	Coffee	13%

Stored product pests thrive in temperatures between 28 and 33°C and relative humidity levels between 60 and 80%. When conditions approach these ideal ranges, a rapid succession of generations can result in mass reproduction .

Mold begins to form at a relative humidity of 65-70%. The higher the relative humidity, the more favorable the conditions for the growth of fungi and mold. The temperature range within which fungi can develop varies depending on the species. This also applies to the production of highly toxic metabolic byproducts, known as mycotoxins, which are associated with fungal infestations

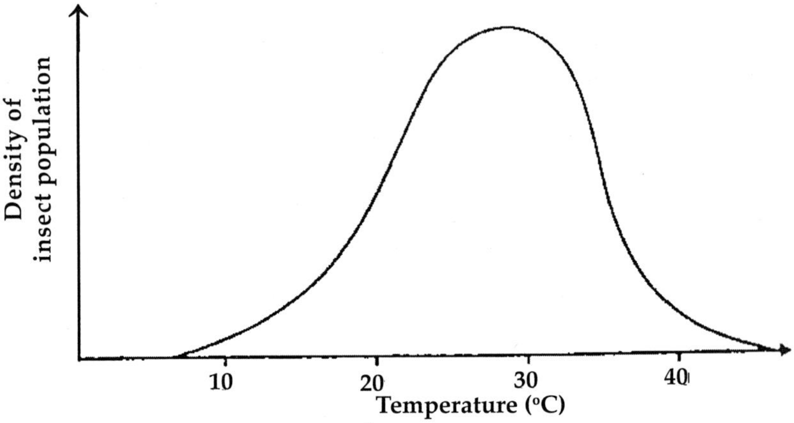

Figure 1.10 : The range of temperature within which fungi can develop

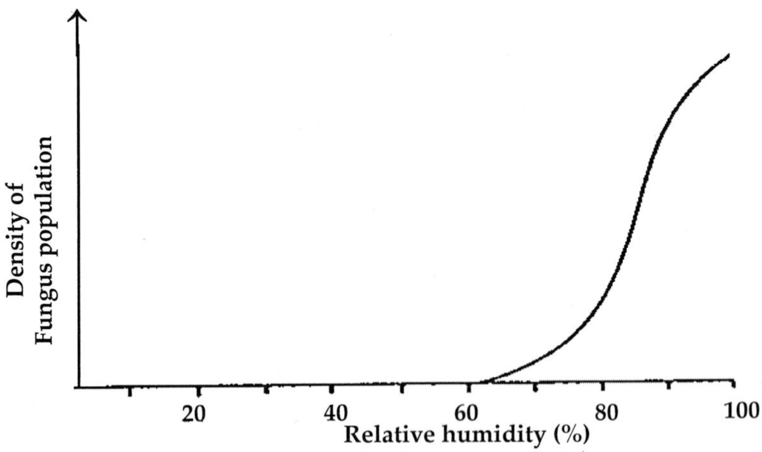

Figure 1.11 : Mould begins with relative hunmidity of density of fungus population

Overview of the Effects of Climatic and Biotic Factors on the Quality of Stored Produce

High temperatures, high relative humidity, and high moisture content in stored produce create favorable conditions for the development of pests. The respiration of pests (and the stored produce) generates moisture and heat, which further enhance the environment for pests, leading to an increase in their population.

Rainfall, ground moisture, and a drop in temperature raise the relative humidity. Rainwater and ground moisture can be directly absorbed by the grain. High relative humidity increases the moisture content of the stored produce, potentially leading to condensation. Without measures to counteract this, significant losses are likely. The quality of the stored produce can only be maintained if steps such as drying the produce, ensuring proper storage hygiene, controlling ventilation, and implementing pest control are taken.

Low, consistent temperatures and low relative humidity are ideal for preserving the quality of stored produce.

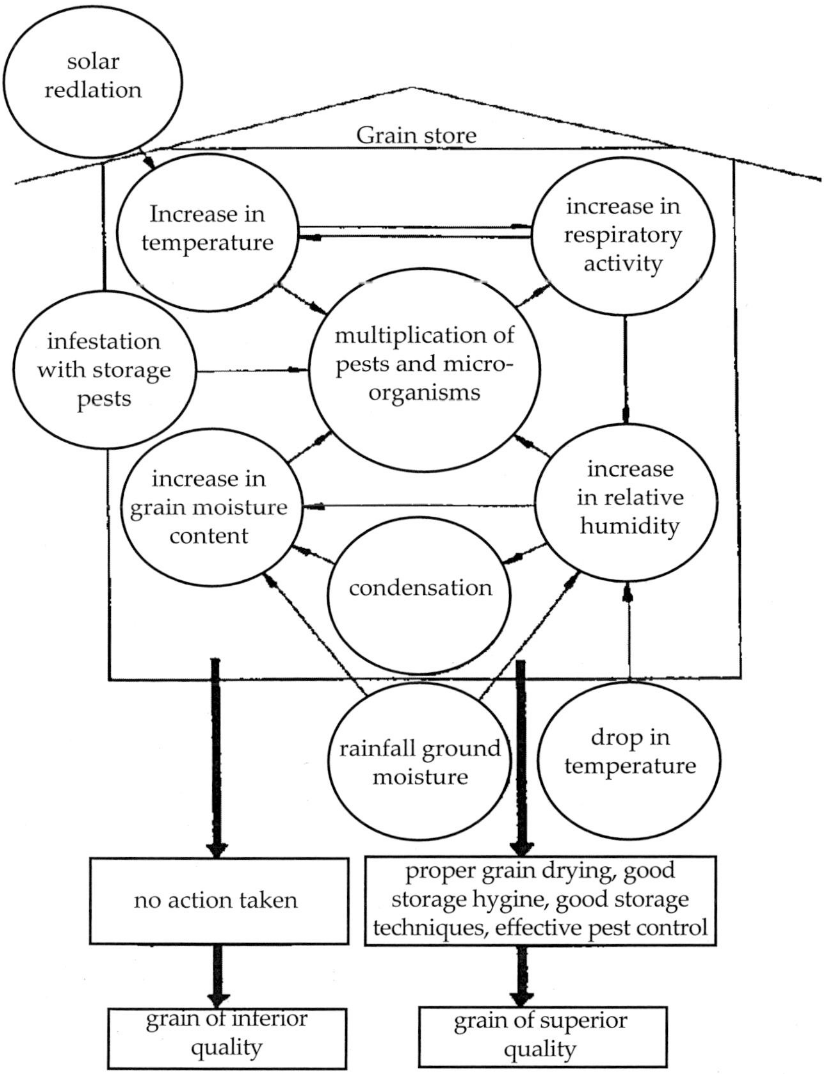

Figure 1.12 : Quality of the stored produce to be maintained only by changing produce Controling ventilation and implementing past control

MEASUREMENT OF GRAIN SAMPLING AND MOISTURE CONTENT

MOISTURE CONTENT OF GRAIN

The moisture content of grains is a crucial factor in storage, as it directly impacts the quality and shelf life of the produce. Excess moisture promotes the growth of various microorganisms, including bacteria, molds, fungi, pests, and insects. To prevent spoilage, grains should be stored at recommended moisture levels and temperatures, and moisture migration should be controlled. For many grains, the recommended moisture content is below 13%.

MONITORING OF GRAIN

Products intended for storage may have characteristics that prevent immediate warehousing. Excessive moisture content or the presence of insects and impurities can negatively impact the long-term preservation of product quality.

For effective technical and marketing management, it is essential to periodically assess the quantity and quality of the stored products. Before storage begins, products should be thoroughly checked to verify weight, moisture content, and the percentage of impurities.

Throughout the storage period, the condition of the products must be regularly monitored. This includes not only checking moisture content and the extent of insect infestation but also periodically measuring the temperature of the grain.

WEIGHING

Weighing is performed when the products first arrive at the storage centers. Depending on the delivery conditions (such as whether the products are delivered in bags or in bulk, and the transport system used), weighing can be carried out using basic mechanical scales or platform scales.

Mechanical Scales

In smaller storage centers, when products are delivered in bags, weighing is typically done using simple mechanical scales. These scales have a capacity of 200 kg, allowing multiple bags of grain to be weighed simultaneously.

A storage center should have enough scales to maintain a consistent, year-round flow of products into the warehouse.

To reduce reception time in some cases, if the bags entering the warehouse have a standard gross weight, partial weighing of the batches can be performed. The total weight is then calculated by multiplying the number of bags by the average weight of the weighed bags.

Platform Scales

Platform scales allow for the weighing of batches by measuring the weight of loaded or unloaded vehicles as they enter and exit the storage centers. Due to their high cost and large load-bearing capacity, these weighing systems are primarily beneficial in large storage centers where products are delivered in bags or bulk by vehicles.

The installation of platform scales requires some construction work. Specifically, a pit needs to be dug and developed to house the platform scale mechanisms. Typically, the pit is 1.60 meters deep, although some specialized platform scale models can be installed in pits as shallow as 90 cm.

Some manufacturers offer open-sky installations that do not require a pit. In these cases, the platform scale is elevated above the ground, necessitating the construction of ramps to allow vehicle access.

It is also important to note that the weight capacity specified by manufacturers refers to the maximum weight the platform scale can support, which includes both the transport vehicle's weight and its load.

SAMPLING

When products arrive at the storage centers and during warehousing, it is essential to assess their quality and condition.

Since it is practically impossible to analyze every batch, a representative sample of the total product must be taken for analysis.

To obtain a representative sample, multiple primary samples need to be collected. Once these are gathered and mixed in a clean container, they form the global sample on which the necessary tests will be conducted.

If the global sample is too large, it must be divided into smaller, yet still representative, portions.

The methods for collecting samples vary depending on whether the products are delivered or stored in bags or in bulk.

SAMPLING OF GRAINS DELIVERED IN BAGS

The number of bags from which samples must be taken for a given batch of grains is determined by the total number of bags, as outlined in the following table:

Table 1.3 : Sampling criteria based on batch composition

Composition of Batch	Bags Sampled
1 to 10 bags	All bags
10 to 100 bags	10 bags chosen at random
More than 100 bags	The square root of the total number of bags

Once the bags are selected, the global sample can be created in two ways: by probing the bags or by emptying the contents of the bags.

Sampling by Probing

Primary samples are collected by inserting hollow probes into the selected bags (such as bag probes or probing rods). Each sample should weigh approximately 50 g per 100-kg bag, and in all cases, there should be enough to create a global sample of at least 500 g. Once collected, the samples must be thoroughly mixed together.

Sampling by Emptying the Bags

The contents of each bag are stirred and spread in a 10 cm thick layer on a clean surface. A primary sample of approximately 1 kg is taken from each layer of grain. These various primary samples are then carefully mixed together to form the global sample.

SAMPLING OF GRAINS THAT IS SUPPLIED IN LARGE QUANTITIES

A sample of grains delivered in bulk can be obtained by taking primary samples either when the product is stationary (e.g., on a truck or trailer) or while it is in motion (e.g., during the filling of a silo).

Sampling of a Stationary Product

A sample of a stationary product is collected by taking multiple samples from within the grain mass and mixing the resulting primary samples. As much as possible, samples should be taken from throughout the entire thickness of the grain layer.

Deep samples, collected using special probes, are preferred over surface samples taken with suction flasks or other small containers. The number of samples and the locations from which they are taken depend on the total quantity of grain, as illustrated in the diagrams below.

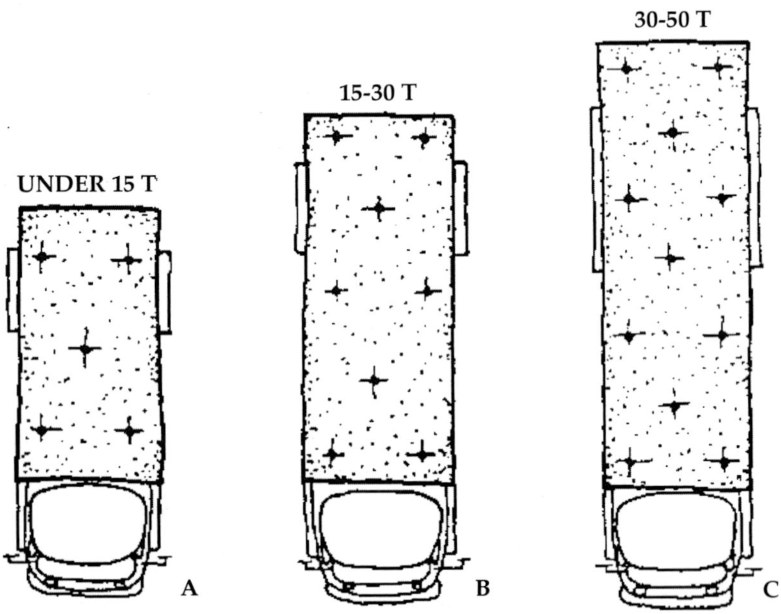

Figure: 1.13 Number of samples: A 5 samples; B 8 samples; C 11 samples.

For highly heterogeneous batches, it is recommended to take samples from every five tonnes of product, with a minimum of 10 samples.

Sampling of a Moving Product

More reliable and precise than the technique of sampling a stationary product, this method involves taking one or more samples at once from the moving grain mass. The samples can typically be collected using simple tools (such as suction flasks or shovels) or by using automatic samplers installed in the ducts where the grain is flowing.

SAMPLE REDUCTION

If the global sample obtained is too large, methods must be employed to reduce it to smaller, yet still representative, samples. One of the simplest methods, though not the most precise, is known as the "cone" method.

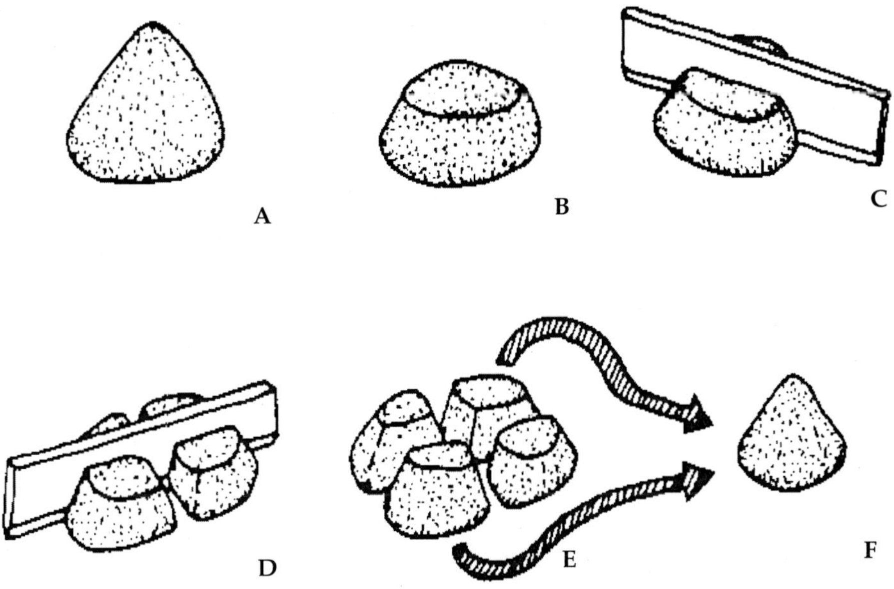

Figure: 1.14 Sample seduction: cone method

Smaller samples can be obtained by dividing the global sample, which has been stirred and piled on a clean surface, into two or four equal portions. Sample reduction can also be achieved using specialized devices such as the conical sample divider, also known as the "Boerner divider," and the riffle divider, which is more commonly used for seeds.

DETERMINING THE PERCENTAGE OF IMPURITIES

Impurities not only affect the storage of products but also influence the overall quality of these products. Therefore, it is essential to determine the percentage of impurities in a batch of grain before storing or trading it.

Common impurities include:

- Plant debris (straw, leaves)
- Mineral matter (earth, gravel)
- Miscellaneous items (metal fragments, string)
- Foreign grains
- Unripe grains
- Germinated grains
- Broken grains
- Damaged grains (caused by insects or rodents)
- Grains that are deteriorated, moldy, or discolored.

The percentage of impurities is determined from samples that typically weigh a few hundred grams. In practice, healthy grains are separated from impurities through visual sorting and sifting. The impurities are then classified and weighed on a scale. The percentage of impurities in the batch is calculated by expressing the weight of the impurities as a percentage of the total sample weight.

DETERMINING THE MOISTURE CONTENT OF GRAIN

Grain with moisture levels exceeding grade requirements can foster an environment that encourages the growth and development of insects and fungi if not properly managed. Unattended grain may experience a rise in temperature, which, in turn, creates convection currents that can lead to surface condensation.

To monitor the moisture content of grain in storage, it is essential to collect samples from the bins every 3 to 4 weeks if the grain is not being actively managed (i.e., no aeration or turning). Samples should be gathered from multiple areas within the bulk and stored in sealed plastic containers before testing.

MEASURING MOISTURE CONTENT

Determining the moisture content of grain is a crucial operation throughout all stages of the post-harvest system.

Before harvest, it allows for an estimation of the grain's maturity level. After threshing, it helps in selecting appropriate drying methods and durations. Prior to product processing, it indicates whether the grain is in suitable condition for treatment.

At the time of marketing, it reveals the amount of dry matter being purchased, which helps establish a fair sales price, as water does not have the same market value as grain.

Before and during storage, it aids in determining the appropriate warehousing conditions and assessing the overall condition of the grain.

Empirical Evaluations

In the field, farmers often rely on empirical methods to estimate the moisture content of grain based on their personal experience. These methods do not provide a true, objective measurement but instead offer a subjective estimation through sensory perception (touch, sight, and smell) of the grain's characteristics.

For instance, some farmers nibble on grains, score them with a thumbnail, or crush them between their fingers to assess their hardness and consistency, which helps estimate moisture content. Others depend on the smell of the grain, whether it is pleasant or unpleasant, while some evaluate the dull or sharp rattle of grains shaken in a metal box. Another method involves assessing the grain's fluidity by attempting to push an open hand into a large mass of grain contained in a bag or spread in a thick layer.

Among these empirical techniques, the salt test is perhaps the least approximate. In this method, a sample of grain is mixed with dry kitchen salt in a glass container. After shaking the container several times, the walls are examined to check whether the salt has stuck. If the salt adheres to the walls, it indicates that the grain's moisture content is above 15 percent.

Although, these empirical methods are still widely used by farmers, they should increasingly be replaced by instruments that provide accurate moisture content measurements. The use of such methods in storage centers or during commercial transactions should be strongly discouraged.

Currently, the methods utilizing appropriate measuring instruments can be categorized into two types: direct and indirect measurement.

Direct Measurement

The sample to be measured is first weighed on precision scales, then dried in a drying room, and weighed again. The difference in weight before and after drying reveals the amount of water contained in the sample.

The technological complexity of these instruments and the detailed measurements require the presence of qualified personnel.

Some of the measuring instruments that work based on the principle of drying the sample include:

- The slow incubator
- The fast CHOPIN incubator
- The infrared lamp

These instruments, which are both precise and complex, are best suited for specialized laboratories responsible for calibrating other indirect measurement devices (such as hygrometers) or determining moisture content in large storage corporations or during commercial transactions.

Indirect Measurement

These methods determine moisture content by measuring the electrical properties of grain moisture.

Some of the instruments that use this principle include:

- Hygrometers that measure the electrical resistance of the grain
- Hygrometers that measure the dielectric constant of the grain

Hygrometers are electronic devices that allow the moisture content of a grain sample to be directly and instantly read on a dial.

Hygrometers that measure the electrical resistance of grain are portable, relatively imprecise instruments, but they are highly practical and affordable. On the other hand, more expensive and sophisticated hygrometers, which measure the dielectric constant of grain, are typically used in large storage centers and for commercial transactions.

TEMPERATURE CONTROL

Temperature control is essential for monitoring the preservation of stored products. An unusual increase in grain temperature can indicate the beginning of deterioration. Therefore, regular inspections must be conducted to prevent significant product losses.

Since grain masses are not uniform, samples must be taken from various points within each stored batch. First, we will examine the characteristics required for effective measuring devices, followed by an overview of the different types available.

Due to the heterogeneous nature of stored grain, measuring devices do not need to be highly precise, as deviations of up to one degree Celsius are insignificant. However, these devices must be highly sensitive to detect even the slightest abnormal temperature change as quickly as possible.

Additionally, they should be easy to read and require minimal handling. To withstand repeated use and potential impacts during handling, they must also be robust and durable.

Different types of temperature monitoring devices operate on various principles and have distinct methods of use. While they are crucial for bulk-storage facilities, they can also be valuable for monitoring bagged storage.

In addition to the sophisticated devices described below, digital thermometers are available as an easy-to-read, cost-effective alternative.

Liquid Thermometers

These devices operate based on the principle of liquid expansion (mercury or alcohol) in response to temperature changes. They are housed within metal probes that can be inserted into bags or directly into the grain mass.

This system is relatively inexpensive and can be used for both bagged and bulk-stored grain. However, its main drawback is the inaccuracy of the readings, as the thermometer must be removed from the measurement point for reading, which can affect precision.

Resistance Thermometers

These thermometers function by measuring the electrical current passing through a filament made of platinum, copper, steel, or nickel, whose resistance changes with temperature.

Encased in a long sheath and suspended from the top of the storage bin, the thermometer is inserted into the grain mass.

A key advantage of this type of thermometer is its ability to provide a single reading that reflects the overall temperature of the stored products, unlike liquid thermometers, which require multiple measurements at different points within the grain mass.

Thermistors or Thermocouples in Probes

These probes are fitted with sensors or sensitive components (such as thermistors or thermocouples) that function as electric thermometers, allowing temperature readings to be taken remotely.

Inserted into the grain after the storage bins have been filled, these probes are electrically connected via telephone cables to either portable reading devices or centralized control panels for monitoring.

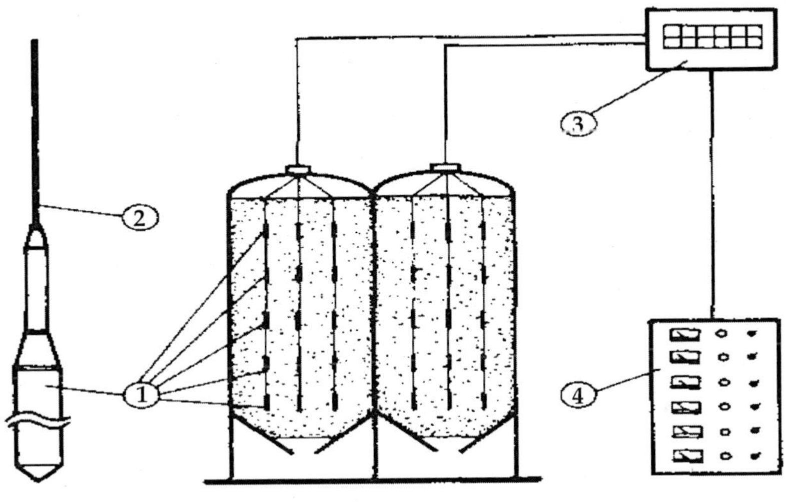

Figure: 1.15 Positions of probes in a silo: 1. Probes; 2. Cable; 3. Connection box; 4. Control panel.

Since temperature varies within the grain mass, sensors must be strategically distributed throughout the stored grain.

In general, they should be positioned as follows:

- One sensor every 3-4 meters vertically
- One sensor every 5-6 meters horizontally

CONTROL OF ENVIRONMENT INSIDE STORAGE

AERATION

Aeration helps maintain the quality of stored grain by ensuring a consistent and cool temperature, making it an essential tool for grain management during harvest and storage. Grain stored with proper aeration can be safely kept at a higher moisture content while preserving its viability and vigor for a longer period.

ADVANTAGES OF AERATION

- Extends the harvesting period for grain and seed crops, reducing delays caused by rain and preventing the downgrading of premium grain due to weather damage.
- Minimizes color deterioration caused by delayed harvest, particularly for premium crops valued based on color, such as shochu barley or pulses.
- Balances the temperature inside silos to prevent hot spots, which can degrade grain quality and create ideal conditions for insect and mold infestation.
- Protects high-moisture grain from mold development during storage.
- Cools stored grain, reducing insect-related damage in high-throughput storage facilities, such as feedlots, where grain is fed to livestock and fumigation opportunities are limited.
- Enables a consistent supply of wheat to millers and manufacturers year-round. Flour milled from wheat stored at cool temperatures retains its baking qualities for a longer period.

The of Aeration Process

Aeration involves passing ambient (unheated) air through bulk grain. If the relative humidity (RH) of the airflow differs from that of the air surrounding the grain, moisture will either be drawn from the grain or absorbed by it until equilibrium is established.

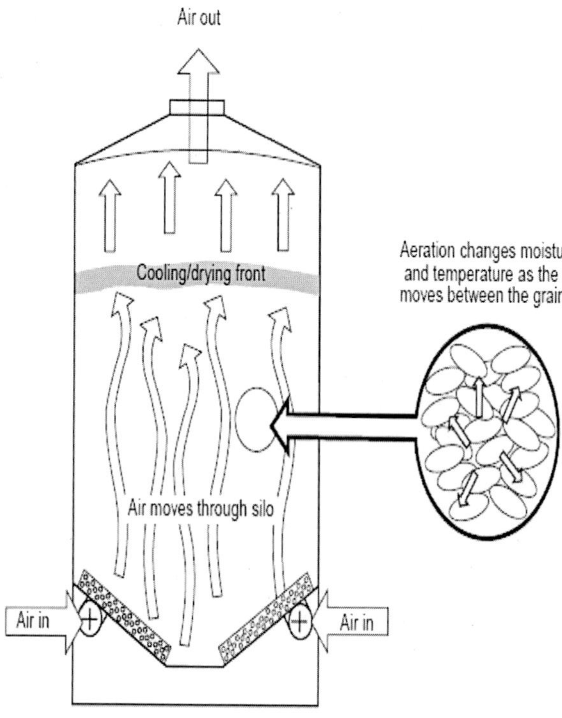

Figure: 1.16 Aeration process

GRAIN WITH LOW MOISTURE CONTENT STORED FOR A LONG TIME

Low Airflow Aeration

Low-flow aeration helps preserve the quality of low-moisture grain for extended storage periods while also slowing the growth of insect populations. To maintain grain in a safe condition for long-term storage, a fan capacity of approximately two liters per second per tonne (l/s/t) is typically sufficient.

For effective aeration, exhaust air must be able to escape freely from the top of the storage. It is recommended to have an opening of at least 0.1 m^2 for every 500 liters per second of air delivered. (For reference, a 30 cm by 30 cm opening is roughly 0.1 m^2). Exhaust vents should be designed to prevent water from entering the silo.

For long-term storage, temperature monitoring and automatic fan control systems are highly recommended. These controllers optimize both the quantity and quality of air used in the system, and certain models also prevent high-humidity air from entering the grain bulk.

STORAGE FOR A BRIEF PERIOD OF TIMEHIGH MOISTURE GRAIN

Medium Airflow Aeration

Harvesting barley and other grains at high moisture levels—above those suitable for delivery and storage—helps optimize quality while reducing the risk of fungal staining, sprouting, and losses caused by wet harvest conditions. To maintain the quality of high-moisture grain before it is dried in a heated air dryer, medium airflow aeration is required.

During aeration, moisture content and temperature are balanced within the grain stack, ensuring a consistent feedstock for the dryer. This reduces the need for frequent adjustments to dryer speed and heat settings. The required airflow rate depends on the grain's moisture content but typically ranges between 4 to 10 liters per second per tonne (l/s/t).

To keep the grain in a safe condition, aim for a maximum moisture content of 15% and a storage temperature of 20°C. When harvesting in the early morning or late evening, moisture from the surface or surrounding air can increase the moisture content of individual grains. An airflow of 4 to 10 l/s/t is sufficient to remove excess surface moisture from each grain.

EQUIPMENT FOR MONITORING, MANAGEMENT

To effectively manage stored grain, the operator must be able to collect samples from the stored grain, measure moisture content, monitor grain temperatures, and maintain simple records of both grain and ambient temperatures.

A deep bin probe should be used to collect samples from various locations within the bin to assess moisture content, the level of fine material, and overall grain condition.

A reasonably accurate moisture tester is necessary, and the operator must be aware of its accuracy under different conditions. Inexpensive electrical testers can provide inaccurate readings under certain circumstances, such as with freshly dried grain, warm or hot grain, and extremely cold grain. The operator can calibrate the tester by comparing its readings with those from a local elevator or more precise testers.

Thermocouple cables installed in larger bins are helpful for monitoring temperatures within the storage to assess the effectiveness of aeration. In bins without these cables, thermometer probes should be used to check temperatures at various points within the bin, aiding in the monitoring of aeration progress and the identification of potential issues. A thermometer to measure exhaust air temperature and another for ambient air temperature is essential for managing fan operations. Maximum-minimum thermometers are particularly useful as they show temperature changes over time. This equipment not only helps the operator manage the grain storage but also provides insights into the functioning of the aeration system and the grain's response to treatment.

How Aeration Systems Work

Aeration systems help preserve stored grain and maintain its dryness by lowering the grain's temperature and reducing moisture migration. Proper aeration can prevent the formation of convection currents and condensation.

When planning aeration and drying, it is essential to consider the physical characteristics of the grain. Factors such as the grain's class and the storage configuration affect the static pressure, which in turn influences the requirements for the aeration fan. Typically, as static pressure increases—such as when the storage height increases or the commodity class changes—the time needed for proper aeration also changes. It is advisable to consult with your aeration system provider to determine the appropriate aeration or drying times for the specific bin type or commodity you are storing.

How to Use Aeration Systems?

Stored grains should be aerated as soon as possible after harvest, especially if aeration can lower the bulk temperature to below 18°C. When the ambient temperature drops below that of the grain bulk, typically during the early evening, night, and early morning, aeration can be used to cool the grain.

However, if you aerate grain when the ambient temperature exceeds 20°C and the grain temperature is above 30°C, the odors produced may attract insect pests. Therefore, sanitation, including cleaning and treating the grain, is crucial to preventing issues.

In addition to preventing insect infestations, aeration is also highly effective in controlling them. Once the grain temperature is reduced to below 18°C, which prevents insect feeding and reproduction, further cooling can be used to induce mortality. Refer to the disinfestation time periods required at low temperatures table in the Physical Control of Grain Insect Pests for guidance.

To maximize the effectiveness of your aeration system, it is important to understand the fan and motor efficiency, as well as the static pressure of the commodity you are aerating. The Prairie Agriculture Machinery Institute provides charts that can help you determine the appropriate aeration time for your stored grain.

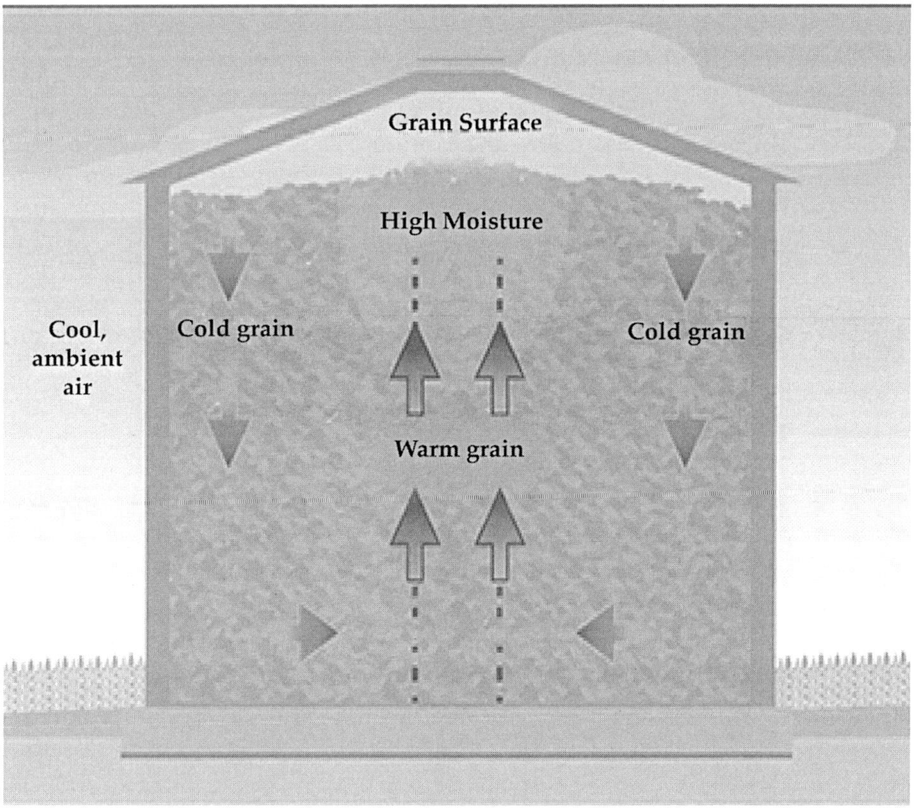

Figure: 1.17 Monitoring grain temperature and aeration grain

Other Cooling Methods

If an aeration system is unavailable, turning the grain outside the bin can serve as an alternative when the ambient air temperature drops below 15°C. The grain should be turned every 2 to 4 weeks until its temperature reaches 15°C. This process involves removing about one-third of the grain from the bin and then placing it back in.

Grain chillers are another option for reducing the temperature of grain when outside temperatures are above 20°C. These chillers lower both the temperature and moisture content of the air used to aerate the grain. Once cooled, the grain retains its lower temperature for extended periods due to its natural insulating properties.

Grain mixing and stirring equipment is also effective for achieving uniform temperature and moisture content in stored grain. These devices gradually move the grain from the lower and central areas of the storage bin to the surface, helping to reduce the effects of moisture and temperature concentration caused by convection. These systems can be used alongside aeration to maintain consistent grain temperature and moisture levels.

QUALITY OF GRAIN

The term 'quality' holds different meanings for those involved in the handling, storage, processing, and use of grain, even though all aim for grain of "good quality." For example, grain-handling agencies seek dry, insect-free, and undamaged grain that stores well; millers want grain that yields a high percentage of finished products; and consumers focus on factors like flavor, appearance, or cooking qualities.

Grain quality varies depending on individual preferences. It can encompass many factors such as aroma, size, cooking characteristics, color, nutritional value, and the percentage of whole grains.

The quality of grain can also differ depending on the variety or type chosen by the farmer, and it is influenced by climatic and soil conditions during the growing season, cultivation practices, weather conditions at harvest, and harvesting methods. Apart from short-term aging or maturation after harvest, quality cannot be improved during storage, handling, or processing. In fact, quality can easily degrade during these stages.

Each type of grain has certain characteristics that contribute to its overall quality. Considering these factors, either individually or together, allows for grading and valuation of the grain, which in turn helps in developing optimal methods for handling, storing, and processing.

Research into methods for identifying grain varieties may play a significant role in future grain grading systems. As consumers are now used to purchasing fruits and vegetables by variety, the same could apply to grain. Several cereal crops have been studied; techniques like polyacrylamide gel electrophoresis (PAGE) have been used to distinguish between wheat varieties, and reversed-phase high-performance liquid chromatography (RPHPLC) may be useful for both wheat and rice.

Consumer preferences, such as a preference for a specific smell or the whiteness of grain, influence purchasing decisions and thus affect market prices. Therefore, it's important to produce what the market demands.

Grain moisture content is the most critical factor in maintaining grain quality. Grain quality cannot be improved after harvest, except perhaps through processes like parboiling to reduce cracking. From the point of harvest onward, grain deterioration can be slowed but not completely stopped. Therefore, it is crucial to have a uniform and timely harvest, followed by an effective post-harvest management system that slows the deterioration of grain quality.

Both good crop management and proper post-harvest handling are essential for maintaining quality, boosting prices, and minimizing losses. Steps to preserve quality include:

Table 1.4 Factors to preserve the quality

Factor	What to do
Variety	Grow varieties that meet market quality demands.
Crop management	Manage your field so that the crop matures uniformly. Good crop establishment, land leveling and uniform water, nutrient and pest management are important for uniform maturing of the crop. Uniformity of maturing is important as the moisture from the harvested less-mature grains can move to the dryer grains and cause grain cracking.
Harvest	Harvest grain at 20-25% moisture. Too wet or too dry leads to grain damage on threshing.
Stacking	Briefly stack harvested rice. If the crop has high moisture and temperatures are high, then rapid yellowing of the grain - even within 24hrs - can occur.
Threshing	Thresh promptly but at the right moisture. Too dry (less than 20%), grain will be broken during mechanical threshing leading to a lower percent of head rice. Too wet (more 25%), grain can be deformed during mechanical threshing. Manual threshing leads to less grain breakage, but can be very slow and other quality losses (e.g. fungal growth) can occur if not threshed and dried quickly.
Drying	Dry grain as quickly as possible to less 14% for medium term storage.
Grain storage	Do not mix wet grain and dry grain less than 16%. Moisture moves from the wet to the dry and this causes the dry grains to crack.
Milling	Mill rice at 12-14% moisture content to reduce cracking.

QUALITY CHARACTERISTICS OF GRAINS

Over the years, consumers have grown accustomed to demanding grain with specific qualities. In local markets, where consumers are closer to the source of the grain, their personal preferences and the laws of supply and demand typically dictate the quality of the grain.

However, when grain is traded over long distances, especially internationally, consumers have no direct influence over its quality. In such cases, regulatory standards must be established and enforced to protect consumer rights. As a result, clear criteria for grain quality must be defined and accepted by all parties involved in the grain trade. These criteria encompass both the intrinsic varietal qualities of the grain and those qualities that are influenced by environmental conditions or processing methods. The key quality criteria relevant to grain grading are discussed in the following sections.

INTRINSIC QUALITIES

Colour

Cereal grains come in a variety of colors, ranging from very light tan or nearly white to black. In cases where extractive milling is necessary, grains with high pigmentation may result in lower yields of white flour.

Composition

The composition of grain, including protein, carbohydrates, lipids, and their breakdown products, significantly influences product acceptability by affecting texture and taste. Quality changes in stored grain occur gradually, while they happen more quickly in milled or processed products.

Certain components of grain, such as the husk, are inedible and have a direct impact on product yield and the overall nutrient content available to the consumer.

Bulk Density

Each type or variety of grain, when in optimal condition and fully mature, has a characteristic bulk density, which is defined as the weight per standard volume, measured in a consistent manner. This characteristic is often referred to as "test weight," "bushel weight," or "specific weight."

If the bulk density fluctuates, it typically decreases, indicating a reduction in the overall quality of the grain. Therefore, it is frequently measured in the grain trade. Common factors affecting bulk density include insect infestations, excessive foreign matter, and high moisture content. In wheat, bulk density is considered a reliable indicator of milling yield.

It is important not to confuse "bulk density" with "specific volume," While the terms are related, the distinction is crucial because it is well-established that grain's "bulk density" increases when stored in large quantities, whether in bags or bulk, due to compaction.

Aroma and Smell

Most types of grain, when fresh, have a distinct natural odor or aroma, which is generally considered a sign of good quality. However, some individuals may prefer grain that has an "old" or even fermented smell. Like other natural products, certain grain varieties are more favored than others based on their aroma. For instance, specific rice cultivars have aromatic qualities that are highly valued by certain consumers.

Dimensions and Form

Rice, as a whole-grain food, is classified based on its size (length) and shape (length-to-breadth ratio). Other grains also have their size considered in their specifications. Generally, a small range in size helps improve processing and handling efficiency.

INDUCED QUALITIES

Age

During the post-harvest phase, grain experiences complex biochemical changes known as 'aging.' These changes affect the carbohydrate, lipid, and protein fractions, leading to effects such as the firming of rice texture during cooking and improved gas-retention ability in wheat flour.

For most consumers, the effects of these changes are viewed as desirable. When plotting consumer acceptability of a grain product against its age since harvest, the product is generally considered to be maturing during the upward curve of the graph, with deterioration occurring only when the curve begins to decline.

Broken Grain

Grain is typically marketed in its whole form and is considered of inferior quality if it is broken. Breakage can occur due to fissures caused by excessive drying or weathering conditions in the field, or during handling. Broken grains reduce quality by lowering acceptability and increasing the likelihood of infestation during storage. Additionally, breakage impacts milling yield by contributing to weight loss.

Chalky or Immature Grain

Sterility, pre-harvest infections, or insect attacks can all result in empty grains. Harvest timing has an impact on the amount of immature grains. The immature grains of rice usually have a greenish hue. Incomplete grain filling, frequently brought on by pests or illnesses, results in thin, opaque white grains.

An incompletely filled starchy endosperm causes chalkiness by obstructing light transmission and producing opaque areas. Chalky portions of most cereals break more easily when handled and show reduced mechanical strength in crush tests. Certain storage pests are more likely to infest the broken areas.

Foreign Matter

Foreign matter diluting the prime product lowers its value and may have an impact on processing and handling. Animal origin (insects and their byproducts, rodent feces, etc.); vegetable origin (straw, weeds, seeds, dust, microorganisms/ toxins); and mineral origin (stones, mud, dust, glass, metals, oil products, pesticide residues) are some subcategories of foreign matter.

All three subclasses may contain components that make the grain unfit for human consumption. Micro-contamination with toxins, chemical pesticide residues, and the bacterial products of inadequate sanitation poses perhaps the biggest risk to human health.

Infected Grain that is Infested

Infestation lowers grain mass and, consequently, yield. Because invasive microorganisms can produce toxins under specific conditions that can cause acute or chronic illness, contamination has both direct and indirect effects on food hygiene.

Mixed Varieties

A mixture of grains indicates poor pre- and post-harvest management and supervision, such as issues with seed selection, lot segregation, treatment, and contamination. Grains that differ in size and other characteristics can impact processing potential. While preference for a specific variety may influence markets on a national or regional level, internationally traded grain is generally recognized by its type rather than its variety, such as yellow or white maize. However, exceptions exist, such as basmati rice, where factors like odor and aroma are important.

Moisture Content

Moisture content of grain is critical in post-harvest processing and is linked to many of the grain's induced characteristics. Water vapor will diffuse throughout the bulk of the grain, causing the moisture content to equalize. 'Hot spots' can develop at locations with increased respiration, which may be caused by sprouting, infestation, or microbial activity. Additionally, condensation can occur on cold grain or containers.

HOW DOES GRAIN QUALITY AFFECT STORAGE METHOD

The best way to understand how storage methods impact grain quality is to examine the properties of different grain types. Quality is influenced by so many factors that generalizing is difficult. For example, the quality of bran and germ is affected by the crop variety, growing conditions, and storage methods. Some grain varieties remain intact during storage, while others may lose more germ and increase bran content.

Proper storage, such as using silos, is a safe method for preserving grain, but it can affect germination rates and overall quality. Additionally, the moisture content of the grain plays a significant role; if the grain is too dry, germination becomes more difficult, while if it is too wet, spoilage becomes more likely.

DIFFERENCES BETWEEN GRAIN STORAGE OPTIONS

There are several key differences between various grain storage methods, and the best approach depends on several factors. First, issues related to age and quality can arise from problems with the storage containers themselves.

Two main concerns often arise when storing grains in containers:

- **Container Age:** This refers to how long the containers have been in use before storing grain. Since grains themselves do not age, the actual age of the containers is difficult to determine. However, using containers that are significantly older than the recommended specifications can lead to corrosion, which can potentially damage the grains.
- **Container Quality:** Not all containers are of the same quality. Over time, some containers may have coatings or sealants that have degraded, which could slightly affect the quality of the stored grains.

WHICH METHOD IS BEST FOR WHICH SITUATION

Different types of grains can be stored in various ways using bulk storage systems, but there are a few general guidelines that apply to most grains:

- **Whole Grains**: like wheat, corn, or oats, can be stored for up to a year. These grains are ideal for use as animal feed, as they don't require milling and can be fed directly to most livestock. Due to their high nutrient density, whole grains can be fed as is, though mixing them with other feed improves digestion efficiency.
- **Pasta-type Grains:** such as couscous, quinoa, or shredded wheat, should be stored in airtight containers. They can be kept for 6-12 months and are perfect as a quick and convenient alternative to traditional grains in cooking.
- **Cereal Grains:** have a shorter shelf life and should be stored in airtight containers for 1-3 months.

THE BEST METHODS FOR STORING GRAINS

- **Air-Tight and Light-Proof Storage Containers:** The optimal way to store grains is in silos that are both light-proof and kept in a dry, dark environment.
- **Keeping Grain in the Dark:** Storing grains in the dark is one of the most effective methods, as it minimizes exposure to sunlight. This reduces the risk of enzymatic breakdown and fermentation of starches in the grains.
- **Cool Temperatures and Moisture:** The ideal storage temperature for grains ranges from 12 to 18 degrees Celsius, with relative humidity between 65 and 80%. This temperature range helps minimize potential quality issues and slows the enzymatic breakdown of starches.

EVALUATION OF GRAIN QUALITY

With over 420 standard test methods, including at least 75 internationally applicable ones, it is clear that there is significant diversity in grain characteristics. This diversity is evident when considering the various uses for grain, such as paddy for producing milled rice, barley for malting, and durum wheat for pasta production.

Many assessments are specific to the commodity, product, or end user. Among the many properties, bulk density and foreign matter are commonly assessed for most grain types. Additionally, the impact of moisture content on other grain qualities, along with the economic implications, make its quantification essential.

Bulk Density

All equipment used to determine bulk density shares common features: (a) the sample material is allowed to fall from a standard container through a defined height into a standard volume weighing bucket, (b) the material's surface in the bucket is leveled without influencing its packing, and (c) the loaded bucket is weighed. However, variations in equipment design and procedural details can lead to different bulk density values, even when the same grain sample is used. Therefore, it is crucial to use only one type of apparatus for bulk density determination. ISO 7971 is the standard reference method, with results expressed as mass per hectolitre.

The bulk density of a grain sample can also be influenced by foreign matter and moisture content (mc). Consequently, it is common practice to remove as much foreign matter as possible by sieving the samples before determining bulk density, and to measure the moisture content of the sieved material.

Foreign Matter

Most grain quality standards specify that the screens in sieves used to assess foreign matter content should be made of perforated metal plates that meet the specifications set by national or international standards organizations. These specifications cover the metal plate's composition and thickness, the shape and size of the perforations, and their arrangement on the plate.

Operating Capacity of Sieves

The efficiency of a sieve is influenced by two key factors: the size of the apertures in the screen and the proportion of material that cannot pass through these apertures. Typically, a screen with smaller perforations has a lower percentage of sieving area compared to one with larger holes, which consequently reduces its sieving efficiency. Additionally, for a perforated metal screen with fixed specifications, the sieving efficiency significantly decreases if the volume of material that cannot pass through the apertures exceeds a certain limit. Table 3.9 provides the recommended volume of grain that should be placed on a screen to maintain optimal sieving efficiency.

Table 1.5 : Grain Sieves, 200 mm diameter, maximum loadings.

Nominal aperture mm	Recommended volume of load cm^3	Typical grain equivalent
8.0	500	300g Maize
4.0	350	250g Sorghum
2.0	200	150g Wheat
1.0	140	100g Millet

Moisture Content

The standard method (ISO 712) for determining moisture content in cereals is through mass loss in a hot-air oven, which can be time-consuming. As a result, several rapid methods have been developed for daily use, ranging from accelerated heating with an infrared source gravimetric test to near-instantaneous readouts with electronic moisture meters. Two common types of electronic moisture meters are resistance meters and capacitance meters.

It is advisable for grain-handling agencies to avoid using a mix of different types of meters, as this can lead to inconsistent results. Instead, the meter best suited to their specific needs should be selected. When choosing a moisture meter, the following factors should be taken into consideration:

- **Resolution:** This refers to the meter's ability to differentiate between moisture contents that are very close. Some meters have non-linear scales, resulting in poor resolution at both high and low readings.
- **Repeatability:** This indicates the meter's ability to provide consistent results when the same sample is measured multiple times. Capacitance meters may show more variation due to differences in grain packing, whereas resistance meters typically produce more reliable results from homogeneous samples.
- **Reliability:** This refers to the consistency of readings across different meters when measuring the same sample. Regular calibration is essential to maintain meter reliability.
- **Stability/Drift of Measurements:** This factor affects how often calibration is needed against the standard test method.
- **Range of Commodity:** Calibrations will be required for various commodities, and the meter must be capable of measuring all relevant products.
- **Range of MC:** Resistance meters typically cannot measure moisture content below 9%, while capacitance meters can measure as low as 1-2%.
- **Sample Size:** Larger samples generally provide more accurate readings and require fewer repetitions.
- **Sample Weighing:** Some capacitance meters require weighing the sample, adding an extra variable and cost.
- **Ambient Effect:** Meter readings can vary with temperature, and adjustments may be necessary. Some meters offer automatic temperature corrections.

MAINTAINING GRAIN QUALITY

Maintaining the quality of stored grain is crucial, not only for its immediate financial impact but also for long-term food security and stability. Here are the essential factors involved in preserving grain quality:

- **Effective Aeration Techniques:** Proper aeration plays a vital role in regulating the temperature and moisture content of the grain throughout the storage facility. Using fans to circulate air through the grain mass helps maintain consistency and prevents overheating, mold formation, and insect activity. It's important to ensure that the airflow is uniform and reaches all sections of the stored grain.
- **Routine Inspections:** Storing grain is not a one-time task; it requires continuous monitoring. Regular inspections are crucial for identifying potential problems such as hot spots, mold, or insect infestations at an early stage. Addressing these issues early on is not only more effective but often less costly.
- **Moisture Management:** Excess moisture is one of the primary threats to stored grain. It can lead to mold growth, which degrades the quality and can

cause severe losses. Employing grain dryers or aerators is effective in reducing moisture. Additionally, it's important to ensure that the storage environment remains dry and doesn't allow external moisture to penetrate.

- **Temperature Control:** High temperatures are ideal conditions for pests and reduce the shelf life of grain. Keeping the grain temperature consistently below 15°C can drastically lower the chances of pest and mold development, extending the grain's shelf life.

Ensuring the quality of stored grain requires a comprehensive, proactive strategy. By combining the right methods with timely intervention, grain can be preserved in optimal condition throughout its storage period.

INITIAL GRAIN CONDITIONS

To ensure that only high-quality grain is stored, the following steps are recommended:

- Clean the storage area thoroughly, removing any old grain, grass, weeds, and other debris.
- Clear any remnants of old grain from the storage and handling equipment.
- Properly adjust the sealing to minimize grain damage.
- Clean the grain before placing it into the bin, ideally using a rotating grain cleaner.
- Cool the grain to match the external ambient temperature before it is stored in the bin.

Insect and Mold Control

Pests and insects generally don't pose a problem for storage lasting less than 10 months to a year. However, if grain is to be stored for longer periods or if the container has had a pest issue previously, special precautions should be taken. These include:

- Spraying the interior of the storage container with protective insecticides 2 to 3 weeks prior to adding new grain.
- Treating the grain with approved insecticides as the container is filled.
- Applying a supported insecticide to the grain surface after the container is filled and the grain is leveled.

Environmental Conditions

Check the grain temperature and condition at least once every month. Use aeration as needed to maintain grain temperatures between 35° and 40°F. During winter, the aeration system should be operated only on a maintenance schedule to manage slight temperature increases. Inspect the grain temperature and condition regularly, and monitor the transition between cooling and warming zones as necessary.

Avoid operating the fan on warm days. When air temperatures exceed the grain temperature, fan operation may cause moisture to condense, potentially leading to freezing on the grain. Insect activity peaks during summer, so frequent monitoring is necessary to control infestations before they become significant problems.

2

Different Factors for Grain Deterioration During Storage

Agricultural professionals continuously confront challenges in preventing pest infestations and managing temperature and moisture levels to protect grains from decay. They recognize the critical importance of safeguarding these valuable resources and rely on quick, dependable solutions to tackle common grain storage issues.

Let's take a closer look at the challenges faced by growers, handlers, transporters, and processors in long-term grain storage, and the strategies they employ to overcome these obstacles.

ABIOTIC FACTORS

There are also abiotic factors, which are non-living elements, that influence the quality of stored grains. Factors such as air, humidity, and temperature play a significant role in grain storage. If these factors are imbalanced in terms of quantity or quality, they can have a detrimental effect on the stored grains.

SPACE CONSTRAINTS

As crop yields continue to rise, farmers face the challenge of finding enough storage space to accommodate the increased harvest. Often, last year's grain still fills storage bins when the new crop arrives, prompting the agricultural industry to seek innovative storage solutions.

The most straightforward solution to a shortage of storage space is to build additional bins. However, this option is not always feasible for smaller farms or processing facilities with limited budgets. As a result, many choose to repurpose existing barns or store surplus grain outdoors in piles. Unfortunately, this outdoor storage method comes with its own set of challenges, including faster spoilage and pest issues. To counter these problems, some facilities use temporary storage options such as grain bagging systems or outdoor storage tents. Mechanical ventilation systems are also employed to ensure proper aeration, reducing the risk of spoilage before the grain is moved to its final destination.

Another challenge faced by grain elevators, cooperatives, feed mills, pet food processors, and other facilities handling dry bulk agricultural materials is silo buildup. Over time, as material compacts against the walls of a storage silo, its effective capacity shrinks. Eventually, this can lead to narrow ratholes of flowing product surrounded by stuck material, causing bridges or clogs that halt production.

Many facilities may not realize how much more efficiently they could operate if their bins were restored to their full capacity. This is where powerful silo cleaning tools come in, allowing facilities to dislodge stuck material without the need for hazardous bin entry, thereby recovering valuable product and restoring storage capacity. Some facilities choose to invest in these practical tools for their personnel, while others opt to hire silo cleaning service crews to handle the task on an as-needed basis.

TEMPERATURE CONSIDERATIONS

High temperatures in grain storage can jeopardize the safety of stored grains and their by-products by causing elevated moisture levels, which promote fungal growth, pest infestations, spoilage, caking, and other forms of damage.

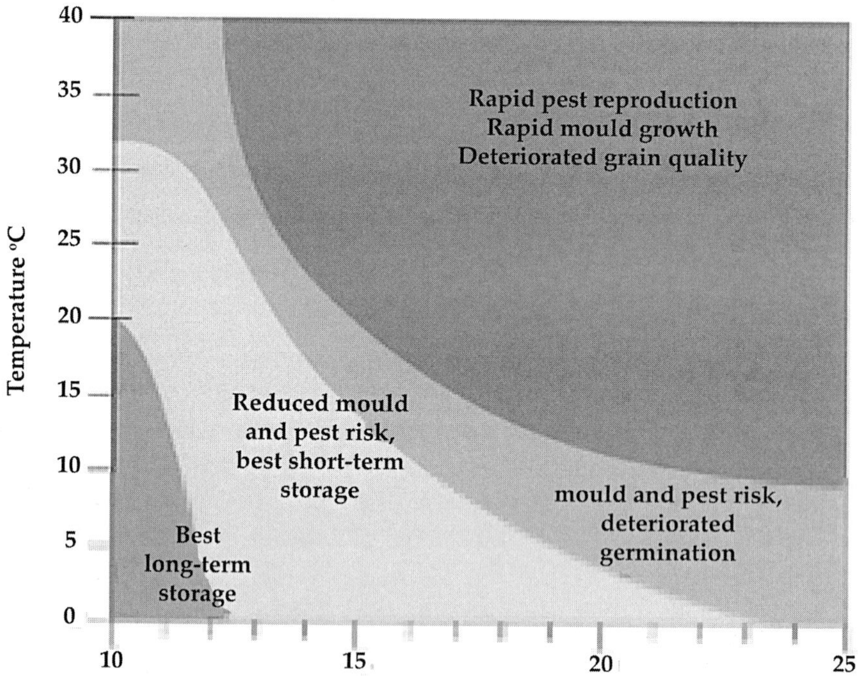

Figure 2.1 : Temperature effects on stored grains

Air vents, power roof exhausters, and various aeration systems are the primary methods used by grain handling facilities to regulate temperature within storage units. For many years, the standard practice was to maintain grain temperature within 10 to 15 degrees of the outside temperature. However, it is now understood that optimal storage temperatures depend on several factors, such as the time of year and the intended storage duration. Common target temperatures include 40°F or 50°F, which are ideal for preventing insect activity.

Regular checks are essential for stored agricultural products, particularly when ambient temperatures fluctuate, as this is when moisture migration is most likely. Signs of moisture movement include frost or condensation on the underside of bin roof panels, or the presence of crusted, wet, or foul-smelling grain.

Many facilities install temperature monitoring cables inside storage containers or opt for portable grain monitoring equipment, which is a cost-effective alternative. Continuous remote monitoring systems offer a convenient and effective way to safeguard valuable stored commodities.

Temperature control is crucial in warehouses and granaries, as it plays a significant role in minimizing losses during food storage. When stored at high temperatures, grain can sweat, which fosters the growth of molds and fungi, rendering the grain toxic. Aeration, or the natural flow of air, helps regulate temperature, prevent sweating, and maintain proper storage conditions. Ensuring the grain is properly cooled before storage is vital to preserving both its quality and quantity.

ISSUES WITH MOISTURE CONTENT

High temperatures in grain storage can jeopardize the safety of stored grains and their by-products by causing elevated moisture levels, which promote fungal growth, pest infestations, spoilage, caking, and other forms of damage.

Air vents, power roof exhausters, and various aeration systems are the primary methods used by grain handling facilities to regulate temperature within storage units. For many years, the standard practice was to maintain grain temperature within 10 to 15 degrees of the outside temperature. However, it is now understood that optimal storage temperatures depend on several factors, such as the time of year and the intended storage duration. Common target temperatures include 40°F or 50°F, which are ideal for preventing insect activity.

Regular checks are essential for stored agricultural products, particularly when ambient temperatures fluctuate, as this is when moisture migration is most likely. Signs of moisture movement include frost or condensation on the underside of bin roof panels, or the presence of crusted, wet, or foul-smelling grain.

Many facilities install temperature monitoring cables inside storage containers or opt for portable grain monitoring equipment, which is a cost-effective alternative. Continuous remote monitoring systems offer a convenient and effective way to safeguard valuable stored commodities.

Temperature control is crucial in warehouses and granaries, as it plays a significant role in minimizing losses during food storage. When stored at high temperatures, grain can sweat, which fosters the growth of molds and fungi, rendering the grain toxic. Aeration, or the natural flow of air, helps regulate temperature, prevent sweating, and maintain proper storage conditions. Ensuring the grain is properly cooled before storage is vital to preserving both its quality and quantity.

- **Corn:** 12–15%
- **Soybeans:** 11–14%
- **Wheat:** 11–14%

For long-term storage (lasting one year or more), the recommended values are as follows:

- **Corn**: 12%
- **Soybeans:** 11%
- **Wheat:** 12%

Several factors influence these numbers, and operators must adjust according to the specific characteristics and storage conditions of the product they are handling. Moisture is a key factor in determining the safety of stored grains. Warm and humid conditions create an ideal environment for various biotic elements such as insects, molds, fungi, and pests to thrive.

Excess moisture leads to grain discoloration and a reduction in quality. It is crucial to frequently monitor the moisture content in stored grains. Nowadays, electronic moisture measuring devices are available, reducing the need for manual checks.

Classification of Storage

Grain storage systems can be classified based on their operating principles. These include:

- **Physical Storage:** This method relies on physical principles and environmental control to prevent deterioration and ensure proper storage of grains. An example is cold storage.
- **Chemical Storage:** This approach involves using chemicals within the storage systems to control pest infestations and preserve the grains. Methyl bromide is a common example.
- **Biological Storage:** This method utilizes biological agents, such as microorganisms, to halt the activities that cause deterioration and extend the storage life of grains.

INITIAL CONDITION OF THE GRAIN

The storage quality of grain can be impacted even before it reaches the storage facility. Factors such as environmental conditions during the grain's growth and maturation, its level of maturity at harvest, harvesting methods, and handling practices at the farm all play a role in determining storage quality. Pest and fungal activity may begin in the field itself. High temperatures and humidity during the maturation of crops like corn are favorable for the formation of aflatoxins. Kernel damage resulting from combined harvesting and handling practices has been linked to the level of fungal infection during storage. Insects, such as the larger grain borer (*Prostephanus truncatus*) and the maize weevil (*Sitophilus zeamais*), which are capable of flying, infest the grain even while it's in the field.

Crops like maize and paddy are often harvested with moisture levels exceeding 15%, making them unsuitable for immediate storage; they need to be dried either artificially or by using sunlight. The condition of the newly harvested grain, including its moisture content, cleanliness, and specific weight, has a direct impact on its storage quality. Therefore, quality tests should be conducted before storing the grain. These tests may include determining moisture content, bulk density, conducting germination tests (such as glutamic acid decarboxylase activity or tetrazolium tests), measuring amylase activity (Hegberge test), checking free fatty acids, non-reducing sugar content, detecting insect infestations, and counting mold levels.

Fungal load can also be assessed using chitin and ergosterol assays. These tests help determine the grain's shelf life potential, making grain quality assessment an essential storage strategy. Among the key parameters, water activity or moisture content is the most significant because it influences the growth of spoilage organisms and the multiplication of insect pests. Moisture content is unlikely to be uniform throughout bulk storage, and it can vary between farms, truckloads, or grain lots, as well as between the inner and outer parts of bags or between the top and bottom layers of bulk storage. The highest moisture level in any part of the grain mass is more important practically than the average moisture content.

PHYSICAL FACTORS

Temperature plays a crucial role in grain storage because pest activity is temperature-dependent. The ideal temperatures for the growth and reproduction of insects, fungi, and mites in stored grain are 25–32°C, 30°C, and 25°C, respectively. When temperatures fall below 15°C for insects and mites, or 5°C for pests, their development slows down. Mold growth, however, only diminishes at temperatures of 0°C or lower. As the temperature increases, so does the respiration rate of both the grain and the pests, leading to increased enzymatic activity in the grain. This heightened biological activity accelerates the deterioration of grain quality at higher temperatures. An interconnected factor is the moisture or water activity of the grain.

Moisture content between 12–14% is ideal for insect development, while a water activity of 0.9 or higher promotes the growth of molds and other microorganisms. When the water activity is lower, pest activity is reduced. Temperature and moisture levels are key determinants of how long grain can be safely stored. During storage, the respiration of both the grain and pests leads to oxygen consumption and carbon dioxide release. The composition of the intergranular atmosphere influences the type of metabolism of both microorganisms and the grain, as well as enzymatic and non-enzymatic reactions. Oxygen and carbon dioxide levels also affect insect populations and mold growth.

The interaction of these physical and biological factors in the grain storage environment leads to changes in the grain's composition and functional properties. As grain lipids break down by lipases, free fatty acids and glycerol are formed, with the free fatty acid content serving as a sensitive indicator of storage deterioration. Carbohydrates in the grain also undergo changes, including a decrease in non-reducing sugars and total sugars. Significant losses in vitamin A activity in yellow corn and sorghum, reductions in water-soluble B vitamins, and increases in phosphorus compounds have been reported during storage. Additionally, functional properties, such as wheat's bread-making quality, rice's milling and cooking quality, barley's malting quality, and corn's starch separation, can also be affected. In some regions of Asia, aged rice is preferred, but storage has been shown to reduce the levels of 2-acetyl-1-pyrroline, a key aroma compound in aromatic rice. Moreover, decreases in free amino acids, non-reducing sugars, and albumin content have been observed in ordinary rice.

BIOTIC FACTORS AND TREATMENT EFFECTS

Biotic factors, including insects, mites, rodents, birds, and microorganisms, contribute to both quantitative and qualitative losses in stored grains. These factors are responsible for contamination, heating, and other storage issues, and in extreme cases, they can pose significant health risks. Biotic components refer to living organisms that cause damage to food crops, such as pests, weeds, insects, and rodents, which are common culprits in grain destruction. Around 100 species of insects negatively impact stored food grains, with crops like wheat, barley, rice, millet, pulses, nuts, maize, and dry fruits being particularly vulnerable to insect attacks from pests like rice moths, beetles, rice flour beetles, and Indian meal moths.

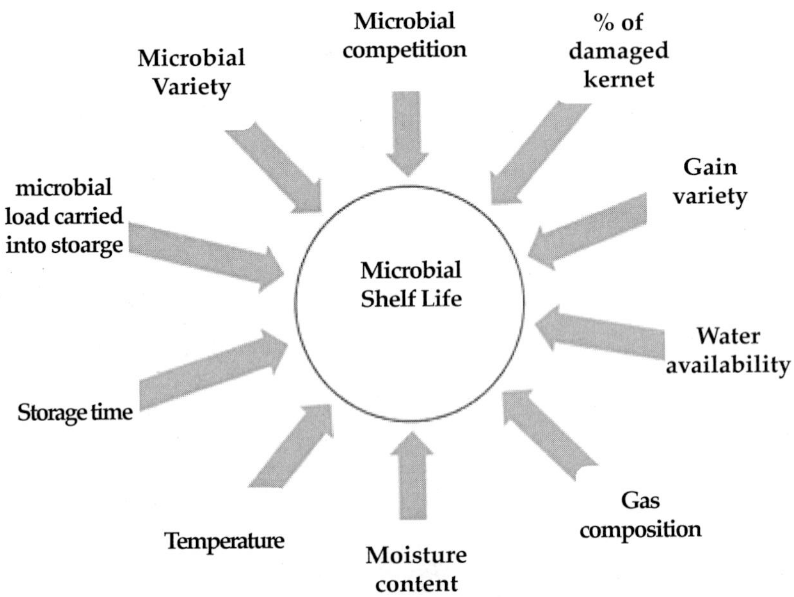

Figure: 2.2 Biotic factors affecting shelf life of grains

Fungi are also major threats to grain storage, as they can severely damage food quality. Certain fungi and molds, such as *Penicillium* and *Aspergillus*, not only harm the crops but also make them toxic by producing harmful toxins that are unsafe for consumption by humans or animals. These toxins cannot be eliminated through any purification process. Additionally, the excretory waste and other residues from insects, if left on the grain's surface, can be extremely harmful.

INFESTATIONS OF INSECTS

Inadequate temperature and moisture control can accelerate the lifecycle of various harmful insects and pests, leading to severe infestations. These pests can cause substantial damage to both crops and grain storage facilities, and once an infestation occurs, the consequences can be irreversible. Some common insects that can contaminate stored grains and agricultural products include:

- Grain weevils
- Grain borers
- Grain and flour moths
- Grain and flour mites
- Grain and flour beetles
- Dermestid, spider, and other beetles
- Mealworms
- Booklice or psocids
- Silverfish
- Cockroaches

By consistently monitoring and controlling temperature and humidity levels in storage containers, the likelihood of a pest infestation can be minimized. Regular temperature checks and product inspections are effective practices to detect and prevent insect infestations in grain bins, helping to address potential issues before they escalate.

Figure: 2.3 The Insects cause the Damage to Stored Grain

Insects typically cause the most damage to stored grain, although rodents can sometimes cause even greater harm in certain regions. Due to their rapid reproduction rate and short development cycle, insects can quickly escalate from a small infestation to a massive one, leading to significant damage. For instance, the multiplication factor of Tribolium is 70, which means that under ideal conditions, a single pair of Tribolium can produce the following:

- **After 1 month:** 2 × 70 = 140
- **After 2 months:** 140 × 70 = 9,800
- **After 3 months:** 9,800 × 70 = 686,000
- **After 4 months:** 686,000 × 70 = 48,020,000

However, after four months, resources for survival and further growth become limited, and overcrowding and competition for food slow down their development.

IDENTIFICATION OF PESTS

Insect species vary significantly in terms of their behavior, the extent of damage they cause, and their response to control methods. Identifying the insects present in storage and understanding their biology is crucial in addressing the following key questions:

Is it a Storage Pest?

Example : Several species of Bruchus are considered pests of pulses and may be brought into storage where they are unable to develop. In such cases, these insects do not pose a threat as storage pests.

Is it an Important Storage Pest?

Example: The Maize weevil (*Sitophilus zeamais*) is a significant storage pest affecting various commodities, particularly cereals in tropical and subtropical areas, while the Depressed flour beetle (*Palorus subdepressus*) typically plays a lesser role.

Is It An Insect Species Which Reveals Problems In Storage?

Example: The Black fungus beetle (*Alphitobius laevigatus*) is primarily found in moldy stock. Its presence indicates that the storage conditions are too moist.

What control Measures Should Be Performed?

Example: Bostrichidae, such as the Lesser grain borer *(Rhyzopertha dominica),* are most effectively controlled by pyrethroids, and less so by organophosphorous compounds.

There are various tools to assist in identifying insects:

- Identification keys, though not ideal for daily practical use in storage environments.
- Illustrations in the form of posters, leaflets, brochures, or books.
- Reference collections of storage pests for direct comparison with those found.

- Every storekeeper should have a hand magnifying glass with eight to twelvefold magnification.

CLASSIFICATION OF STORAGE PESTS

The largest group of storage pests is beetles (Coleoptera), followed by moths (Lepidoptera). Other pests, such as dust lice (Psocoptera), cause minimal damage to stored produce but may become a hygiene issue if present in large quantities.

In addition to insects, mites (Acarina), which belong to the order Arachnida, also occur as pests in grain and, particularly, in flour.

DEVELOPMENT OF INSECTS

Like other insects, beetles and moths undergo several developmental stages. The adult insects lay eggs, which hatch into larvae. These larvae cause the most damage due to their intense feeding on stored produce. The larvae go through multiple growth stages known as instars before pupating, with the adult emerging from the pupa. This cycle of development is called complete metamorphosis. The length of this cycle varies by species and is heavily influenced by external factors.

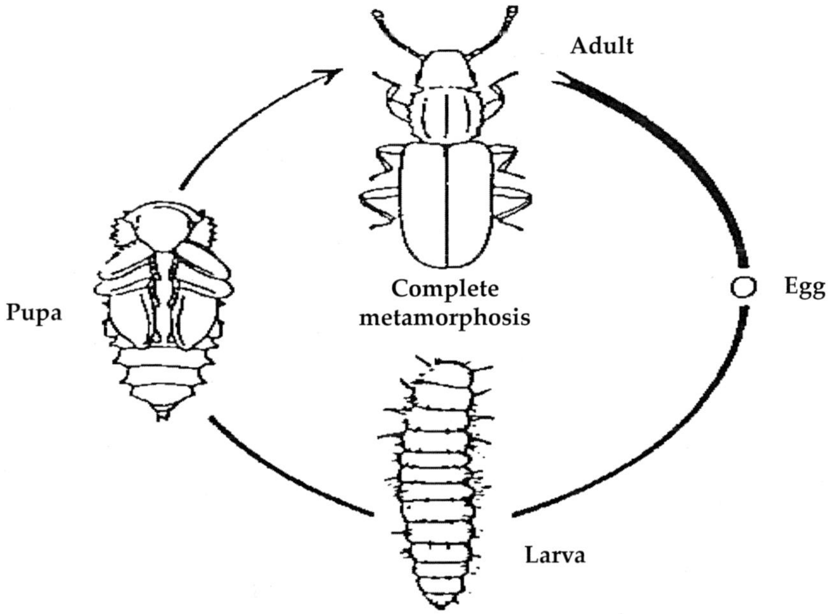

Figure: 2.4 Manual of the preuention of post-harvest grain losses.

Additionally, there are often species-specific differences in egg-laying locations (on or in the grain), larval development sites (inside or outside the grain), and pupation locations (inside or outside the grain).

MOLDS AND MYCOTOXINS

Mycotoxins are harmful chemicals produced by certain mold species. If ingested, these toxins can negatively affect the health of both humans and animals.

Unfortunately, the fungal microorganisms responsible for producing these dangerous substances often infest agricultural crops. Some of the primary groups of mycotoxins include:

- Aflatoxins
- Ochratoxin
- Citrinin
- Ergot
- Patulin
- Fusarium

Similar to insects that thrive in poorly stored grain, fungal infestations and the subsequent production of mycotoxins can contaminate crop yields, resulting in severe consequences. Therefore, controlling temperature and moisture levels, along with ensuring proper aeration, is crucial in preventing mycotoxin contamination during long-term grain storage.

INSECT PESTS OF GRAIN STORAGE

Biology of Storage Insects

Insects develop in a temperature range of 17°C to 35°C, with an optimal temperature of around 30°C and 75% relative humidity for most storage insects. These insects are more sensitive to high temperatures, with most being killed at temperatures above 40°C. While stored grain insects can survive freezing temperatures for several days, they are killed when exposed to 65°C for just a few minutes.

The number of significant storage insect species is relatively small, with about 30 species in total. Most of these insects have a short life cycle, lasting 4-6 weeks, and exhibit a broad preference for various types of produce. Some storage insects lay eggs directly on or near the produce, and once the larvae hatch, they enter the grain to develop. Others develop and pupate on or between the grains.

Adult storage insects vary in lifespan, with species like Bruchids and moths living up to 3 weeks and laying most of their eggs during the first week of adulthood. Other species, such as Sitophilus and Tribolium, can live from 6 to 12 months and lay eggs over an extended period. The development and reproduction of storage pests are influenced by several factors, including the type and condition of the produce, its moisture content, and climate. For instance, at 25°C and 70% relative humidity, the development of Ephestiacautella takes about 30 days on grains, 43 days on groundnuts, and 53 days on cocoa beans.

Storage pests are classified as primary or secondary. Primary pests, like Sitophilus and Ephestia species, can develop on undamaged produce, while secondary pests require produce that has already been damaged by other insects or mechanical processes. As a result, a specific succession of pests may occur in stored produce. In this section, the biology of some major insect pests will be briefly outlined.

The Rice Weevil ***(Sitophilusoryzae L.)***

Order Coleoptera, Family Curculionidae

The weevil is a small insect, brown to black in color, with two lighter reddish-brown patches on each elytra, and measures 2-3 mm in length. The female weevil lays approximately 200 eggs in the grain, where the larvae feed and pupate. The incubation period lasts about 36 days, while the larval and pupal stages take 20-30 days and 3-7 days, respectively. The entire life cycle of the weevil is completed within 30-40 days.

The Red Flour Beetle ***(Triboliumcastaneum Hbst.)***

Order Coleoptera, Family Tenebrionidae

The beetle is reddish-brown, flat, and measures between 2.3 to 4.4 mm in length. Its eyes are large and emarginate, with clavate, 11-segmented antennae. The eggs are white, oblong or pear-shaped. A female beetle lays between 15 and 72 eggs in rice, with the incubation period lasting 3-7 days. The larvae are whitish and worm-like, going through 6-7 instars. The larval period lasts 21-40 days, followed by a pupal period of 3-7 days. The complete life cycle takes between 26 and 48 days.

The Angoumois Grain Moth ***(Sitotrogacerealella Oliv.)***

Order Lepidoptera, Family Gelechiidae

The small moth, with a wingspan of approximately 1/2 inch, is identifiable by its pale brown color and the sharply pointed, elongated apices of its hind wings. A female lays between 30-78 white, oblong-shaped eggs, either singly or in small clusters. After hatching, the whitish larva bores into a single grain and completes its entire life cycle inside it, eventually pupating within. The incubation period lasts 4-6 days, while the larval stage takes 26-35 days. The pupal period spans 3-6 days, and the moth's lifespan ranges from 37 days.

The Almond Moth ***(Ephestiacautella W.)***

Order Lepidoptera, Family Phycitidae

The moth is greyish or pale grey, with two zigzag lines across its forewings, and has a wingspan of about 12-16 mm. A female lays up to 205 eggs in cracks or crevices on the grain, after which she dies shortly afterward. The eggs hatch within 3-6 days. The whitish larvae molt 3 times and complete their life cycle in 27-83 days.

The Rice Moth ***(Corcyra cephalonica Staint.)***

Order Lepidoptera, Family Galleriidae

A medium-sized moth with a wingspan of 20-25 mm, the forewings are uniformly pale brown, with slightly darkened veins. A female lays 44-364 whitish eggs, with an incubation period of 4-5 days. The larva is white to whitish-grey. The larval period lasts 28-41 days, with 5-7 larval instars. The pupal period is 6-13 days, and the moth can survive for 4-6 days.

THE COWPEA BEETLE AND SOUTHERN COWPEA BEETLE *(CALLOSOBRUCHUSCHINENSIS L. & C. MACULATUS F.)*

Order Coleoptera, Family Bruchidae

These two species resemble each other in appearance and occasionally feed on food together. The Cowpea beetle is slightly smaller than the Southern Cowpea beetle (2.0-3.5 mm vs. 3.0-4.5 mm). It is a small, oval brown beetle with or without black markings on the elytra. A female lays more than 10 yellowish eggs (with an average of 50 eggs) on grain, with an incubation period of 3-6 days. The larva feeds and pupates inside the grain before emerging as an adult. The larval and pupal periods last 18-20 and 3-7 days, respectively. The full life cycle is completed in 18-33 days, and the beetle can survive up to 12 days.

PRIMARY GRAIN PESTS

Lesser Grain Borer (*Rhyzopertha dominica*)

It is a dark brown cylindrical beetle, approximately 3mm long, with the head concealed by the thorax when viewed from above. Females lay up to 500 eggs, which are scattered loosely throughout the grain. The eggs hatch into curved white larvae with brown heads and three pairs of legs. The larvae burrow into slightly damaged grains and consume the starchy interior. After pupation, adults emerge from the grain, leaving behind large, irregular exit holes. The life cycle lasts between 3 to 6 weeks, depending on the temperature, and adults can live up to two months.

Figure: 2.5 Lesser grain borer *(Rhyzopertha Dominica)*

Adult lesser grain borers chew grain indiscriminately, causing damage that could lead to a secondary pest infestation. It can quickly spread from infected grain to start new infestations elsewhere because it is a powerful flyer.

Granary weevil (*Sitophilus granarius*)

It remains motionless for several minutes when disturbed. In holes chewed in cereal grains, an adult can lay up to 450 eggs on its own. The white, legless larvae that emerge from each egg consume the grain from the inside out. The adult chews its way out of the grain after the larva pupates inside. Weevil damage can be identified by the exit holes. In the summer, the life cycle lasts roughly a month, and adults can live for an additional eight months.

About 4 mm long and dark brown-black in color, the granary weevil has a distinctive rostrum (snout) that protrudes from its head. It has two club-like antennae and parts of its mouth that bite at the front of the rostrum.

Figure: 2.6 Granary weevil *(Sitophilus granarius)*

Rice weevil (*Sitophilus oryzae*)

Up to 450 eggs can be laid singly by an adult in holes made in cereal grains. After hatching, each egg becomes a white, legless larva that consumes the grain from the inside out. After pupating inside the grain, the adult larva chews its way out. A telltale sign of weevil damage is the exit holes. Adults may live for an additional eight months, and the life cycle takes roughly a month during the summer. The rice weevil is approximately 3 mm long, with a distinctive rostrum (snout) extending from its hThe distinctive rostrum, or nose, protrudes from the head of the rice weevil, which is approximately 3 mm long and has four orange-brown patches on its wing cases. It features two antennae that resemble clubs and parts of its mouth that bite at the front of the rostrum. The rice weevil has wings, unlike the granary weevil, and can occasionally fly.

Figure 2.7 : Rice weevil *(Sitophiluso ryzae)*

Angoumois Grain Moth (*Sitotrogacerealella*)

The angoumois moth has darker markings and is yellow-brown in color. It has a 12–20 mm wingspan. Up to 250 eggs are laid by females on or close to the surface of grain that has been stored. After hatching, the caterpillar burrows into grain kernels and stays there until it is fully grown. After that, it eats its way out of the grain, leaving the grain surface with distinctive exit pin holes.

No surface web forms, in contrast to the majority of other moth pests. In as little as five weeks, the life cycle could be finished. Infestations of Angoumois moths not only cause the grains to lose weight, but they also give the cereal an unpleasant taste and odor.

GRAIN STORAGE SECONDARY PESTS

Rust-Red Flour Beetle (*Tribolium castaneum*)

The rust-red flour beetle is commonly found on farms in WA. It is a reddish-brown beetle, approximately 3 mm in length, with the final three segments of its antennae significantly enlarged to form a club shape. Young adults are pale brown in color and darken as they mature. Females lay up to 1,000 eggs, which are loosely scattered throughout the infested grain. The cream-colored larvae, with biting mouthparts and three pairs of legs, hatch and remain free from the grain, feeding on cereal dust and damaged grains. A generation typically takes about one month to complete in summer, but longer in cold weather. Adults can live for up to a year, and they are winged, allowing them to fly.

Figure: 2.8 Rust - red flour beetle *(Tribolium castaneum)*

Confused Flour Beetle (*Tribolium confusum*)

The confused flour beetle closely resembles the rust-red flour beetle in both appearance and life history, with the main difference being that its antennae lack the distinct three-segmented club at the end. This beetle is more commonly found in flour mills than on farms, as it prefers more finely divided materials.

Figure: 2.9 Confused flour beetle *(Tribolium confusum)*

Saw-Toothed Grain Beetle (*Oryzaephilus surinamensis*)

The saw-toothed grain beetle is commonly found on WA farms. The adults are dark brown to black, characterized by six tooth-like projections on each side of the thorax. They lay up to 500 eggs, which are loosely distributed throughout the infested grain. Upon hatching, the larvae feed externally on grain dust and occasionally on wheat embryos. The mature larvae pupate within a silken cocoon. A full generation can develop in as little as three weeks, although the adults can live up to nine months. They often hide in cracks and crevices within buildings and machinery.

Figure 2.10 : Saw - toothed grain beetle *(Oryzaephilus surinamensis)*

Flat Grain Beetle (*Cryptolestes* spp.)

Flat grain beetles are small reddish-brown insects, measuring approximately 1.5mm in length, with long antennae and a flattened body. They lay their eggs throughout the stored grain, which develop into tiny larvae that have distinct tail horns, biting mouthparts, and three pairs of legs. The larvae feed on damaged grain and wheat embryos. Pupation occurs within a cocoon. A full life cycle takes about 4 to 5 weeks, and the adults can survive for up to one year.

Warehouse Moth (*Ephestia* spp.)

The warehouse moth is a dull grey moth with a wingspan of 10-12 mm. It typically infests only the surface of stored grain. Moths live for about two weeks, during which time they lay up to 200 eggs, which are loosely scattered over the grain surface. The larvae hatch from the eggs and move across the grain, leaving a trail of silk that may eventually form a thick mat on the surface of the infested grain. The mature larvae pupate in a silk cocoon either among the grain or on the walls of the building. The entire life cycle takes at least four weeks.

Figure 2.11 : Warehouse moth (Ephistia sp.)

Indian Meal Moth (*Plodia interpunctella*)

The adult Indian meal moth is gray, with distinctive brownish-red tips on the forewings. The female lays up to 200 eggs near the surface of the grain, moving slowly from grain to grain while spinning a silk thread. In cases of severe infestation, a surface web may form on the grain heap. The larvae attack the wheat germ and then pupate in a cocoon, often found in cracks and crevices of buildings. The insects quickly emerge as adult moths. Under warm conditions, a generation can complete in as little as four weeks.

Figure 2.12 : Indian meal moth (*Plodia interpunctella*)

Warehouse Beetle (*Trogoderma variable*)

The warehouse beetle was first identified in WA in 1989, and that infestation was eradicated. However, it has since spread to about a dozen locations in WA but has never reached damaging population levels. While the warehouse beetle is a pest of stored grain, its greater concern lies in its potential to mask an incursion of the khapra beetle, the world's worst pest of stored grain. Distinguishing between the warehouse beetle and the khapra beetle requires microscopic examination. The khapra beetle is not present in Australia, and its introduction would severely impact international trade.

Eggs are typically laid in crevices and beneath the surface of loose food, hatching in about a week. The larval stage is the only phase that damages grain. It is commonly found in seeds, groceries, and used sacks. The larvae are distinctly hairy and usually live for about five weeks but may enter a dormant phase (diapause) lasting more than two years. Larvae can molt up to ten times.

Figure 2.13 : Warehouse beetle *(Trogoderma variable)*

After pupation, adults emerge. They are less noticeable than the larvae and do not damage grain. Adults live for up to five weeks, during which females lay up to 80 eggs. Warehouse beetles cannot fly and are spread only through infested commodities and old sacks.

A notable feature of warehouse beetle infestations is the accumulation of shed larval skins. Hairs shed by larvae can cause asthma, skin, or gastric issues. It is impossible to distinguish T. variabile from several harmless native species without a microscope. Any hairy larvae found in grain stores should be sent to DPIRD for proper identification.

Figure 2.14 : Warehouse beetle larvae

RESISTANCE TO INSECTICIDE

Over time, many insect populations have developed resistance to insecticides due to their widespread use in pest control. In some instances, insects exposed to a single insecticide also develop resistance to other related compounds. Developing and testing new insecticides takes years and significant financial investment, making it crucial to prevent the spread of insecticide resistance. To achieve this, it is essential to use pesticides responsibly and maintain good farm hygiene. This involves thoroughly cleaning all machinery and storage facilities, from the harvest equipment to the port terminal, to prevent contamination and the spread of resistant pests.

STORAGE LOSS

Storage is just one component of the post-harvest system that food products move through from the field to the consumer. Losses that occur during this post-harvest phase are finite, and unlike crop losses during growth, they cannot be replenished by further plant development. The extent of storage losses is influenced by conditions during the pre-storage stages, such as harvesting, threshing, and drying. Likewise, losses after storage may also be impacted by how the storage process is managed.

The term "loss" has been widely debated and often confused with "damage." Loss refers to a measurable reduction in the foodstuff, whether in quantity or quality, and should not be mistaken for damage, which refers to visible signs of deterioration (e.g., broken grains) that may eventually lead to loss. While damage hinders usage, loss completely prevents it.

DIFFERENT TYPES OF LOSS

Loss can be evaluated in terms of either quantity or quality. Quantitative loss refers to the physical reduction in substance, which is observed as a decrease in weight or volume. This type of loss is the easiest to measure and assess in terms of value.

On the other hand, qualitative loss is more challenging to quantify and is often best identified by comparing the affected product to well-established standards. Quality loss can include aspects like nutritional loss and the degradation of seed quality.

Weight Loss

A reduction in weight is evident, but it doesn't always signify a loss. This could be attributed to a decrease in moisture content, which is accounted for with a shrinkage factor. Weight loss may occur due to the consumption of grains by insects, rodents, and birds, or from spillage caused by improper handling and pest activity. Changes in moisture levels could potentially increase weight, and in some cases, water produced by insect infestations might partially compensate for weight loss. In many situations, weight loss might go unnoticed as trade occurs by volume.

In commercial storage, weight is a critical factor and may lead to unethical practices, such as adulteration with water, stones, or soil to cover up the loss. Typically, minor moisture fluctuations are allowed for, and standard weight packages are employed.

Loss in Quality

Quality is typically evaluated and products are graded based on characteristics such as appearance, shape, size, and sometimes smell and flavor. However, foreign matter content and contaminants are significant factors that impact quality. Foreign matter can include insect fragments, grass, rodent hairs and droppings, weed seeds, plant parts, earth, stones, glass, and more. Contaminants that are harder to remove include pest excretions, oils, pesticides, pathogenic organisms from rodents, and toxins resulting from fungal infestations.

Chemical changes, such as those found in oilseeds, can also be crucial. For instance, groundnut infestation can lead to an increase in free fatty acids, causing rancidity in the oil, similar to what happens in maize meal.

Nutritional Loss

Food loss during storage results from both quantitative and qualitative losses. While weight loss (excluding moisture loss) can indicate food loss, the qualitative losses may be more significant due to selective feeding by pests. Rodents and moth larvae often target the germ of the grain, removing much of the protein and vitamin content, while weevils mainly consume the endosperm, reducing the carbohydrate content. Many pests also consume the bran of cereals, diminishing the vitamin content, such as thiamine.

Additionally, factors like moisture levels and fungal infections can further affect the vitamin content. For beans, particularly, protein loss is critical, as up to 25% of the dry matter may consist of crude protein.

Loss of Seed Viability

Seed germination loss is associated with several factors, including light, temperature, moisture, excessive respiration, and pest infestation. Seed grain is typically stored more carefully due to its higher value. Changes in environmental conditions or improper infestation control methods can lead to this loss. Insects that specifically target the germ of the seed cause a more significant reduction in germination compared to other pests.

Commercial Losses

Commercial losses can stem from a variety of factors, including the need for preventive or corrective measures, and the associated costs of equipment. These losses often arise from a lack of knowledge, experience, or management skills.

Monetary Loss

Weight loss and any reduction in product quality result in economic loss. Any corrective action necessary to make the commodity saleable also counts as an economic loss. Additional costs include losses in packaging, repacking due to rodent or handling damage, repairs, machinery downtime, and damage to storage facilities, all of which can be consequences of infestation.

Loss of Goodwill

While not directly measurable, loss of goodwill is significant, particularly as quality standards rise. An initially costly control measure that leads to customer retention or better customer relations is often more beneficial than no action, which may result in losing customers. This is especially critical in export markets where a reputation for high-quality goods significantly benefits a country's economy.

Loss Due to Legal Action

This category includes damages awarded for harm caused to human or animal health, expenses incurred by third parties from infestation linked to a particular shipment, and legal actions arising from contamination issues.

ASSESSMENT OF STORAGE LOSSES

Due to the challenges in accurately estimating the amount being lost, there has been a great deal of conjecture regarding the extent of losses that occur after harvest, especially during storage. It is widely acknowledged that estimating storage loss is challenging, especially when considering rural areas in developing nations, but it is necessary.

The degree of loss is significant, but not the only one; other economic, social, and political aspects must be taken into account when choosing strategies to lessen loss. Therefore, measuring storage loss necessitates a comprehensive, multidisciplinary approach. The following components should be included in any project that estimates losses:

1. **Clearly Defined Objectives:** Loss measurements should be conducted with the goal of reducing losses in mind. After implementing corrective actions, subsequent loss measurements using the same method will allow for evaluating the effectiveness of these measures.
2. **Reproducible Methods***:* The methods employed should be well-documented so they can be replicated by others for similar assessments in the future. Potential sources of error should be identified and recorded as they arise. The techniques used should be simple, requiring minimal and robust equipment, especially if the method is applied in the field with untrained personnel.
3. **Representativeness:** This pertains to selecting the area to be studied, choosing stores within the area, and sampling those stores. Various factors, such as climate, traditions, and extension influence, can affect the "typical" nature of the area, so a balance between the ideal and the practical must be struck. Factors like climate and whether the farm is subsistence or commercial should guide the sampling approach. Stratified random sampling is often used, though other methods may be suitable depending on the situation, which can be found in sampling textbooks. Caution must be exercised when interpreting data to avoid biases or preconceived notions; it's crucial to acknowledge the inherent limitations of such data.

BASIC FRAMEWORK

All loss estimations should follow a structured process: conducting a survey, employing a sampling method, and analyzing the sample to determine the loss.

Survey

The survey allows for an in-depth examination of the area being investigated, identifying factors that influence storage. This ensures that the selection of storage sites reflects these variables. During this initial phase, field testing of questionnaires or sampling techniques should be done to address any practical challenges. Criteria for determining loss should be established, and once storage sites are selected, any background data needed for loss assessment should be gathered.

Sampling

Sampling involves taking grain samples from the storage. If regular visits are planned for monitoring, a large sample should be collected when the grain is first stored, serving as baseline data for future comparisons. Sampling once a month, along with records of grain consumption and disposal, will help accurately estimate losses throughout the storage period.

If frequent sampling isn't possible, at least three samples should be taken: one at the time of storage, one midway through the period, and one about a month before the store is emptied. These samples should be representative of the entire store to understand the infestation pattern. The method of grain removal and consumption pattern should also be noted.

Sampling throughout the store can alter the infestation pattern, so it shouldn't be done if monthly sampling is planned. However, it's necessary if only a few samples will be taken.

Analysis of the Sample

Testing for seed grain loss typically involves a simple germination test using sub-samples. Quality loss analysis is best conducted using a local grading system to assess the extent of deterioration, considering factors like defective and damaged grains, and foreign matter.

Nutritional loss requires specific analysis for the targeted substance, comparing its concentration at storage to the current level. Weight-to-weight comparisons may be misleading since insect-damaged grains might have initially weighed more. A volume-to-volume comparison or using a fixed number of grains taken randomly is a more accurate method. Protein measurement using nitrogen determination might be prone to error, as insects contain non-protein nitrogen. Additionally, when grains are cooked whole, insect-damaged grains might lose more nutrients than intact grains.

Weight loss in samples removed for analysis can be estimated in several ways, but before these estimates, dust and insects should be sieved off, as they are generally removed under field conditions before consumption. The proportion of dust and insects can contribute to the weight and quality loss. Identifying the insects present can help in selecting control measures and understanding the significance of each species.

There are three primary methods to measure weight losses caused by insects:

1. **Volumetric:** Also known as bushel weight or bulk density methods, these techniques rely on obtaining an accurate standard volume of grain using basic apparatus. This equipment typically uses fixed drop heights into a standardized volume measure, making it a straightforward process for assessing weight loss by volume.
2. **Gravimetric:** This method focuses purely on weighing and counting, requiring smaller samples compared to volumetric techniques. A maximum of about 1,000 grains is sufficient, making it an efficient and quick field method for assessing weight loss. It is widely used for its practicality and speed in real-world settings.
3. **Indirect:** Indirect methods rely on a factor related to weight loss that is easily measurable and can then be converted into an estimate of loss using a graph or formula. A laboratory experiment is typically conducted first to determine the relationship between the factor and weight loss. Once established, the results are applied to field samples of the same variety affected by the same pest. The most commonly used factor is the percentage of damaged grain, as it is simple to measure. However, this approach can become complicated in larger grains, as multiple infestations may lead to several emergence holes per grain, causing variations in weight loss. This issue can be mitigated by using the number of emergence holes per 100 grains instead of measuring the percentage of damaged grain.

Losses Caused by Fungi

A significant portion of the grain rejected by farmers is often discarded due to mould, and the presence of infected grain leads to a decrease in quality grading. To estimate the impact of fungal infection on grain loss, it is necessary to separate mould damage from other types of damage during the analysis process. This differentiation allows for a clearer understanding of the specific losses attributed to fungal contamination.

Losses Brought on by Pests Vertebrates

Vertebrates, including rodents and birds, often remove entire grains from storage, and the losses attributed to them are typically calculated by subtraction. Any remaining unaccounted-for losses are usually attributed to these pests. Efforts have been made to estimate these losses through population censuses and feeding trials.

However, both rodents and birds consume stored food as part of their overall diet, which can result in overestimating the actual consumption of stored grain during feeding trials.

USES OF DIFFERENT TYPES OF SIVES IN GRAIN STORAGE

HAND-HELD SIEVES

Hand-held sieves are frequently used to assess the foreign matter content in small grain samples. Sieves with round frames, typically measuring 300 to 310 mm in diameter, are most commonly preferred, although square-framed sieves with sides of 300 to 310 mm can also be used. Each sieve should be paired with a bottom pan (receiver) to collect the material that passes through the screen, as well as a lid to prevent spillage during the sieving process.

For results to be comparable, uniformity in the manufacture of hand-held sieves is essential. It is crucial to ensure that sieves are made by a factory whose products are certified by an approved standards organization.

To maintain consistent results, sieves should be used in a uniform manner. First, the sieve should be held level with both hands directly in front of the body, with elbows tucked into the waist. Then, using a steady motion, the sieve should be moved approximately 25 cm to the left and back through the center, smoothly moved 25 cm to the right, and returned to the center position. This motion should be repeated exactly 30 times, taking about 30 seconds to complete. Movements should avoid any forward and backward or up and down motions. A final gentle tap of the sieve will help clear any material stuck in the perforations before removing the bottom pan. When sieves with slotted screens are used, it's crucial to ensure that the long sides of the slots are aligned parallel to the direction of the sieve's movement.

SACK SIEVES

The foreign matter content in grain is more precisely measured when whole sacks of grain are screened, though this method is obviously more time-consuming than hand-sieving smaller samples.

A sack sieve should have two key features: a hopper to gradually feed the grain onto the screen and a screen that moves during the sieving process. The slope of the moving screen should ensure that the grain continuously moves towards the discharge end. Lateral movement of the screen, as seen in rotary-type sieves, is more effective at separating foreign matter compared to end-to-end movement of other mechanical sieves.

Therefore, it is advisable to check samples of the grain against standard sieves with varying specifications before purchasing a quantity of sieves for grain quality assessment.

CARE AND MAINTENANCE

Standard quality sieves are precision instruments that require careful handling and maintenance to ensure their accuracy. They should always be kept clean and dry. After use, a proper sieve brush should be employed to remove dust and other materials. Never push debris through the perforations from the top surface, as this can distort the holes and compromise the sieve's accuracy. Instead, the sieve should be turned upside down and tapped gently, or material should be pushed out of blocked perforations using a fingertip.

Newly manufactured sieves are typically coated with a thin layer of oil or wax, which should be removed with warm water and detergent before they are used. If a sieve is not going to be used for an extended period, it should be thoroughly cleaned, coated with oil, and stored properly to prevent deterioration. Prior to reuse, the sieve must be cleaned again.

Despite careful handling, sieves will experience wear and tear over time. They should be periodically checked for accuracy by comparing them with standard sieves. This is generally the responsibility of a national standards organization or central laboratory that oversees grain quality matters.

CONTROLLING PEST AND DISEASE IN GRAIN STORAGE

Grain storage is susceptible to various pests that, if left uncontrolled, can cause significant damage to the stored produce. Common pests include weevils, beetles, and moths. Effective management strategies for pest control include:

- **Early Identification of Pests:** Conducting regular inspections is essential for detecting any early signs of pest infestation. Physical barriers, such as insect screens, can be used to prevent pests from entering storage areas.
- **Mold and Fungus Control:** Maintaining low moisture levels is the best defense against mold and fungal growth. Utilizing desiccants or grain dryers helps regulate moisture content, ensuring that the grains remain dry and less prone to fungal contamination.
- **Consistent Fumigation:** Regular fumigation is key to controlling pest populations. Whether using natural repellents or chemical treatments, timely fumigation ensures that pests are eliminated, helping to preserve the quality of the stored grain.

SAFETY MEASURES FOR STORING GRAIN

Ensuring the safe handling of grain is crucial not only for maintaining its quality but also for protecting the well-being of those working within and around storage facilities.

- **Grain Dust Explosion Prevention:** Grain dust is highly combustible, and the risk of explosion can be minimized by regularly cleaning storage areas and maintaining equipment properly to reduce dust accumulation.
- **Adequate Ventilation:** Proper ventilation is essential for dispersing gases from fumigation or natural grain respiration, while also lowering humidity levels, which helps prevent mold growth.
- **Safe Handling and Transport:** Using equipment such as conveyors and elevators facilitates the safe movement of grain within storage facilities. It's important that workers are trained in proper handling techniques to avoid accidents.

By implementing a systematic pest management plan and prioritizing safety measures, grain storage can be both efficient and safe for all involved.

3

Warehouse Equipment and Different Storage Structures

Warehousing is a critical national strategy for conserving food grains. The proper storage and maintenance of notified commodities, primarily food grains, alongside safeguarding them from adverse weather, rodents, and natural decay, are vital for fostering the growth and development of the agricultural sector.

Post-harvest losses contribute to approximately 10% of total food grains, primarily due to improper storage methods, insects, rodents, microorganisms, and birds. The Punjab State Warehousing Corporation (PSWC) takes on the responsibility of storing, handling, and warehousing notified commodities, including agricultural produce, industrial raw materials, finished goods, and various perishable and hygroscopic items. PSWC provides scientifically designed warehouses that protect both the quality and quantity of stored goods, aided by trained personnel.

At PSWC warehouses, stored products are safeguarded from rodents, pests, and moisture, ensuring their preservation. The provision of scientifically managed storage facilities for food grains, from procurement to distribution, is a vital function carried out by PSWC. PSWC has made significant strides in creating warehousing facilities throughout the state, constructing numerous warehouses in key rural and urban areas.

Rail-side warehousing facilities have also been established, offering cost-effective and efficient storage solutions under a unified approach. Additionally, PSWC helps prevent distress sales, enabling producers to hold their products until favorable market conditions arise, thereby securing the best possible value for their goods.

Horizontal sheds are commonly used to offer low-cost, large-volume storage, and the Food Corporation of India (FCI) has also built very large sheds for storing grains and other products. These sheds typically feature steel or corrugated sheet construction with flat concrete floors, while grain loads are supported by girts and robust vertical buttresses designed to withstand bending. Roofs are supported by a network of purlins and rafters. For larger sheds with a capacity of 50,000-60,000 tonnes, suspended drag-chain conveyors are used for efficient operation.

Modern storage bins offer several advantages, including:

- Low cost, ease of handling, and enhanced quality control.
- Minimal space requirements.
- Savings on packaging costs.
- Access to modern automation and mechanization technologies for faster handling.
- Protection from birds, rodents, and environmental factors.

PREVENTIVE MEASURES FOR THE LOSS OF GRAINS IN STORAGE

BELOW ARE THE PREVENTIVE MEASURES FOR THE LOTS OF GRAINS IN STORAGE

- **Heating:** Pests can be eradicated by exposing them to temperatures of 60°C for over 10 minutes or 50°C for 2 hours.
- **Radiation:** Beta or gamma rays are utilized to cause physical damage, reduce reproductive ability, and ultimately eliminate pests. Gamma rays have deeper penetration power, although they are more expensive compared to beta rays.
- **Aeration:** This involves circulating air through processed grain at low flow rates to enhance and preserve its quality. It cools the grain, slows insect activity, prevents the development of odors, reduces moisture build-up, and regulates temperature and relative humidity (RH). Combining fumigation with aeration proves to be an effective method.
- **Fumigation:** Fumigation involves applying chemical agents through spraying or dusting. The goal is to control pests by exposing the grains to lethal concentrations of a toxic gas for a sufficient duration. The three main types of fumigants are:
- **Ethylene Bromide:** A liquid fumigant with a higher boiling point.
- **Methyl Bromide:** A gaseous fumigant with a lower boiling point, used for quick pest elimination and requiring subsequent aeration.
- **Phosphine Tablets:** Solid fumigants that react with atmospheric moisture to produce hydrogen phosphide gas, which is lethal to pests and microorganisms.

EQUIPMENT FOR WAREHOUSE MATERIAL HANDLING: RAISING, MOVING, AND STORING

Pallet Jacks

Pallet jacks facilitate the transportation of bulky items that are stacked on pallets. Under the pallet, they have two twin forks that slide. With a manual pallet jack, the pallet is raised by a hydraulic action that requires the user to pump force up and down the handle.

Figure: 3.1 Pallet jacks

Hand Trucks

Similar to pallet jacks, hand trucks facilitate the movement of bulky items throughout the warehouse. A hand truck's handles, toe plate, and frame are all made of metal. The operator can wheel an object to a different location in the warehouse by sliding the toe plate underneath it and tilting the handles back. Hand trucks don't use hydraulic action and are better suited to moving smaller items than pallet jacks.

Figure 3.2 Hand trucks

Order Picker Forklift

Operators can pick and move materials needed to finish an order with the aid of an order picker forklift. The operator is raised to the same level as the inventory by the forklift. Compared to using manual equipment like a ladder, which must be moved constantly and can easily shift on the operator, this makes order picking safer and more efficient.

Side loader Forklift

A forklift made specifically for use in confined areas, like narrow aisles, is called a side loader. It is typically less agile than conventional forklifts, though. The operator either stands or sits inside the machine, depending on how it is designed. Side loaders run on electricity, diesel, or propane and can be used indoors or outdoors.

Figure 3.3 : Side loader forklift

Automated Guided Vehicles

An automated guided vehicle (AGV) is a type of warehouse material handling equipment designed to operate autonomously within a warehouse. AGVs are used to carry out tasks typically performed by forklifts, conveyor systems, or even manual carts. There are various types of AGVs, including:

- **Automated Guided Carts (AGCs):** The simplest form of AGVs, with basic features, used to transport materials in applications like cross-docking, sorting, and storage.
- **Forklift AGVs:** These AGVs function like human-operated forklifts but do not require an operator.
- **Towing AGVs:** Also called tugger AGVs, these are used to pull one or more load-carrying vehicles behind them, similar to a train. They are typically employed to transport heavy loads over long distances.

- **Unit Load Handlers:** These AGVs are designed to carry single units or objects, such as pallets.
- **Heavy Burden Carriers:** Used in tasks involving large assembly or plate transport, some of these AGVs are equipped with self-loading capabilities.
- **Autonomous Mobile Robots (AMRs):** Considered the most advanced type of AGV, AMRs often come with intelligent navigation systems that enable them to dynamically navigate around a warehouse and obstacles.

Figure 3.4 : Automated guided vehicles

Cranes

Cranes are widely used in warehouses for material handling, with various types chosen based on specific needs. Common crane types include stacker bridge cranes, gantry cranes, and jib cranes.

- **Bridge Cranes:** Are used to move large and heavy objects. These cranes span a gap between two runway tracks, with the hoist moving along the bridge. This design allows the hoist to access and reach objects along three axes of movement.
- **Jib Cranes:** Are more stationary than bridge cranes. These have a hoist mounted on a jib or boom attached to a stationary structure, like a wall. If the boom is fixed, the crane lacks lateral rotation capability.
- **Gantry Cranes:** Operate by floating back and forth along a gantry, which is an overhead frame structure that supports the equipment. Gantry cranes offer more flexibility than bridge cranes since they are supported by their own frames and are typically mounted on wheels or a track system.

Figure: 3.5 Cranes in a warehouse

Platform Trucks

A platform truck consists of a flat metal sheet with wheels at the bottom and a handle at one end, allowing the operator to push or pull the truck. Some platform trucks are capable of carrying more than 2,500 lbs. While operating the truck, it's important for the operator to push the truck itself rather than the merchandise resting on it. Pushing the merchandise directly can cause it to fall off, potentially leading to broken items or accidents.

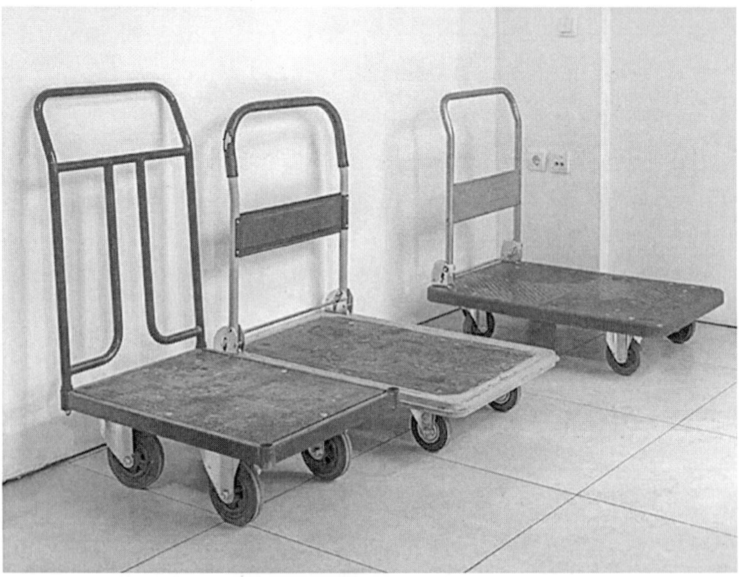

Figure: 3.6 Platform trucks

Conveyor Belts

A conveyor belt is a belt that is powered by a motor and is a component of a larger conveyor system. Items are loaded onto the belt by operators. Items are moved to their final destination in the conveyor system by the rotating belt.

Figure: 3.7 Conveyor belts

Reclaimers

A conveyor system also includes a reclaimer. At one end of the conveyor system is a machine that has a rotating scoop. Small, loose objects are collected by the reclaimer and put back on the belt to continue traveling.

Figure: 3.8 Reclaimers

Hoppers

Hoppers are used to handle small, loose objects and have a funnel-like appearance. The hopper's top is filled with items. They sink to the bottom due to gravity. Hoppers are frequently used for recycling and waste disposal. Certain hoppers have technology that enables them to empty loads automatically.

Figure: 3.9 Hoppers

Bucket Elevators

Grain legs, also known as bucket elevators, are used to move small objects vertically. Similar to a miniature ski lift, material is collected and transported to the top by means of small buckets that are fastened to a belt. The buckets may need to be raised by hand cranking the elevator or by using a motor.

Figure: 3.10 Bucket elevators

Silos

Grain and silage are stored and shielded from the weather in agricultural settings using silos. In other contexts, they are employed to store goods like food items, wood, and coal. Silos aid in shielding these priceless resources from the weather.

Figure : 3.11 Silos

WAREHOUSE MATERIAL HANDLING EQUIPMENT: SAFETY AND FALL PROTECTION

Personal Protective Equipment (PPE)

Warehouse environments can be highly hazardous due to the constant movement of trucks and people, the use of various equipment, and the presence of potentially dangerous elements like heat, electricity, and chemicals. The proper use of personal protective equipment (PPE) plays a crucial role in safeguarding workers and minimizing the risk of severe injuries. PPE encompasses a wide range of protective gear, including hard hats, masks, gloves, and protective clothing, all designed to protect workers from these potential hazards.

Figure: 3.12 Personal Protective

Industrial and Portable Stairs

Prefabricated industrial stairs that meet Safety standards are essential for ensuring worker safety. These stairs are equipped with important features such as handrails, guardrails, and slip-resistant decking, all of which help minimize the risk of falls and injuries, promoting a safer working environment.

Figure: 3.13 Industrial and portable stairs

Handrails

A portable aluminum safety railing system is an effective way to protect employees from falls when working at elevated heights. Additionally, they should be designed with non-penetrating features for easy installation and removal, ensuring flexibility and safety.

Figure: 3.14 Handrails

GRAIN HANDLING AND CONVEYING REQUIREMENTS IN INDIA

India's agriculture and food supply chain depend on effective grain handling and conveying systems to move grains from farms to facilities for distribution, processing, and storage in a safe and effective manner. An efficient grain handling infrastructure is essential to reducing post-harvest losses, preserving quality, and satisfying domestic and export demands because India is one of the world's top producers of rice, wheat, maize, and pulses.

REQUIREMENTS FOR GRAIN HANDLING AND CONVEYING

1. Effective systems for handling: Mechanized systems are necessary for grain handling in India in order to decrease manual labor, increase productivity, and minimize losses. Grain can move smoothly between stages with the help of common handling systems like bucket elevators, belt conveyors, pneumatic conveyors, and screw conveyors. Grain handling automation lowers damage, spills, and contamination.
2. Appropriate transportation and storage: Grain must be stored correctly after harvest to avoid spoiling, pest infestation, and moisture absorption. To maintain grain quality, India needs godowns, temperature-controlled storage facilities, and contemporary silos. In order to maintain hygienic standards and guarantee safe transportation from farms to storage facilities, processing mills, and retail markets, conveying systems must be designed.
3. Observance of food safety rules to ensure food safety and hygiene: The food corporation of India (FCI) and other regulatory agencies require that grain handling and transportation adhere to FSSAI standards. To preserve grain purity and avoid contamination, proper conveyor design and material selection are essential (for example, stainless steel for food-grade applications).
4. Reducing losses after harvest: Due to ineffective handling and inadequate storage facilities, India experiences significant post-harvest losses. Grain vacuum conveyors and automated bagging systems are examples of mechanized handling systems that can be implemented to drastically cut waste and increase operational effectiveness.
5. Cost-effectiveness and energy efficiency: Grain conveying systems should be economical and energy-efficient due to rising energy prices. In order to lower operating costs, contemporary solutions like gravity-fed systems and solar-powered conveyors are becoming more popular. India needs to implement contemporary grain handling and conveying systems to guarantee food security, lower losses, and boost productivity.

India's agricultural infrastructure will be strengthened and the overall effectiveness of the grain supply chain will be increased by investing in mechanization, automation, and adherence to safety regulations.

STORAGE STRUCTURES

Storage plays a vital role in preserving grain quality after harvest by achieving two key objectives:

- **Ensuring a consistent supply of grain:** Proper storage helps maintain an uninterrupted grain supply throughout the year, allowing for steady availability.
- **Capitalizing on higher prices:** Storing grain allows farmers and sellers to wait for market conditions to improve, potentially selling at higher prices later on.

TWO METHODS OF GRAIN STORAGE

There are two primary methods of grain storage:

1. Bag storage
2. Loose bulk storage

The choice between these methods depends on several local factors, including:

- The type of grain being stored
- The intended duration of storage
- The value of the grain
- Climatic conditions
- The available transport system
- The cost and availability of labor
- The cost and availability of storage bags
- The presence of rodents and specific insect species

Table 3.1 : Difference between Bag and Bulk Storages

Bag Storage	Bulk Storage
Flexibility of storage	Inflexible storage
Partly mechanical	Mechanical
Slow handling	Rapid handling
Considerable spillage	Little spillage
Low capital cost	High capital cost
High operating cost	Low operating cost
High rodent loss potential	Low rodent loss potential
Reinfestation occurs	Little protection against reinfestation

TRADITIONAL STORAGE STRUCTURES

BUKKHARI TYPE

- The structure is cylindrical in shape
- Made from mud or a combination of mud and split bamboo

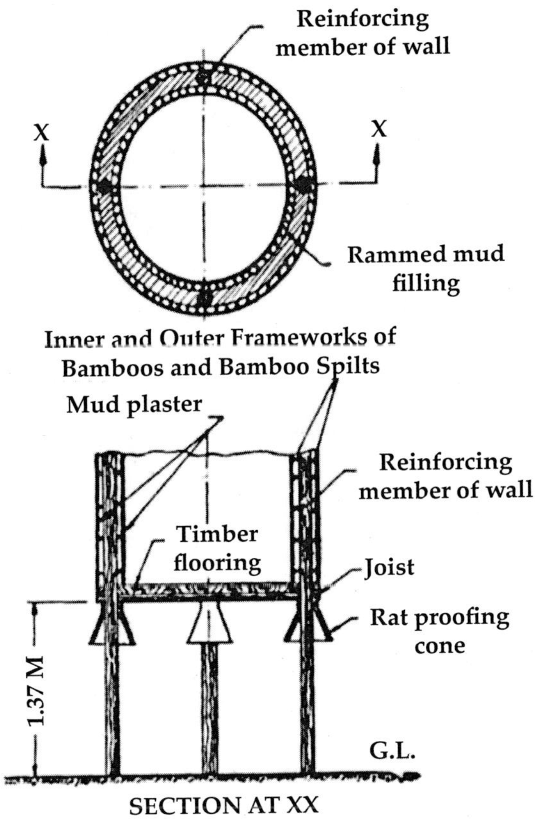

Figure: 3.15 Bukhari type grain storage structure

- Raised above the ground on a wooden or masonry platform
- Floor
- Walls
- Roof
- Improved type – same structure
- Rat proofing cones
- Suitable for storing grains like wheat, gram, paddy, maize, and sorghum
- Capacity–3.5–18 t

KOTHAR TYPE

- Store –sorghum, paddy, maize, wheat
- Capacity: 9-35 t
- Structure: box
- Improved Kothar made from 5 cm thick wooden planks and beams
- No gap between the planks

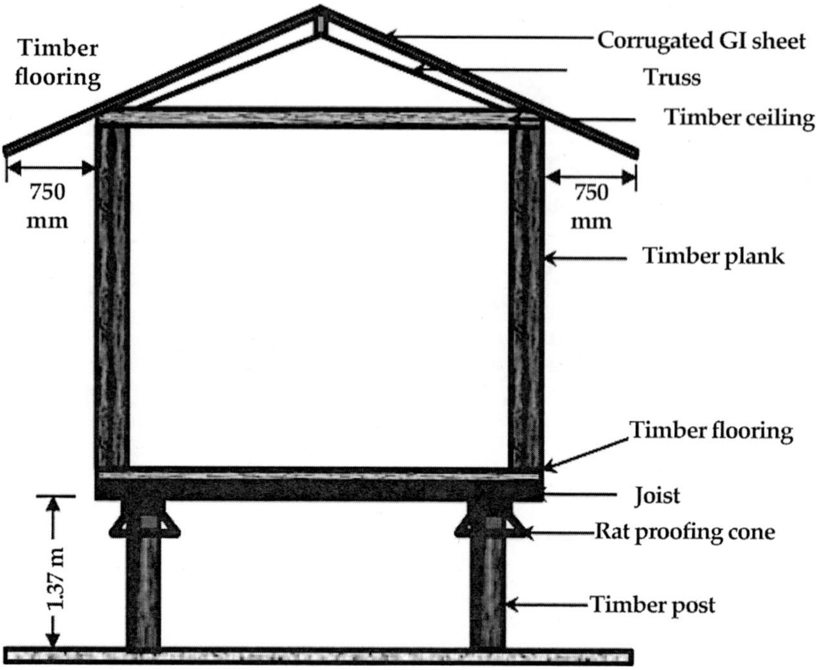

Figure: 3.16 Kothar type grain storage structure - Vertical Section

MORAI TYPE

- **Grains:** Paddy, maize, sorghum
- **Capacity:** 3.5 – 18 t
- **Shape:** Inverted truncated cone

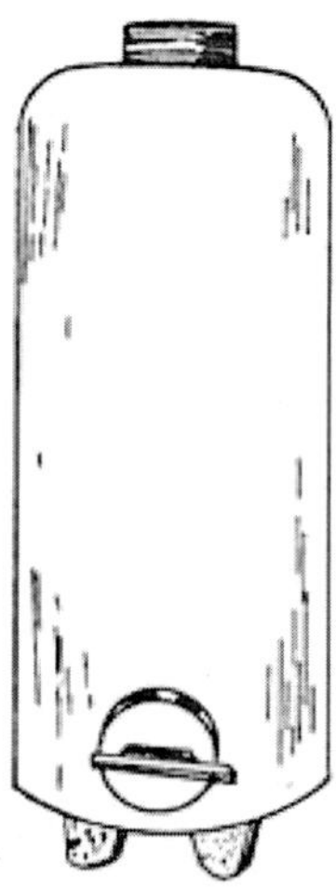

Figure: 3.17 Morai type

- Bagged storage system
- Silo storage system
- Air tight storage system
- Aerated storage system
- Low temperature storage system
- Controlled atmosphere storage system
- Damp grain storage system with chemicals

BAGGED STORAGE SYSTEM

- Storage capacity ranges from 25 tones
- Length is typically about twice the width or more

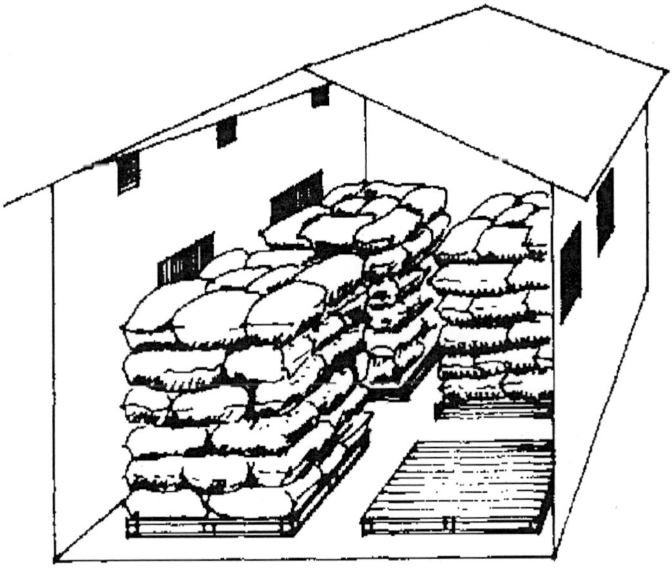

Figure: 3.18 Storage system of bagged

- The entire structure should be moisture-proof
- Large size doors of 2.4 × 2.4 m and top ventilators
- Each door is fitted with a light overhanging hood
- Should be equipped with ventilators that have wire netting and shutters

DAMP PROOF FLOOR

- A 15 cm thick layer of gravel and sand, well-rammed at the bottom
- A 12.5 cm thick layer of stone or brick ballast, or a double layer of brick
- A 10 cm thick layer of cement concrete (1:4:8)
- A 1.25 cm thick layer of bitumen mixed with sand
- A 4 cm thick layer of cement concrete (1:2:4)

- A 2.5 cm thick layer of cement concrete (1:1 1/2: 3)

The walls are constructed from bricks or stone, laid in either lime mortar (1:2) or cement mortar (1:6)

The thickness of the wall is either 37.5 cm or 45 cm

The height of the walls on which trusses are placed is 5.5 m

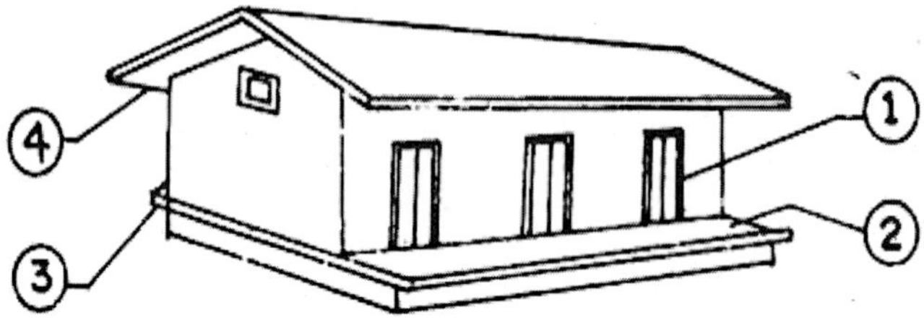

Figure: 3.19 Modern Storage Godown: 1. Sealed door, 2. Floor, 3.Rat proof slab, 4. Air proof roof.

Roof

The roof can be either gabled or flat:

- Gabled roof is covered with corrugated sheet
- Flat roof is more durable, constructed from either reinforced brick or concrete, with a thickness of 10 to 12.5 cm

The terracing on the roof is made from brick ballast, surkhi, and lime in a ratio of 3.5:1:1.

4

Cleaning, Drying and Aeration of Stored Products

Cleaning, drying, and aeration are essential processes in the management of stored agricultural products to maintain their quality and reduce the risk of spoilage. These practices are particularly important in preventing the growth of molds, the infestation of pests, and the deterioration of the product during storage.

Cleaning is the first step in the storage process. It involves removing any debris, dust, dirt, and residues from both the stored products and storage facilities. Proper cleaning eliminates potential sources of contamination, such as pests, molds, and bacteria, which can thrive in the presence of organic matter. It also ensures that the grain or other stored product is free from contaminants that could affect its quality and marketability.

Drying is equally crucial to prevent moisture-related issues. Excess moisture can lead to mold growth, fungal infections, and insect infestations. Drying reduces the moisture content of the grain or product to safe levels, typically below 14% for grains, which helps preserve their quality during storage.

The drying process can be carried out using natural sunlight or mechanical dryers, depending on the volume of the product and available resources. Properly dried products are less prone to spoilage and can be stored for longer periods.

Aeration involves the circulation of air through stored products to maintain optimal temperature and humidity levels. By controlling the environment, aeration helps prevent the buildup of heat and moisture, both of which can lead to product deterioration.

It also reduces the risk of insect infestations by keeping the grain cool and dry. Aeration systems typically use fans or ventilation channels to ensure continuous airflow, especially in large-scale storage facilities. Together, these processes form a comprehensive approach to maintaining the quality and safety of stored agricultural products.

CLEANING OF GRAINS AND APPLICATION OF INSECTICIDE

DEFINITION

Some of the controls mentioned earlier primarily focus on determining the condition of the grain when it arrives at a storage facility. These controls help not only in accurately assessing the market value of the product but also in identifying the necessary treatments the grain requires before storage, marketing, or further processing.

For instance, if the grain contains impurities, it must be cleaned appropriately. If the moisture content is too high, drying must be done immediately. In the case of insect infestation, prompt measures are essential to eliminate the insects.

While drying operations have already been discussed, we will now focus on the processes of cleaning and insect control.

CLEANING OF GRAINS

After threshing, grains (or shells, in the case of groundnuts) become contaminated with various impurities such as earth, small pebbles, plant debris, insect waste, seed cases, etc. These impurities interfere with the drying process, making it longer and more expensive. Even after drying, especially with traditional methods like open-air drying, the grain may still contain these impurities.

These contaminants not only reduce the quality of the grain but also serve as a breeding ground for potential infestations during storage.

"Cleaning" refers to the process or series of operations in the post-harvest system that removes these impurities mixed with the grain mass. This step, which may also involve sorting the products by quality, is crucial before storage, marketing, or further processing.

Additionally, cleaning is essential as a preliminary step before artificial drying in dryers. It would be both costly and inefficient to waste resources on drying impurities along with the grain.

TRADITIONAL METHODS OF CLEANING

The most basic cleaning technique, known as winnowing, involves tossing the grain into the air and allowing the wind to blow away the lighter impurities.

While this method is commonly used in farming, it is not effective in removing heavier impurities such as gravel, foreign grains, and earth.

CLEANING DEVICES

To ensure the desired product is completely free of impurities and suitable for extended storage, the use of appropriate cleaning equipment is essential. This may include winnowers, pre-cleaners, and cleaner-separators.

Winnowers

These machines, with some models capable of reaching an output of up to one ton per hour, can greatly enhance product quality and marketing, particularly in production areas. While some winnowers are manually operated, many are motorized. These simple machines typically consist of a hopper to receive the grain, a fan, and a set of sieves.

The process begins by passing the grain through a current of air produced by the fan to remove the lightest impurities. The sieves then finish cleaning the grain while sorting it by size.

Pre-cleaners

These motor-driven machines are typically used to pre-clean grain that has been harvested while still moist, before it is sent to the artificial dryer. There are several types of pre-cleaners available:

- **The circular pre-cleaner:** This model uses suction to remove impurities and can handle an output of about 150 quintals per hour.
- **The drum pre-cleaner:** This type eliminates the heaviest impurities by passing the grain through the drum's mesh and removes the lighter impurities via suction, with an output of about 10 to 50 tonnes per hour.
- **The clodder:** In this machine, bulky impurities are removed using a coarse, vibrating sieve.

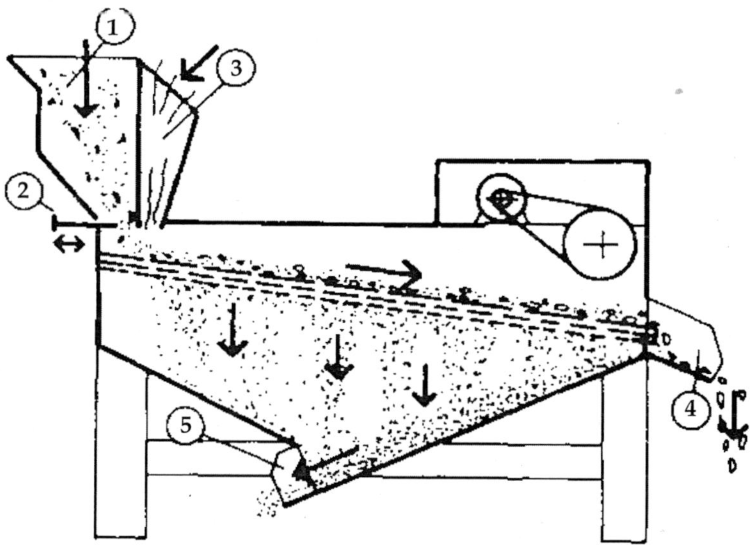

Figure: 4.1 Diagram of a clodder: 1 Grain entry; 2 Adjustment; 3 Suction; 4 Impurities exit; 5 Grain exit.

Cleaner-separators

These machines, with a large output capacity of up to 20 tonnes per hour, are among the most efficient tools for cleaning grain, and it is highly recommended that all storage facilities are equipped with them. Cleaner-separators are motorized machines primarily composed of a reception hopper, a fan, and a set of vibrating sieves. The cleaning process involves repeatedly using suction to remove the lightest impurities, followed by sifting the grain.

The sieve set consists of a coarse sieve (clodder) for removing bulkier impurities and a fine sieve (sifter) for eliminating finer impurities. These sieves should be selected with care, based on the shape and size of the grains being cleaned. Typically, a set with oblong perforations is used for long grains, while round grains require a clodder with round perforations and a sifter with oblong perforations.

For the machine to operate optimally, it is essential to make proper adjustments to factors such as the grain flow, suction intensity, and possibly the sieve vibration speed.

GRAIN INSECTICIDE TREATMENTS

Efforts to protect grain from insects can be approached in two ways:

1. Preventive measures before the grain is stored, starting from the moment it is received, even if no visible insects are present.
2. Curative measures applied during or even before storage, if necessary.

In both cases, the goal is to eliminate insects without compromising the quality of the food product. To achieve this, certain hygienic practices and treatment protocols for the storage premises must be followed.

There are several insect-control methods for grain, including biological, physical, mechanical, and chemical approaches. Among these, chemical control is the most commonly used today and can be categorized into two main types of treatment:

1. Contact insecticide treatment,
2. Fumigation treatment.

TREATMENT OF PREMISES

Before applying insecticides to storage buildings (such as warehouses or silos), it is essential to thoroughly clean the entire premises. The variety of insecticide products available allows for treatment of different surfaces based on their characteristics.

For uneven surfaces like bricks, breeze blocks, or raw wood, a powder mixed with water is sprayed until it becomes runny. In contrast, for smooth, non-porous surfaces like metal or polyester, a stickier concentrate is preferred for spraying.

Ambient treatment aims to eliminate flying insects by dispersing aerosols in sealed premises. This treatment should ideally be carried out in the evening, when flying insects are most active.

TREATMENT OF GRAIN WITH CONTACT INSECTICIDE

This process involves covering the grain with a layer of insecticide that works upon contact with insects, with varying effects in terms of speed and persistence. These products come in different forms, such as powders for dusting, powders to mix with water, liquid concentrates, or fumigants, and the choice dictates the application method.

For bulk grain storage, the insecticide is applied directly to the grain before filling the silos. In bagged storage, after cleaning, the grain is mixed with powder or sprayed before being bagged. To prevent reinfestation in bagged grain, additional dustings or sprayings are applied while stacking and during the storage period.

The equipment used for dusting can range from simple mechanical dusters to motorized ones; however, this type of equipment may not provide uniform treatment, leading to uneven dust distribution. Spraying methods can be mechanical (pressure sprayer), pneumatic, or thermal, offering better product distribution. In larger storage facilities, to ensure even distribution and a thorough insecticide coating, fine spraying is performed using a compressor with a mist nozzle.

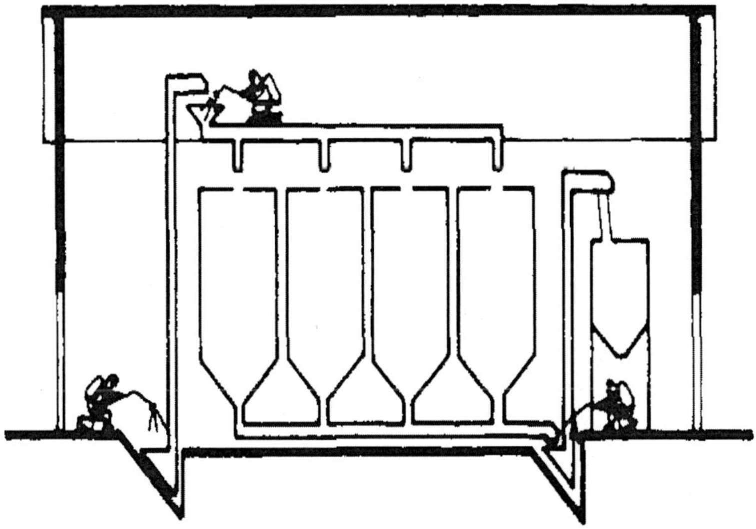

Figure: 4.2 Misting grain before silo storage

On fully grown insects, contact treatment systems are unquestionably effective, but they have little to no effect on the eggs or larvae. Additionally, some product residues may remain in food items even though they are not extremely harmful.

TREATMENT OF GRAIN BY FUMIGATION

Fumigation is a method that eliminates insects from stored grain using a toxic gas known as a fumigant. This gas, when produced and concentrated, is lethal to specific pest species. Unlike contact powders, fumigants penetrate the grain mass and reach hidden stages of insect development, such as eggs and larvae.

The fumigant spreads throughout the area it is released into, so the space must be completely sealed off. For bulk grain, bins need to be airtight, while for bagged grain, the bags are typically covered with a tarpaulin, with the edges sealed against the ground or walls.

The effectiveness of fumigation depends on the concentration of the fumigant and the duration of exposure. Fumigation using methyl bromide generally takes 24 to 48 hours, while phosphine requires a minimum of five days. Phosphine is more commonly used due to its ease of application, typically in pellet form spread throughout the grain mass.

Since fumigants are highly toxic to humans, workers must receive proper training in their application. Strict adherence to safety precautions such as wearing masks and gloves, washing hands, and ensuring the proper sealing of fumigant containers is essential. It's also crucial to remember that fumigation is a curative measure with no long-lasting effects, so combining contact insecticide and fumigation methods is recommended for more effective pest management.

DRYING GRAIN

Food must be available year-round, extending beyond the harvesting season, and therefore, it is crucial to store it properly to maintain its optimal quality. Drying grains is one of the most effective primary methods for food preservation. Improper drying before storing grain is a significant cause of post-harvest food loss during storage.

India holds the top position globally with the largest net cropped area, producing hundreds of millions of tonnes of food grains annually. While production has steadily increased over the past two decades due to advancements in agricultural technology, food losses have remained unchanged. Consequently, as food production rises, the loss of food grains continues to increase, primarily due to improper storage practices.

There is a need for greater awareness among crop owners regarding the different grain drying methods, their proper usage, and the advantages they offer in improving storage and marketing. Despite the high initial capital investment required, investing in proper drying and storage techniques will significantly reduce food loss.

Drying is the process of removing moisture from agricultural products. It involves exposing the grains to air with low relative humidity, causing the moisture within the grains to evaporate and be removed. This process ensures the preservation of grains, foods, fruits, and vegetables, making long-term storage possible while maintaining high nutritional value.

Common agricultural commodities that are dried include:

- Rice
- Wheat
- Maize
- Groundnuts
- Soybeans
- Coffee
- Berries

RICE DRYING

Traditionally, sun drying rice does not present major challenges. In tropical regions, the average insolation level exceeds 0.5 kw/m^2, which, over 12 hours of sunshine, provides a heat quantity of 21.6 MJ/m^2. This amount of energy is sufficient to evaporate 9 kg of water.

For rice harvested during the dry season, the main issue lies in controlling the drying process to avoid overheating and excessive moisture stress on the grain.

For rain-fed rice harvested during periods of high humidity, some development projects have investigated and introduced models of drying floors made from various materials. The grain is carefully spread on limited surfaces of specially designed drying floors, and the drying process is carefully monitored. Studies have shown that paddy can be dried from 24-26% moisture content to 14% moisture content in beds 50-100 mm thick at a rate of 3.3 kg/m^2/h if the grain is regularly turned, or 1.9 kg/m^2/h if it is not turned.

In conditions of maximum sunlight, the grain temperature can reach 60°C, and the drying rate is high enough to cause cracking and milling losses. To prevent this, the drying rate should be slowed by covering the grain between midday and 3 pm, as observed by the IRRI, reducing cracking by 25%.

MAIZE DRYING

Maize drying occurs during the middle of the rainy season, when the relative humidity stays around 80% for several weeks post-harvest. As a result, without the addition of heat, it becomes nearly impossible to reduce the moisture content of the maize to the 13-15% required for safe storage.

The issue of humidity is further complicated by an increase in the quantity harvested, which often exceeds the drying capacity of the producers. A drying phase of varying duration typically takes place in the field, while the maize is still on the stalk. However, this method leads to losses from pests.

Additionally, after harvest, delays in transport to the homestead often result in further loss as the grain remains exposed to moisture for too long, causing significant damage from fungal infestations.

Maize Dryer

Corn, another name for maize, is a staple crop that is grown all over the world. The Maize Dryer Machine is an automatic dryer that runs continuously. Food processing, animal feed production, warehousing, stock, oil mills, the maize starch industry, poultry feed producers, cow feed manufacturers, and other businesses related to maize drying are just a few of the industries that use it. However, maize needs to be properly dried in order to lower its moisture content and guarantee long-term storage stability before it can be used efficiently.

Capacity of maize grain dryer

The ability of the maize grain dryer to adapt to varying production volumes is one of its main benefits. The maize dryer's capacity is as follows:

- Belt Dryer: 50-500 TPD
- Vertical Flow Dryer: 50-150 TPD
- Conical Dryer: 5-500 TPD

Maize dryer machine can be operated throughout the year even during off season.

Operation

Our maize dryer's sophisticated operating system, which combines state-of-the-art technology with intuitive controls for peak performance, is its brains. In India, the maize dryer machine uses a convection drying system. The maize travels over a thin air permeable belt through hot air distribution slits, where it is continuously dried and cleaned by a flow of hot air with a specific temperature, speed, and retention time. The operating system is made to give users exact control over important variables like humidity, airflow, and temperature, guaranteeing reliable and consistent drying outcomes.

WHY IS DRYING GRAINS IMPORTANT?

All grains naturally contain moisture, but dry grains store more effectively and safely than wet grains for several reasons:

- Wet grains lack a strong seed coat, which allows insects and molds to penetrate, leading to spoilage.
- Wet grains respirate at a faster rate, causing an increase in temperature, which attracts insects and molds.
- If the grains are warm and moist enough, they may even start to germinate within the storage area.

Therefore, drying grains is vital to ensure:

- The moisture level remains optimal.
- Protection against contamination from insects, pests, and mold growth.
- The ability to store grains for extended periods after harvest, before they are sold or utilized.
- Prevention of crop loss.
- Retention of the grain's aroma, flavor, taste, and nutritional value.
- Helping farmers obtain the best possible price for their produce.

FUNDAMENTALS OF DRYING GRAINS

Proper drying is crucial for ensuring food security, as it directly affects grain quality and seed viability. Understanding the basics of grain drying is essential.

- **Moisture Removal:** Grains have moisture at two levels: surface moisture and internal moisture within the kernel. Surface moisture evaporates quickly when exposed to hot air, but internal moisture takes longer to evaporate, as it needs to move from the kernel to the surface.
- **Drying Rate:** The drying rate refers to how quickly the moisture content decreases during the drying process. Surface moisture and internal moisture dry at different rates, each requiring distinct drying periods.

- **Temperature:** Most agricultural products require heated air with temperatures between 45-60°C for safe drying. The maximum safe temperature varies depending on the drying method, the type of crop, the moisture content, and the final use of the product.
- **Uniform Drying:** Moisture content varies from one grain to another during drying, and this variability should be minimized for optimal grain and seed quality. Achieving uniform drying involves frequent stirring during sun drying, turning the grain in fixed-bed dryers, or using circulation in recirculating batch dryers.
- **Tempering:** Tempering is a process where drying is paused temporarily, allowing moisture to equalize within and between grains. When drying resumes, the rate of moisture loss is higher compared to continuous drying. Therefore, incorporating tempering periods is important for effective drying.

DIFFERENT METHODS OF DRYING GRAINS

The fastest method to dry grains involves exposing them to air that is:

- **Dry:** This allows the air to absorb moisture from the grain.
- **Warm:** Heat speeds up the drying process, making it quicker.
- **Moving:** Moving air helps carry the moisture away from the grain, promoting faster drying.

There are two main types of drying methods: natural and mechanical.

NATURAL DRYING OR SUN DRYING

This is the oldest and most traditional method for drying grains. It harnesses solar energy, allowing the grain to absorb heat while releasing its surface moisture into the surrounding air. The process involves spreading wet grain on the ground or on plastic sheets (to prevent contamination from dirt) and turning the grain periodically to ensure moisture is effectively removed.

Sun Drying Grains

The drying period can range from 5 to 45 days, depending on the type of crop being dried.

The benefits of sun-drying include:

- Free airflow throughout the entire field.
- The task can be carried out by unskilled labor.
- There is no cost involved.
- It can be done anywhere.

Sun-drying is the most commonly used method for drying grains in India, largely due to the low level of mechanization in agriculture and the high levels of crop production. However, the method has several drawbacks:

- The drying process is slow.
- It is weather-dependent, as it can only be done during the day.
- It can reduce the quality and quantity of the product.
- Achieving uniform drying can be challenging.

Mechanical Drying of grains

Mechanical drying utilizes thermal energy collection devices and dryers that remove moisture from wet grains by circulating heated air through them. The drying process continues until the grain reaches the desired moisture content. Various types of solar dryers exist, which differ based on their reheating methods and how heat is used. Some dryers also utilize propane or natural gas to heat the air, which is then pushed through the grain by large fans.

The benefits of mechanical drying include:

- Faster, safer, and more effective compared to traditional sun drying.
- High drying rate.
- Drying can be done at any time of the day or night.
- Improved control over temperature and moisture levels.
- Produces better-looking, tastier, and more nutritious food.
- No loss of product, and faster reloading in a few hours.
- Consistency in drying and tempering.

However, these dryers are often not readily available to farmers, and the drawbacks include:

High cost, particularly the significant initial investment required for the equipment.

TIPS FOR DRYING

To achieve the best results with any drying method, follow these key tips:

- Clean and prepare the grains before drying. Remove any contaminants such as leaves, rocks, plastic, or other foreign materials.
- Assess the storage period to determine the ideal moisture content for drying. The longer the storage, the lower the moisture content should be.
- Allow enough time for the drying process, particularly if sun drying is used.
- Ensure the temperature is set within safe limits to avoid over-drying or overheating, which can damage the grain.
- Regularly monitor the moisture content of the grain, even after the drying process is complete.
- Consider utilizing modern technologies and commercially available dryers for more efficient drying before storage.

Once drying is complete, proper storage is essential to preserve the grain and maintain the quality of the drying process.

Table 4.1 : Store preparation: hazards and management

Key hazards	Risk score	Management		
		Preventative measures	**Monitoring procedures**	**Corrective actions**
Fungi with potential to cause mycotoxins	**	Clean equipment and store	Inspect cleanliness	Targeted cleaning
Insects and mites	**	Clean equipment and store	Use traps	Apply pesticide at recommended rate
Pesticide residues	*	Use approved products in recommended manner	Check records of pesticide application	Review applications and practices
Rodents and rodent faeces	*	Clean store, remove (where possible) potential places of shelter and prevent entry	Check for rodent presence	Use rodenticides in recommended manner; targeted cleaning and proofing
Birds and bird faeces	*	Clean store and prevent entry	Check for bird presence	Targeted cleaning and proofing
Glass	*	Glass control procedures	Check for compliance with procedures	Remove and replace or protect glass

PRODUCTS AERATION IN STORAGE

Many issues with stored grain, such as mold, insects, fungi, and spoilage, are either caused by or exacerbated by improper moisture and temperature levels. Internal air currents, driven by temperature differences within the grain, cause moisture to migrate to the top and center of the grain mass, leading to mold growth and providing a breeding ground for insects. Aeration is a method used to regulate temperature and maintain consistent moisture levels in stored grain. It involves using a fan to pump external air through the grain mass, allowing the grain temperature to stabilize to that of the air circulating through it. Without aeration, temperature differentials can develop within the grain, increasing the likelihood of mold and insect infestations.

Different types of grain have specific requirements for storage temperature and moisture content, requiring distinct aeration protocols.

CHOOSING AIRFLOW RATE

The airflow used in aeration is typically measured in CFM/Bu (cubic feet of air per minute per bushel of stored grain). The aeration rate generally starts at about 0.05 CFM/bu and increases depending on specific requirements, as outlined in.

The appropriate airflow rate should be selected based on the intended use of the aeration system. If the grain is stored at a safe moisture content and the primary function of the aeration system is to prevent moisture migration, a light aeration system may suffice. However, if the grain is stored with moisture levels 1% or 2% higher than the recommended safe levels, closer control of grain temperature is necessary, and a more robust aeration system with greater capacity is recommended. In general, when rapid cooling of the grain is needed, a higher airflow rate should be chosen.

Table 4.2 : Aeration time required to cool wheat and corn versus CFM/bu.

Time (hours) Grain Condition			
CFM/Bu.	**Clean**	**High F.M.**	**Classification**
0.05	240	300-350	Light
0.1	120	150-175	Light
0.2	60	75-85	Medium
0.3	40	50-60	Medium
0.4	30	35-40	Fast
0.5	24	30-35	Fast
0.6	20	25-30	Fast
0.8	15	18-20	Fast
1	12	14-16	High Speed
2	6	42957	High Speed
3	4	42861	High Speed
5	2.5	42798	High Speed

Light aeration systems, 0.1 CFM/bu or less, require long operation times to lower grain temperatures and are best suited to cooler climates.

Time Required For Cooling

The time needed to cool grain to match the ambient temperature is primarily influenced by airflow rate, the presence of foreign materials in the grain, and the amount of evaporative cooling (drying) occurring. Many on-farm aeration fans are designed for about 0.1 CFM/bushel airflow, which requires approximately 120 hours (five days) of continuous operation for clean grain, or around 150 to 175 hours (six to seven days) for grain with high levels of foreign material (f.m.).

To make the most of brief periods of cool weather in early fall, it's recommended to use automatic aeration controllers and higher-capacity fans that provide at least 0.2 CFM/bushel airflow. This can cool the grain in under 60 to 85 hours. The additional cost of these systems can often be recovered within one or two seasons through savings on grain damage, moisture loss, and expenses related to protectants and fumigation.

Airflow Direction: Pressure Vs. Suction

- Many grain storage managers prefer pressure (upward) airflow over suction (downward) airflow for several reasons as follows:
- Aeration fans are optimized to generate maximum airflow against pressure, enabling them to push cooler, denser air more effectively than warmer, lighter air;
- Pressure fans ensure more uniform airflow throughout the grain mass compared to suction systems;
- With pressure airflow, condensation on top of the grain is visible and typically dries up by the end of the aeration cycle, making the problem observable and fixable, whereas condensation damage at the bottom caused by suction fans is hidden until the bin is emptied;
- Pressure fans prevent winter roof collapse in bins, as roof vents may freeze over during suction cooling.

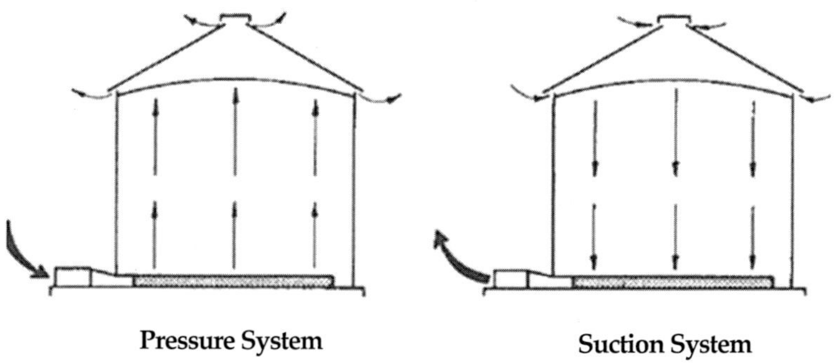

Figure: 4.3 Direction of airflow in aeration systems

NOTE: Axial (Propeller) fans can typically be reversed by simply rotating the fan housing and rebolting it. However, for most fans, reversing is not a feasible option.

Construction of Grain Bin and Additional Factors

Grain bins equipped with fully perforated drying floors are excellent for aeration, but cleaning beneath the floor can be challenging, and the installation costs tend to be higher. An alternative to perforated floors is removable floor ducts, which are available in various patterns such as large square, cross, Y, or U shapes.

Cross-flow aeration systems help reduce the resistance to airflow in tall grain bins. This leads to lower power consumption, thereby reducing operating expenses and capital costs.

Bins need proper roof exhaust vents to minimize condensation and enhance airflow. For every 1,500 CFM of airflow, there should be at least one square foot of roof vent opening. If permanent roof openings aren't available, temporary solutions like opening roof fill caps and access doors can allow air to escape during aeration fan operation.

Aeration fans can draw rain and snow into the grain bin. Short-duration storms (3-6 hours) generally don't pose moisture problems, but during longer storms or persistent foggy weather, it's advisable to stop aeration until conditions improve. The best practice is to cover the fan intake when the aeration fans are not in use.

NATURAL VENTILATION

Natural ventilation involves the movement of air into and out of an indoor space without the use of mechanical systems, as illustrated in Figure. It relies on external air flow that is driven by differences in pressure or temperature. There are two main types of natural ventilation in buildings: wind-driven ventilation and buoyancy-driven ventilation. Wind-driven ventilation is primarily influenced by wind, while buoyancy-driven ventilation occurs due to the buoyant force caused by temperature differences between the interior and exterior of the building.

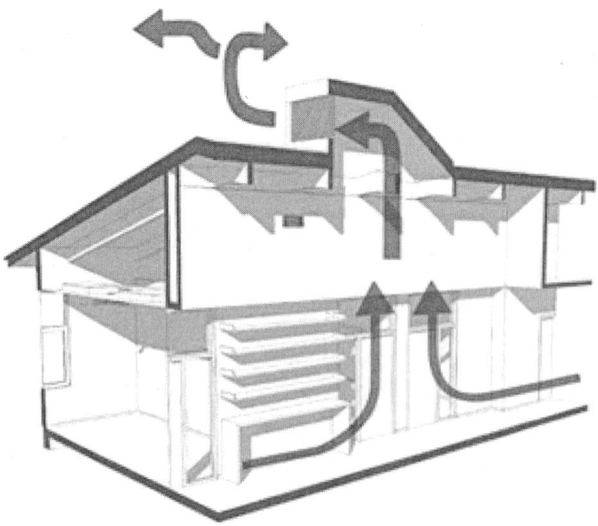

Figure: 4.4 Natural ventilation

Figure illustrates an example of natural ventilation structures designed for the storage of grains in bags.

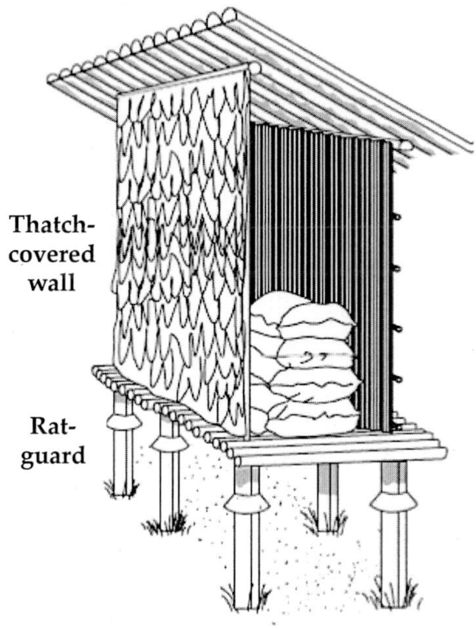

Figure: 4.5 Natural ventilated for storing grain in bags

Static pressure refers to the pressure within a freely flowing air stream, represented by isobars on weather maps. Variations in static pressure occur due to thermal effects at both global and microclimate levels, which in turn generate wind. Dynamic pressure, on the other hand, is the pressure exerted when the wind interacts with an object, like a hill or building, and is described by the following equation:

$$q=\frac{1}{2}pv^2$$

where,

- q = dynamic pressure, Pa
- p = fluid (air) density, kg/m^3
- v = fluid velocity, m/s.

Wind impact on a building influences both ventilation and infiltration rates, affecting the building's heat losses or gains. Wind speed typically increases with height and decreases near the ground due to frictional drag. The wind's effect on the building shape creates areas of positive pressure on the windward side and negative pressure on the leeward and sides. Consequently, the building's shape and local wind patterns are crucial in generating the wind pressures that drive air flow through openings.

In practice, wind pressure can fluctuate significantly, creating complex air flows and turbulence as it interacts with natural elements (like trees and hills) and urban structures (such as buildings and other man-made structures). Traditional and vernacular buildings across various climatic regions often rely on natural ventilation to maintain thermal comfort in enclosed spaces.

GUIDELINES FOR THE NATURAL VENTILATION STRUCTURES DESIGN IN BUILDINGS

The following design guidelines are typically recommended by the Whole Building Design Guide, a program by the National Institute of Building Sciences:

- To enhance wind-induced ventilation, position the ridge of a building perpendicular to the prevailing summer winds.
- The width of naturally ventilated zones should be narrow {max 13.7 m (45 feet)}.
- Each room should have two separate openings for supply and exhaust. Position exhaust vents high above the inlet to optimize the stack effect.
- Windows should be oriented across the room and offset from each other to improve air mixing and reduce airflow obstructions.
- Ensure that window openings are operable by the building occupants.
- Consider incorporating clerestories or vented skylights into the design.

MECHANICAL VENTILATION

Using mechanical systems to supply and remove air is known as mechanical ventilation.

Both vertical and horizontal storage spaces can have mechanical ventilation systems installed. It has been determined that the following set of fundamental design parameters is appropriate for mechanical ventilation cooling of dry grains.

Air flow rate:

- Silos: 0.8 litres per second per tonne
- Sheds: 1.6 litres per second per tonne
- Maximum duct velocity: 10 m/s
- Maximum entry velocity of air into the grain: 0.15 m/s

The typical air flow rates for aerating paddy range between 0.07 and 0.28 m^3/minute per tonne of paddy. These air flow rates for aeration are only a small fraction of the air volume required to dry grains. From the provided parameters, the fan output, duct size, and duct surface area can be calculated.

Air can be either pulled or pushed through the grain in storage. It can be moved from top to bottom or from bottom to top of the bin. In tropical climates, aeration should be done from the bottom to the top. This is because any air trapped under the roof of the storage structure tends to be at a high temperature. This warmer air can be easily forced out from the top, while the cooler air from the bottom helps to cool the warmer grain stored in the bin.

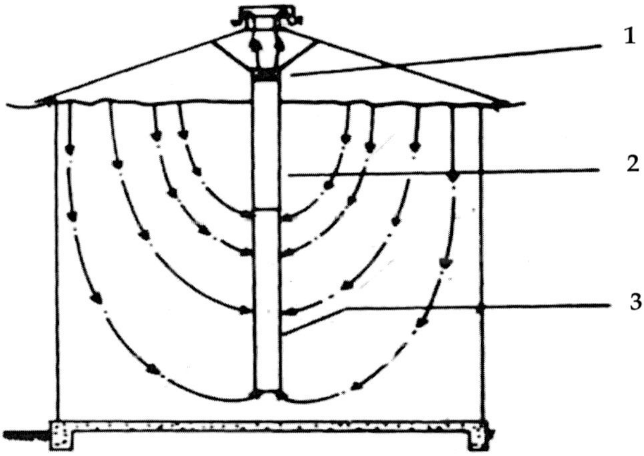

Figure: 4.6 Central ventilation/aeration system in vertical silo. 1. Fan, 2. Solid duct, 3. Perforated section.

Axial fans are typically used for aerating sheds, while non-overloading centrifugal fans are recommended for vertical storage due to the higher pressure requirements. In the case of overloading fans, it is advised to use a manually adjustable throttle valve in the inlet duct to regulate the airflow, especially when aerating partially filled silos.

The main components of an aeration system are: ans to move the air, and ducts to carry air from the fans to the storage system.

Different ducting configurations can be used for air distribution within the grain mass. The most common ventilation systems for silos include: the central vertical system floor ducts, and perforated floors.

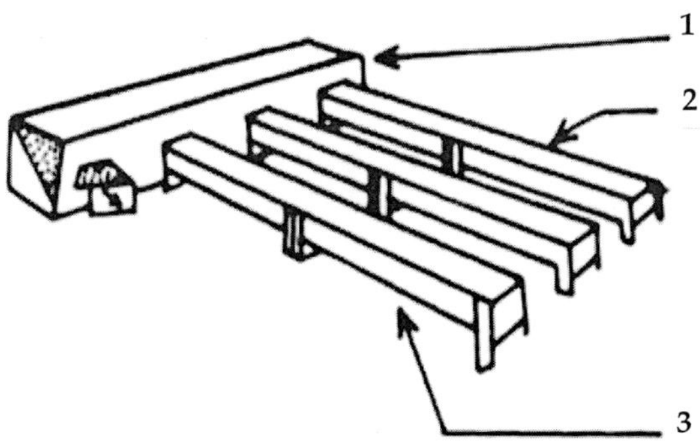

Figure: 4.7 Floor ducts for aeration. 1. main duct 2. transferable lateral ducts 3. interspace on floor

In a vertical duct system, the top portion of the central duct is solid, while the lower half is perforated. A fan at the top of the duct draws air through the grain and perforations. The air is then blown out of the bin by the fan. When on-floor ducting is employed, it's often necessary to design it for removal to allow for floor sweeping. For this reason, full-round ducting is typically used in sheds with moderate grain loads. Both longitudinal and cross-floor ducting can be utilized in sheds. Generally, ducting is constructed from galvanized steel sheet with 2.5 mm perforations spaced 6 mm apart.

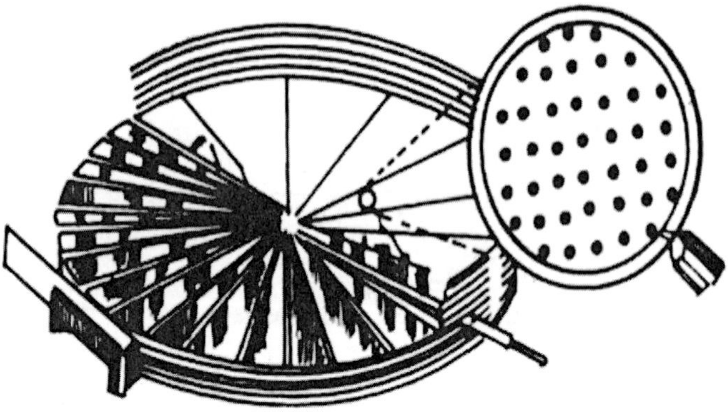

Figure: 4.8 Perforated floor cross-section for aeration

Ducting in silos faces significantly higher grain pressures. In-floor ducting requires flat perforated sheets, which increases the system's cost due to the need for a structural frame beneath the perforated sheet for support. An alternative is perimeter ducting, which uses quarter-round corrugated ducts.

Perforated ducts can take various shapes, including circular, semicircular, rectangular, or inverted V-shaped. The required cross-sectional area of a duct can be determined using the following expression.

ARTIFICIAL DRYING OF GRAIN

Unlike sun drying, artificial drying offers the advantage of being able to set ideal drying conditions and allows the drying process to take place at any time of the day or night. Using artificial drying can also help reduce labor costs, particularly if automatic grain turning or stirring is incorporated, as seen in re-circulating dryers.

In general, grain dried artificially tends to have better quality than sun-dried grain. Artificial drying promotes more uniform drying, leading to higher milling yields and better head recovery. Additionally, grain recirculation ensures even drying, and the use of automatic temperature control for the drying air prevents overheating or over-drying.

Two common types of grain dryers in Asia are the flatbed dryer and the re-circulating batch dryer. Both of these are batch-fed dryers, meaning that a specific amount of grain is loaded and dried before the dryer is unloaded and another batch is processed.

FLATBED TYPE DRYER

Flatbed dryers have a simple design where the grain is spread out on a perforated screen and dried by forcing air through it from below, as illustrated in

Figure. The drying air is typically provided by a basic axial flow fan powered by either a diesel or electric motor. The heat for drying comes from a kerosene burner or a biomass-fueled stove. These dryers can have a capacity ranging from one ton to eight tons. While most drying floors are flat, some models feature reclining sections to aid in unloading or vibrating sections to assist with stirring the grain. The typical layer height is around 40 cm.

Smaller dryers, typically with a capacity of one to three tons per day, require six to twelve hours for drying. For paddy drying in tropical climates, the air temperature is usually set to 40-45°C, with a heater raising the air temperature by 10-15°C above the ambient temperature. For the drying of paddy, the air velocity is around 0.15-0.25 m/s, with fan power requirements ranging from 1.5-2.5 kW/ton. The efficiency of these dryers is enhanced by stirring the grain during the drying process.

Figure: 4.9 Flatbed type of dryer

RE-CIRCULATING BATCH DRYERS

Re-circulating batch dryers consists of two concentric circular cylinders made of 2 mm perforated mild steel sheet of 20 gauge, spaced from 15 to 20 cm apart. These cylinders are supported by four channel sections, and the entire frame is either placed on a suitable foundation or bolted to a frame made from channel sections. A bucket elevator, with the appropriate capacity, is used to feed and re-circulate the grain through the dryer. A centrifugal blower forces hot air into the inner cylinder, which serves as a plenum. The hot air passes through the grain, moving downward by gravity, and exits via the perforated outer cylinder. A torch burner provides the necessary heat, using kerosene oil as fuel. Dryer designs are available with ½, 1, and 2-tonne holding capacities, with the 2-tonne dryer shown in Figure:

The grain is introduced at the top of the inner cylinder, and as it descends through the annular space between the two cylinders, it comes into contact with a cross-flow of hot air supplied by the perforated inner cylinder. Exhaust air escapes through the perforations in the outer cylinder, and the grain is discharged through the outlet of the hopper. The feed rate of the grain is controlled by adjusting the gate at the outlet pipe of the discharge hopper. The grain continues to circulate until it reaches the desired moisture level.

The main advantages of the re-circulating dryer include:

- Compact size and shape, requiring very little floor space, allowing for easy placement inside a grain store or warehouse.
- Affordable price.
- Simple design compared to other flow-type dryers.
- Easy operation.
- Usability on farms and in rice mills.
- Low operating cost when using a husk-fired furnace.

However, the process of loading, unloading, and circulating the grain can create dust, which requires a collection system. It is also advisable to pre-clean the grain before loading and drying. Like flatbed dryers, re-circulating dryers are available in various capacities, ranging from 2 tons (for seed production stations) up to 20 tons (for cooperative drying stations).

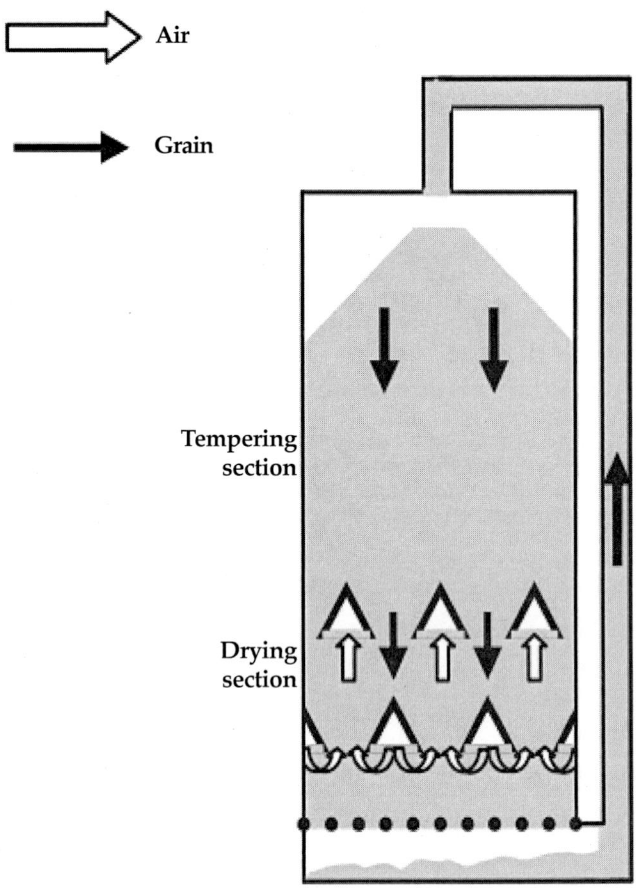

Figure: 4.10 Recirculation of drying system

GENERAL PRECAUTIONS IN USING ARTIFICIAL GRAIN DRYERS

- Prior to loading the dryer, ensure the grain is cleaned by removing fines and green, immature grains. Fines obstruct air flow through the rice, leading to longer drying times and the formation of wet spots.
- Avoid mixing dry rice with wet rice in the dryer. As the drying air passes through the rice, it absorbs moisture, which could cause the dry rice to crack.

5

Determination of Dimension of Warehouse for Bag Storage

The quantity of space available for product storage is referred to as warehouse capacity. Understanding the distinction between theoretical working capacity and storage capacity can be aided by warehouse capacity. In warehouses and other storage facilities, space is perhaps the most valuable resource for online retailers. By making the most of their warehouse space, businesses can significantly increase the quantity of goods they can store there. Having more things in storage at once can save them money on transportation and other expenses.

It also makes it easier for the warehouse KPI staff to access the products, which helps them process orders faster and deliver the goods to customers sooner. Because space can be limited in a warehouse setting, warehouse managers and business owners should take the time to assess how much space they have and how well they're using it.

STEP TO CALCULATE WAREHOUSE STORAGE CAPACITY

Understanding your warehouse's current capacity is the first step in determining how to increase it. This brief guide will show you how to calculate a warehouse's capacity in feet:

- Calculate the total square footage of your warehouse complex. Let's assume that it is 10,000 square feet in this case.
- Determine the total amount of space devoted to non-storage purposes, such as offices, loading areas, restrooms, and break rooms. Assume for the moment that this is equivalent to 2,000 square feet.
- Subtract the total square feet of non-storage space from the total square feet of your warehouse to determine the usable space. The following is the equation:

USABLE SPACE-TOTAL SQUARE FEET – NON-STORAGE SPACE SQUARE FEET

Determine the total usable storage space by identifying the maximum stack height or clear height. This should account for the lowest-hanging overhead obstructions, such as lighting fixtures or warehouse racks. For example, if the clear height is 30 feet, this will be the maximum stacking limit.

To calculate the total storage capacity in cubic feet, multiply the maximum stack height by the total available usable space:

STORAGE CAPACITY MAXIMUM HEIGHT OF STACK IN FEET MULTISIGN USABLE SPACE IN SQUARE FEET

This method provides a general guideline for calculating your warehouse's storage capacity. However, it's important to consider facility-specific factors such as designated workspaces for packing and picking. By accurately assessing warehouse capacity, you can optimize space based on your business's storage needs, including the number of units and unique SKUs, as well as the required equipment and fulfillment areas essential for efficient warehouse operations.

DETERMINE YOUR WAREHOUSE SPACE UTILIZATION

Maximizing efficiency is crucial for business growth, and that includes making the most of your available warehouse space. By calculating your warehouse space utilization, you can determine the percentage of usable space currently occupied.

Here's an important insight: your goal should not be a perfect 100% utilization. Surprising as it may seem, aiming for a lower percentage is more practical. We'll explain why after demonstrating how to measure warehouse space utilization.

Using the previously calculated total storage capacity of 2,000,000 cubic feet, follow these steps to determine how much of that space you're actively using:

- Measure the footprint of all pallet racks.
- Calculate their total vertical storage capacity.
- Multiply the true capacity of each pallet rack by the total number of racks in your warehouse.

The result represents your warehouse's storage cube size. For example, if your calculations total 500,000 cubic feet, and your total storage capacity is 2,000,000 cubic feet, your utilization rate is 25%—which is an efficient and effective percentage.

ASSESSING THE EFFICIENCY OF YOUR SPACE USE

Why is a 25% utilization rate something to celebrate? Shouldn't you aim for a number closer to 100%? Surprisingly, the answer is no. If your warehouse utilization falls below 22% or exceeds 27%, it may signal inefficiencies in your warehouse design and layout.

A utilization rate above 27% often means your space is overcrowded, making it difficult to move around efficiently. Picking and restocking products could take longer, increasing labor costs. Think of it like cramming furniture into a small apartment—sure, everything fits, but navigating the space becomes a challenge. Similarly, stacking products from floor to ceiling may save on storage costs but can lead to inefficiencies in daily operations.

On the other hand, if your utilization is below 22%, you may not be making full use of your valuable warehouse space.

Once you analyze your warehouse utilization, you can focus on optimizing capacity. Implementing strategic layout changes can increase efficiency, saving both time and money while improving overall operations.

MAXIMIZE YOUR STORAGE CAPACITY

Below are the essential tips to help you maximize the storage capacity of your warehouse:

Choose the Right Storage Solutions

Selecting appropriate storage solutions is crucial for maximizing warehouse space. Opt for systems that align with the warehouse layout and the type of products being stored. Popular options that enhance space utilization include pallet racks, mezzanines, flow racks, and stacker cranes.

Optimize Space Organization

Once the ideal storage solutions are in place, focus on efficient organization. Group similar-sized items together to maximize available space, ensuring they fit seamlessly like puzzle pieces. Adjusting aisle widths slightly can create additional storage rows, but it is essential to maintain enough space for equipment and personnel to operate safely and efficiently.

Plan for Future Expansion

Maintaining storage utilization below 27% allows room for future growth, new product launches, and seasonal inventory changes. If storage is at full capacity, it may be a signal that expansion is necessary. Being prepared for increased demand ensures smooth operations and prevents disruptions caused by storage limitations.

Imagine your product getting a major boost—an endorsement from a social media influencer or a feature on a popular industry website, instantly reaching millions of potential customers. It could go viral overnight, creating a surge in demand. While this is an exciting opportunity, without sufficient storage space and infrastructure, fulfilling orders efficiently could become a challenge. If you're unprepared, delays and stock shortages may negatively impact customer satisfaction and harm your company's reputation. High demand is a valuable opportunity, but only if you have the necessary space, tools, and technology to manage it effectively.

STORAGE IN BAGS

Using this method, dried and cleaned grain is stored in plastic or plant fiber bags, which are then neatly stacked in areas that have been prepared. While this approach is widely used in developing nations, it is rarely utilized in developed nations. It is cost-effective and perfectly suited to regional grain transportation and marketing circumstances.

Grain can be stored in bags in a variety of ways. The grain bags can be put inside storehouses, sheds, or warehouses, or they can be stacked outdoors under tarpaulins. Grain is occasionally kept in bags in refrigerated warehouses, particularly for seeds.

Filling the Bag

Taking the time to fill storage bags correctly ensures easier emptying, minimizes maintenance, and reduces spills or machinery realignment during storage:

- Maintain even and straight filling to prevent creases, as mice often target these weak points.
- Regularly adjust brakes and direction in small increments for precise alignment.
- Avoid overfilling, as excessive stretching increases the risk of holes, splits, and tears.
- Keep in mind that polyethylene bags stretch more on hot days when filled with warm grain.
- While bags can be filled directly from the harvester, rushing the process can lead to improper filling, increasing the chances of accidents or equipment damage.
- Stop filling with at least four meters of bag remaining to allow proper sealing and attachment to the emptying machine.
- Seal the bag end by heat-sealing or clamping it to prevent moisture ingress. Tuck any excess material under itself and cover with soil to prevent flapping in the wind.

Emptying the Bag

When making the initial cut for out-loading, apply a strip of tape horizontally across the bag just below its tightly stretched top. Then, make the first cut perpendicular to the bag, just below the tape. Avoid cutting parallel to the bag, as this could cause it to split along its entire length, exposing the grain and making collection more difficult.

As with filling, frequent small adjustments to the machine and roller speeds are more effective than large corrections. When the bag is nearly empty and its weight is reduced, the unloading machine may pull the bag toward itself, leading to tears from ground friction or overstretching. To prevent this, drive the tractor slowly in reverse as the last portion of the bag is emptied.

Clean Up

To prevent reinfestation with insect pests in the next season, clean grain residues thoroughly from all machinery used for grain handling. Structural treatments should be considered as part of a complete clean-down process.

An inert dust, like diatomaceous earth (DE), can be blown into the machinery to prevent insects from harboring during the off-season.

Proper site clean-up is crucial for success. Spilled piles of grain and leftover small grain bags provide an ideal environment for insects to live and breed.

Safety Around the Grain Bags

Filling and emptying grain bags come with several safety risks, which are often heightened during harvest when people are fatigued and in a hurry. Always follow the machinery manufacturer's instructions and consult your State's occupational health and safety authority for advice.

- Treat all operating machinery with respect—keep a safe distance and always ensure there's space to step away if necessary.
- Think carefully before making any adjustments or movements on machinery.
- Make sure everyone on-site is standing clear of the filling machine and tractor before adjusting the brakes, as it can move unexpectedly. Small adjustments help reduce the risk of the machine lurching.

Outdoor Storage

Open-air storage systems are those in which bags are not stacked in solidly constructed buildings. The primary methods of open-air storage include:

- Storage in pyramids
- Storage in flexible silos

The advantage of these systems is their ability to be set up quickly and easily, making them ideal for situations where storage needs are specific and urgent.

Storage in Pyramids

This system is commonly employed for short-term storage in dry regions. It involves stacking bags in pyramid shapes on platforms that can be covered in case of adverse weather.

The platforms used for stacking bags must effectively protect the grain from termite damage. These platforms are typically covered with concrete, tar, or a layer of building blocks, and are topped with tarpaulins or plastic to prevent exposure to rising damp.

To ensure proper storage, the location of the storage areas must be carefully chosen, and drainage ditches should be dug around the platforms to direct rainwater runoff. Additionally, tarpaulins should cover the pyramids of bags to shield the grain from rain. This technique is commonly used for storing groundnuts.

Storage in Flexible Silos

Flexible silo storage is commonly used to establish a security reserve, and it closely resembles pyramid-style storage, though it involves a more complex facility.

A flexible silo typically consists of a concrete platform, often circular in shape. Around the platform, walls made of galvanized screening, usually about 2.5 meters high, are erected, with the interior lined with a thick plastic film. Surrounding the silo, about 50 cm away from the walls, galvanized metal sheets approximately 1 meter in height provide protection against rodents.

The bags of grain stacked within the silo are covered by a conical tarpaulin that is fastened to the walls and secured with a system of ropes.

As these silos are nearly airtight, it is crucial to ensure the grain is very dry when stored. Flexible silos typically hold 500 tonnes, though some can store between 250 and 1,000 tonnes. While the cost to build these silos is relatively low, their lifespan is limited, generally not exceeding five years.

Warehouses and Storehouses

Storage buildings, whether they are basic huts repurposed by farmers or modern, well-equipped warehouses, must fulfill several essential requirements:

- Protect the grain from moisture.
- Shield the grain from excessive temperatures.
- Keep insects, rodents, and birds from accessing the storage area.
- Allow for the monitoring of grain preservation.
- Enable timely insecticide treatments for both the bags and the storage environment.
- Support the maintenance of equipment used for handling and transporting the bags.

THE BUILDING'S POSITION AND ORIENTATION

To ensure effective protection of stored grain from atmospheric factors (such as sun, rain, and humidity) and to ensure smooth operation of storage systems, it is crucial to carefully choose the location and alignment of the buildings. The storage facilities should be:

- Situated in relatively dry areas that are not prone to flooding; avoid low-lying locations, clayey or poorly drained soils, and areas near streams and lakes whenever possible.
- Positioned away from urban areas, ideally equidistant from agricultural production zones and close to transportation routes.
- Located near electricity and water supply systems, where feasible.

Aligned along a north-south axis, ensuring that the sides with the smallest area receive the most sunlight.

BUILDINGS DIMENSIONS

Storehouses are typically rectangular in shape, with a length approximately twice their width. To determine the suitable dimensions of these buildings, the following factors should be considered:

- The type, quantity, and specific volume of grain to be stored in bags.
- The maximum height of the bag stacks.
- The number of batches to be separated and the width of the access corridors.
- The size and layout of service areas.

Specific Volume

Specific volume refers to the space occupied by one tonne of a particular type of grain when stored in bags. It is measured in cubic meters per tonne of product (m^3/t).

The table below provides the specific volumes for various products stored in bags:

Table 5.1: Specific volumes for various products

Grain Stored in Bags	Specific Volume
Milled rice, wheat, coffee	1.6 m^3/t
Maize, sorghum, groundnuts	1 8 m^3/t
(shelled)	
Beans, peas, lentils	1.3 m^3/t
Sunflower seeds	2.8 m^3/t
Soybeans, cocoa	2.0 m^3/t
Millet	1.25 m^3/t
Cottonseed	2.5 m^3/t
Wheat flour, maize flour	2.1 m^3/t

To determine the volume (in m^3) occupied by the bags in the storehouse, multiply the specific volume (in m^3/t) by the quantity of grain (in t) to be stored.

Height of the Stacks

The maximum height of the grain stacks depends on the type of bags used for storage. For bags made of plant fibers (such as jute or sisal), the maximum height can reach 5-6 meters, while for plastic bags (woven polythene), the height should not exceed 3 meters. Additionally, sufficient space must be left between the roof of the building and the top of the stacks to allow for easy movement of workers.

Passages and Corridors

The width of the passages between the batches can range from 2 to 4 meters, while the corridors between the walls and the batches should have a minimum width of 1 meter.

Service Areas

The size and layout of service areas depend on the overall size of the storage system. In addition to the storage spaces, the following provisions should always be made:

- An office, which may be equipped with laboratory tools for quality control.
- A shed for storing bags, equipment, tools, and chemicals.
- A work area, possibly roofed but without walls, for receiving, checking, and reconditioning grain if needed.

CONSTRUCTION DETAILS OF STOREHOUSE

Floor

The storehouse floor must be designed to prevent rising damp. This can be achieved by placing a waterproof layer (such as asphalt, tarred cloth, or plastic film) beneath the cement flooring.

Walls

Walls are typically constructed using bricks or breeze-blocks, but corrugated metal is also an option. The walls should be rough-plastered on both sides and finished with light-colored paint.

Roof

The roof should have an overhang, extending one-quarter to one-third of the height of the walls, to protect the storehouse from rainwater entering through the vents.

Vents

Vents should be appropriately sized and positioned at the top of the walls, under the overhang on the long sides of the building. These vents provide aeration, ventilation, and partial lighting. To prevent the entry of birds, rodents, and insects, these vents should be fitted with screens or mosquito nets.

Doors

The doorways must be wide enough for easy passage of people, equipment, and products. Double metal doors that open outward are preferred, and the doors should be sheltered by a porch-roof to protect against rain.

BUILDING UPKEEP

To ensure optimal storage conditions and extend the building's lifespan, regular monitoring and prompt maintenance are essential. Routine maintenance tasks may include:

- **Roof Repair:** Repositioning displaced roofing materials, replacing nails, sealing holes or cracks, and replacing damaged roofing sections.
- **Wall Maintenance:** Repairing the stucco and repainting the walls as needed.
- **Door-frame Repairs:** Fixing any damage to the door frames.
- **Ventilation System Upkeep:** Cleaning and repairing the ventilation systems to ensure proper airflow.
- **Floor maintenance:** Ensuring the floor remains in good condition.

Maintaining good sanitation also requires systematically clearing the premises and surrounding areas.

EQUIPMENT FOR STORAGE MANAGEMENT

Effective storage management requires equipping storehouses with appropriate tools. While some equipment is essential for maintaining proper storage conditions, others enhance efficiency and reduce workload. Depending on the scale of the storage system, the following equipment is recommended:

- **Reception and Inspection Tools:** Devices for measuring weight, humidity, and temperature.
- **Handling Equipment:** Tools that facilitate the movement of bags.
- **Reconditioning Equipment:** Tools for repackaging and restoring product quality.
- **Insecticide Treatment Equipment:** Necessary for treating grain, bags, and storage areas.
- **Storage Accessories:** Bags and pallets for organized and efficient storage.

Equipment for Handling

Grain bags are typically handled and carried manually. To facilitate this process, two-wheeled trolleys are commonly used for transporting individual bags. It is important to avoid using hooks, as they can cause significant damage to the bags.

In large warehouses, bag stacking is often done with the assistance of a bag-conveyor belt. However, in smaller storage facilities, a mobile bag-lift is generally preferred due to its compact design, which occupies minimal floor space. While the mobile bag-lift raises bags one at a time, the conveyor belt offers the advantage of continuous operation, enhancing efficiency in larger storage environments.

Equipment for Reconditioning Products

If the quality of incoming grain appears questionable, reconditioning may be required. In such cases, a grain-reconditioning unit is essential. This unit typically consists of two feed augers with a hopper, a cleaner-separator, an insecticide treatment device, a weighing and bagging system, and a bag-stitching machine to ensure proper sealing and packaging.

Bags and Pallets

Grain is stored in bags, and a well-stocked supply is essential for any storehouse. These bags can be made from plant fibers such as jute or cotton, or from plastic materials like polythene. The type of bag used plays a crucial role in determining the maximum stacking height.

To prevent direct contact with the floor, bags are placed on wooden platforms known as pallets. These pallets are essential in protecting the grain from moisture that may rise through the floor. Choosing or constructing lightweight pallets is advisable, as they can be moved more easily within the storehouse, enhancing flexibility in storage management.

Bag-storage Management

To ensure efficient reception and storage of grain delivered or stored in bags, the following key guidelines should be followed:

- Avoid accepting more grain than the storehouse can accommodate, considering both total capacity and the number of individual lots to be stored.

- Only store grain that is thoroughly dry and clean to maintain quality.
- Recondition any products if bags are damp, torn, or if the grain's quality appears uncertain.
- Construct stable, well-organized stacks of bags that are easily accessible.
- When stacking, allocate separate sections for different product types, quality levels, and dates of entry into storage.
- Follow the "First In, First Out" (FIFO) inventory management principle to maintain freshness.
- Keep the premises, equipment, and stored products in clean and well-maintained condition.
- Plan ahead to ensure an adequate supply of fuel, bags, insecticides, and other necessary materials.

Stacking the Bags

To ensure organized storage, each type of product should have a designated space within the storehouse:

- Lines can be painted on the floor to demarcate storage areas, keeping inspection corridors open between the walls and stacks of bags, as well as ensuring clear handling passageways near the doors.
- Before stacking, pallets should be inspected to ensure they are in good condition, with no protruding nails or damage.
- For stability, each bag should be stacked so that it is covered by two others.
- Stack walls should slope inward, especially for slippery bags like plastic, to prevent shifting or collapsing.
- Bags can also be arranged in pyramid formations for added stability.
- The maximum stack height should be determined based on the bag type (plant fiber or plastic), the fragility of the stored product, and the dimensions of the storehouse. The height should not exceed the width of the stack.
- Using uniform bag types and maintaining equalized stacks allows for quick and accurate inventory checks. By multiplying the number of bags in a single layer by the number of layers in a stack, the total count for each batch can be easily determined.
- Once stacking is completed, the contents must be verified and documented. Forms should be completed and regularly updated with details such as the number of bags, reception date, stacking date, and any insecticide treatments applied.
- These records must be made in duplicate—one copy for the storehouse administration and another attached to a bag within the corresponding stack for easy reference.

Inspections

Storehouses require frequent inspections to monitor both the condition of stored products and the integrity of the building structure.

Alongside daily visits, more comprehensive inspections should be conducted every one to two weeks to prevent losses caused by rodents, insects, and mold.

These inspections, ideally carried out at the end of the day, should include:

- Examining the condition of stacked bags, checking for issues such as torn stitching, leakage, insect presence, mold growth, damp spots, and rodent activity.
- Assessing the contents by taking grain samples to check moisture levels and signs of infestation.

Additionally, a thorough, overall inspection of both the facility and stored products should be performed on a monthly basis to ensure optimal storage conditions.

WHAT MAKES WAREHOUSE CAPACITY IMPORTANT?

Businesses can reduce operating costs and optimize warehouse space utilization with the aid of an accurate warehouse capacity. For a variety of reasons, you should be aware of how much you can store. Managing seasonal variations in the need for storage capacity is one of the reasons. Warehouse managers and buyers can place the proper inventory orders during these shifts by knowing these figures.

A simple pallet storage company is another example of why warehouse capacity matters. Without knowing your total pallet space capacity, how will you know when to refuse additional inventory? Last but not least, you are losing money if you don't have enough materials to use what your warehouse can hold. On the other hand, storing and maintaining the same inventory in a smaller warehouse becomes more costly if you have more storage space than you require.

WAREHOUSES (SHED) DESIGN

The following key factors should be considered when designing godowns:

- The side walls of the godown are constructed using brick or stone masonry, while the sloped roof is made of asbestos or Corrugated Galvanized Iron (CGI) sheets supported by steel trusses.
- A standard godown typically has a storage capacity of 5,000 tonnes, divided into three compartments, each with a minimum span of 21.7 meters and a clear height of 5.4 meters.
- Air circulation is facilitated through steel ventilators and air inlets made of rolled steel sections.
- The estimated requirement for construction materials includes approximately 50 metric tonnes of steel and 300 metric tonnes of cement.
- Bagged food grains are stacked with a base size of 6 meters × 9 meters, with stack heights varying between 4 and 5 meters. Around 27% of the total floor area is left as free space for alleyways.
- A minimum clearance of 2 meters should be maintained between stacks, while a space from 0.8 and 1.0 meters should be left between the walls and the stacks to allow easy movement for inspection.

- The structure should feature two large doors, each measuring 2.4 meters × 2.4 meters, positioned opposite each other, along with top ventilators to maintain airflow.
- Each door is equipped with an overhanging hood measuring 3.6 meters in length and 2.4 meters in width.
- A ground ventilator with an opening of 30 cm × 30 cm is placed below each top ventilator. The top of the ventilator is positioned 60 cm above the floor level and is secured with iron rods, wire netting, and shutters.
- The walls have a minimum thickness of 37.5 cm and a maximum thickness of 45 cm.
- The walls supporting the trusses are generally built to a height of approximately 5.5 meters.
- The roof can be either gabled or flat. The gabled roof is covered with corrugated metal sheets and is carefully sealed to prevent leaks. The flat roof, made of reinforced brick or reinforced concrete, is more durable and has a thickness from 10 to 12.5 cm.
- Under dry climatic conditions, wheat stored in bags can be preserved for up to two years, whereas in humid conditions, the storage period is reduced from 8 to 12 months.
- When stored in bulk, wheat can be preserved for up to five years in any location.

A Problem Regarding Design of Storage Structure

Create a structure for storing bags that can hold 250 tons of paddy. When required, make reasonable assumptions about the data.

Solution

The storage structure's design capacity = 250 T = 250,000 kg

A bag's capacity is 100 × 60 × 30 cm = 75 kg of Paddy

Therefore, the quantity of bags needed to store 250 T of paddy, or 250,000 kg of paddy

$$= \frac{250,000}{75}$$

= 3340 bags required for storage of 250 T paddy.

Bags are arranged in number of Stacks.

Assume that a stack of 10 bags has ten bags in length and 10 bags in width.

So, No of bags/layer = 10 × 10 = 100

The total number of bags in a stack with 12 layers

= 100 × 12 = 1200

Thus, the quantity of stacks needed

$$= \frac{3340}{1200} = 2.78 \approx 3 \text{ Stacks required for storage of 250 T of paddy}$$

Space required by each stack is as follows:

Length of stack $l = 10 \times 1.0 = 10.0$ m

Width of stack $w = 10 \times 0.6 = 6.0$ m

Height of stack $h = 12 \times 0.3 = 3.6$ m

The clear distance between the walls and the end of stack = 0.8 m

The clear distance between the stacks i.e., between two stack = 2.0 m

Hence, the length of floor L is as follows:

$L = (3 \times 6.0) + (2 \times 2.0) + (2 \times 0.8)$

$= 23.6 \text{ m} \approx 24.0 \text{ m}$

The width of floor W is given below:

$W = (10 \times 1.0) + (2 \times 0.8)$

$= 11.6 \text{ m} \approx 12.0 \text{ m}$

Thus, it is possible to assume that the godown's overall measurements are 24.0 m in length, 12.0 m in width, and 5.0 m in wall height above the floor.

The following figure displays the godown's floor plan.

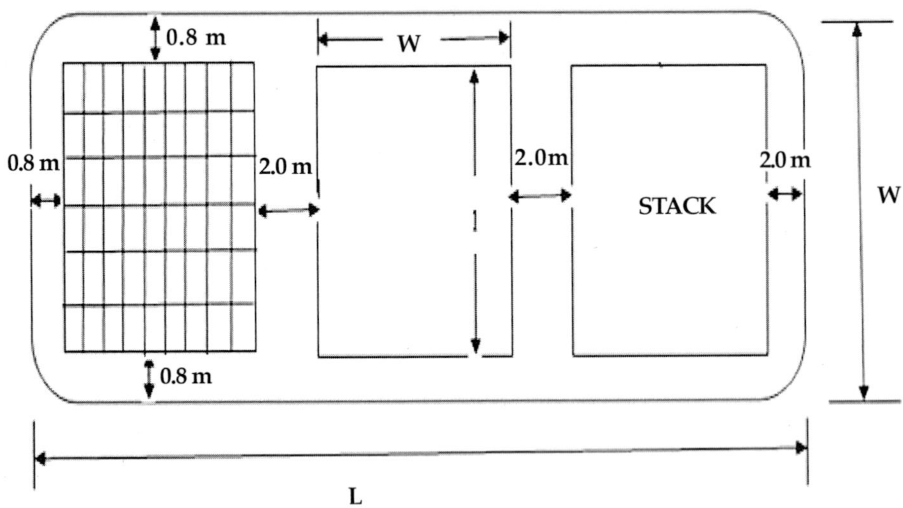

Figure : 5.1 Floor plan of the godown

CONTROL OF ENVIRONMENT

The management of the storage environment involves regulating the atmospheric gases within the storage structure. There are various modified and controlled atmosphere storage methods available. In controlled atmosphere storage, the oxygen levels are reduced to between 2-5%, while the carbon dioxide levels are elevated. This reduction in oxygen slows down the respiration rate of the stored grains, and the increased carbon dioxide concentration helps in eliminating insects.

Controlled Atmosphere Storage (CAS) systems rely on continuously monitoring the composition of the storage environment and injecting the necessary gases to maintain the required levels. These systems are equipped with advanced instruments to measure gas levels and require refrigeration units, nitrogen (N_2) generators, and equipment to evacuate oxygen (O_2) and ethylene. The N_2 generator extracts nitrogen from the atmosphere and pumps it into the storage chamber. A pressure relief valve helps maintain the desired pressure within the container by releasing excess air. This process is repeated until the oxygen level is lowered to the desired amount. The respiration of the stored produce also contributes to reducing the O_2 levels. Depending on the O_2 levels, periodic injection of air or nitrogen may be needed.

The CO_2 concentration is continuously monitored, and when it exceeds the preferred levels, the excess is passed through hydrated lime scrubbers to remove the CO_2. The air is also passed through ethylene absorbers to eliminate excess ethylene. The humidity inside the storage chamber is also closely monitored and maintained. While CAS does not stop deterioration entirely, it helps extend the shelf life of stored produce, ranging from a few days to several months, depending on the type of produce.

Three main techniques are generally used to create controlled atmosphere conditions within a storage facility: conventional CA, liquid N_2 systems, and N_2 generator systems. Conventional CA relies on the respiration of the stored commodity to produce CO_2. The CO_2 concentration is regulated using wet scrubbers, hydrated lime, or inert adsorbents. This storage method requires the room to be airtight, as any leakage can lead to an increase in oxygen levels beyond safe limits.

6

Constructional Features and Maintenance of Warehouses

The design and structure of a warehouse should facilitate proper ventilation, temperature control, and protection from pests. This includes features like smooth floors, durable walls, and proper drainage systems to prevent water accumulation. The warehouse should also be insulated to protect stored goods from extreme temperatures and humidity fluctuations.

Regular maintenance is essential to keep the warehouse in good condition. This involves routine checks for structural integrity, such as inspecting for cracks, leaks, or signs of pest infestation. Equipment like ventilation fans, conveyors, and lighting should be regularly serviced to ensure optimal functioning.

Sanitation and hygiene are equally important in preventing contamination and pest issues. The warehouse should be thoroughly cleaned to remove any dust, dirt, or residues that could harbor pests or mold. All surfaces, including walls, floors, and storage bins, should be disinfected regularly. Proper waste disposal systems should be in place, and areas where food products are stored should be kept free from garbage or organic waste that could attract pests. Ensuring a clean and well-maintained warehouse helps preserve the quality and safety of stored goods.

SELECTION OF STORAGE TYPE

Some basic Guildelins or Principles are Given as Follows:

ROUND OR RECTANGULAR STORAGE

In terms of structural cost per tonne of storage, round storage buildings are generally more cost-effective than rectangular ones. The reasons for this are straightforward:

First, grain exerts horizontal pressure on the structure that contains it. A round storage unit can resist this pressure through hoop tension forces, which are efficiently counteracted, such as with steel reinforcement. In contrast, a rectangular structure must resist grain loads through bending stresses, which are less efficient because both tensile and compressive forces must be managed. Additionally, in the case of a rectangular horizontal storage building, the walls serve as retaining walls, and their foundations must resist overturning moments caused by the grain load. In contrast, the foundations of cylindrical structures mainly need to resist the vertical loads from the walls.

Second, the roof of a rectangular structure must bear its load through bending, while the roof of a cylindrical structure can be designed as a shell (such as a cone), which distributes the load through direct compression and tension.

Cylindrical structures also have fewer joints. In silos where the bins are independent (not connected to one another), there is a joint between the wall and the floor, as well as between the wall and the roof. Sealing these joints to make the structure airtight and suitable for fumigation is usually a straightforward process. Ideally, the roof should be rigidly attached to the wall to facilitate sealing and to significantly enhance the wall's resistance to bending stresses. Silicone-based sealants can be used to seal the roof-wall joint, while bituminous mastic sealants are effective for sliding joints between the surfaces.

On the other hand, rectangular buildings have more joints (such as at the corners), and due to their design, sealing for fumigation tends to be more complex.

Horizontal storage systems also have a disadvantage in that they require more elaborate and extended conveying systems to distribute grain. Typically, an internal conveyor and a tripper (or similar device) are needed to spread the grain across the floor. In contrast, a cylindrical store only requires a central point for filling.

TALL OR SHORT STORAGE

In flat-bottomed storage systems, structural efficiency is improved by reducing the height of the structure. For a given storage volume, a lower wall height increases the grain pressure applied directly to the floor, reducing the load on the walls. Additionally, minimizing the structural surface area (and therefore the cost) for a specific volume of grain is achieved with relatively low walls. For instance, in a cylindrical storage tank with a conical roof, the minimum surface area of both the walls and roof occurs when the wall height is approximately half the radius of the bin. Therefore, it is no surprise that the most cost-effective stores are typically squat cylindrical "tanks," where the walls are relatively short in comparison to the diameter.

For example, consider a rectangular warehouse or shed with an 8-meter wall height and a length about two and a half times the width. To store 12,000 tonnes of corn (or roughly 16,000 cubic meters) with a repose angle of 30°, it might be calculated that the shed would need to be about 60 meters in length and 24 meters in width. In contrast, a cylindrical tank with the same volume and wall height would have a diameter of around 41 meters. Comparing the structural surface areas of both options yields the following results:

Table 6.1 : Comparison of structural areas for 12,000 tonne stores.

Area	Warehouse	Tank
Wall Surface	1510 m^{2*}	1000 m^2
Roof Surface	1660 m^2	1524 m^2
Floor Surface	1440 m^2	1320 m^2
Total Area:	4610 m^2	3844 m^2
* Including 'gable' end walls.		

Since the structural components are determined by the surface areas, this comparison can serve as an initial indicator of relative cost. As noted earlier, the walls and roof of a tank store are generally lighter and more cost-effective compared to those of a warehouse.

However, tank storage isn't suitable for every situation. For example, when high throughput is needed, a self-emptying bin with a sloped floor is often preferable. In such cases, it's more cost-effective to design taller walls with a smaller diameter to minimize the cost of hopper bottoms (which are typically suspended above ground level), reduce the risk of groundwater infiltration, and simplify conveyor design and installation. In areas where land values are high or space is limited, tall bins, even with flat floors, may be the best option to optimize space utilization.

The primary disadvantage of flat-bottomed stores lies in the difficulty of emptying them and removing "dead" grain that does not discharge by gravity. There are several methods to address this issue, such as using portable conveying equipment, pneumatic systems, or front-end loaders. Another popular option is the sweep conveyor (usually a screw or auger), which automatically rotates around the center of the bin to move grain toward the discharge point. Sweep conveyors are often buried under the grain when the bin is full and operate after gravity discharge is completed. In some cases, they are suspended above the grain surface and lowered with winches to perform their function. It should be noted that investing in permanently installed sweep conveyors can be costly and may not be justified if they are only used once or twice a year.

However, when low throughput is needed, such as when a store is filled and emptied only two or three times per year, the lower capital investment in a large-diameter flat store generally outweighs the additional capital and operational costs for emptying it. To determine the most cost-effective solution, it is usually necessary to analyze both capital and operational costs, particularly if the store will be emptied more than five times per year.

CONSTRUCTION MATERIALS

The choice of construction material typically comes down to steel and concrete, although timber or masonry are still used in some regions. The decision between steel and concrete is influenced by a variety of factors, with capital and operational costs being the most significant. In many countries, both materials are widely used, indicating that their costs are generally comparable.

When price is not the primary factor, the following points may help guide the choice:

- Steel silos tend to be quicker to construct than concrete ones, although this is not always the case.
- Steel silos are highly effective for storing dry grain. However, when the grain has high moisture content, there may be a higher risk of moisture migration. This is because the heat conductivity of steel can cause temperature gradients between the inside and outside of the grain mass, leading to moisture condensation on the grain's surface.
- Welded steel silos are gas-tight throughout their lifespan since they are not prone to cracking or differential movements. However, they are susceptible to corrosion and need maintenance to maintain the effectiveness of their paint coatings. The choice of coating system is crucial as it impacts both capital and maintenance costs. It is important to select paint systems tailored to specific needs, and expert advice should be consulted, especially in environments prone to corrosion.
- Proprietary bins made from light-gauge bolted steel panels are a cost-effective storage solution. However, sealing these bins for fumigation can be challenging due to the large number of bolts (8,000 to 10,000 in a 1000-ton silo). With light-gauge steel panels, there is a risk of distortion at the bolt holes and relative movement between panels when the silo is under load. Choosing the right sealing washers under bolt heads and nuts is critical. Felt washers impregnated with materials tend to perform better than unreinforced neoprene types, which may distort under pressure. Silicone sealants are effective for creating a seal between panels, and specially formulated high-build acrylic sealants, often reinforced with fiberglass or similar fabrics, are useful for sealing joints between the roof, walls, and floor.

UNDERGROUND STORAGE STRUCTURES

Subterranean storage facilities are well-like dugouts with cowdung plastered on the sides. They could also be lined with cement and sand or stones. They could have a rectangular or circular shape. The structure's size affects its capacity.

Advantages

- The underground storage space can be temporarily used for other purposes with slight modifications;

- The underground storage structures are easier to fill up because of gravity; and
- They are safer from threats from various external sources of damage, such as theft, rain, or wind.

SURFACE STORAGE STRUCTURES

There are two methods for storing food grains in a ground surface structure: bulk storage and bag storage.

Bag Storage

- Bags are simpler to load and unload; each bag has a specific quantity that can be easily purchased, sold, or shipped.
- Having identifying marks on the bags makes it simpler to maintain distinct lots.
- Because the bag's surface is exposed to the atmosphere, the issue of grain sweating does not occur; additionally, bags that are found to be infested upon inspection are easily removed and treated.

BULK OR LOOSE STORAGE

Advantages

- The exposed surface area per unit weight of grain is reduced, which minimizes the risk of damage from external sources.
- Pest infestation is minimized due to nearly airtight conditions in the deeper layers.
- The Government of India has taken steps to encourage the development of better storage facilities at the farm level.

Improved Grain Storage Structures

- For small-scale storage
- PAU bin

This structure is made of galvanized metal iron and has a capacity ranging from 1.5 to 15 quintals. It was designed by Punjab Agricultural University.

- Pusa bin

This storage structure is constructed using mud or bricks, with a polythene film integrated into the walls.

- Hapur Tekka

It is a cylindrical structure made of rubberized cloth, supported by bamboo poles placed on a metal tube base. The structure features a small hole at the bottom for grain removal.

- For large scale storage
- CAP Storage (Cover and Plinth)

This method involves building brick pillars up to a height of 14 inches from the ground, with grooves designed to hold wooden crates for stacking bags of food grains. The structure can be constructed in under three weeks and offers a cost-effective solution for large-scale storage.

- **Silos**

  In silos, bulk grains are unloaded onto conveyor belts, where mechanical operations transport them into the storage structure. Each silo has a storage capacity of approximately 25,000 tonnes.

WAREHOUSING

Warehouses are specialized storage facilities designed to safeguard the quantity and quality of stored products.

Importance

- **Scientific Storage:** This ensures the protection of the product against both quantitative and qualitative losses by employing necessary preservation techniques.
- **Financing:** Warehouses provide financial support to those storing products. Nationalized banks offer credit against the warehouse receipt issued for stored goods, typically up to 75-80% of their value.
- **Price Stabilization:** Warehouses contribute to the stabilization of agricultural commodity prices by reducing the tendency of farmers to sell their produce immediately after harvest.
- **Market Intelligence:** Warehouses provide access to market information for those holding their products within the facility.

Working of Warehouses

- **Acts:** The warehouses (CWC and SWCs) operate under the Warehousing Acts established by the Central or State Government.
- **Eligibility:** Any individual can store notified commodities in a warehouse, provided they agree to pay the specified charges.
- **Warehouse Receipt (Warrant):** This is a receipt or warrant issued by the warehouse manager or owner to the person storing their produce. It contains details such as the name and location of the warehouse, the issue date, and a description of the commodities, including the grade, weight, and approximate value based on current market prices.
- **Use of Chemicals:** The produce stored in the warehouse is scientifically preserved and protected against rodents, insects, pests, and other infestations. Periodic dusting and fumigation are carried out at the warehouse's expense to ensure the protection of the goods.
- **Financing:** The warehouse receipt acts as collateral for securing credit.

- **Delivery of Produce:** The warehouse receipt must be surrendered to the warehouse owner before the withdrawal of goods. The holder may also take delivery of a portion of the stored produce after paying the applicable storage charges.

TYPES OF WAREHOUSE

On the Basis of Ownership

- **Private Warehouses:** These warehouses are owned by individuals, large businesses, or wholesalers for the storage of their own inventory. They may also store goods for others.
- **Public Warehouses:** These warehouses are government-owned and designated for the storage of goods for the public.
- **Bonded Warehouses:** These warehouses are specifically constructed at seaports or airports and are used to store imported goods until customs duties are paid by the importer. Licensed by the government, these warehouses hold "bonded goods". The services provided by bonded warehouses include:

  The importer can avoid paying the full customs duty upfront, as they can take delivery of the goods in parts.

  Regular maintenance services such as spraying and dusting are carried out to preserve the quality of the goods.

  They facilitate entrepot trade, which involves the re-export of imported goods.

  On the basis of Type of Commodities Stored

- **General Warehouses:** These are standard warehouses used for the storage of various goods such as food grains, fertilizers, and other general products.
- **Special Commodity Warehouses:** These warehouses are specially designed for storing specific types of commodities like cotton, tobacco, wool, and petroleum products.
- **Refrigerated Warehouses:** These warehouses maintain controlled temperatures as per the storage needs of perishable goods such as vegetables, fruits, fish, eggs, and meat.

VARIOUS TYPES OF IMPROVED STORAGE STRUCTURES

PUSA BIN

The Pusa bin is a traditional storage structure made from mud, with an added feature for moisture protection. To prevent moisture, a plastic film is placed on the inner side of the bin. The construction begins with a mud brick platform, on top of which a 700-gauge plastic sheet is spread, overlapping the platform by at least 6 cm. A layer of 7 cm thick "kachcha" bricks is laid on the plastic sheet.

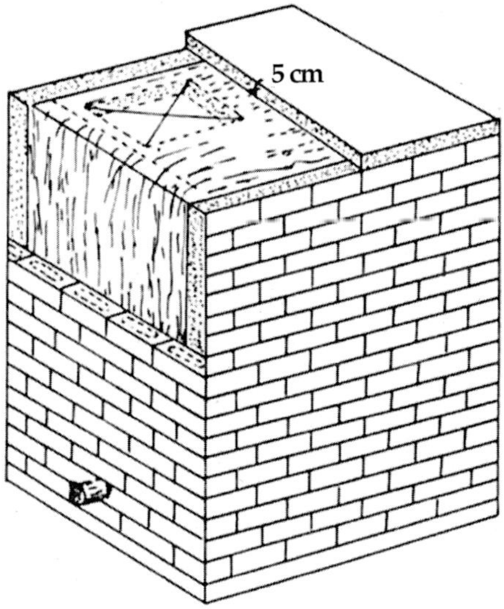

Figure: 6.1 A Pusa bin Design

The walls are constructed from "kachcha" bricks, sealed with mud plaster, and raised to the required height. A wooden frame is then placed on top of the walls. The roof is made from burnt bricks.

For unloading, an inclined wooden or steel pipe is installed, allowing the grains to exit by gravity, with the mouth of the pipe closed by a cover. The inside walls and roof of the bin are also covered with plastic sheets. A 50 cm × 50 cm open space is left at the top for grain loading, which is sealed with mud after filling the bin. Once filled, the top open space is covered with a plastic sheet to prevent air from entering. A typical Pusa bin design is illustrated in Figure.

BRICK AND CEMENT BIN

These storage structures are highly durable, making them largely unaffected by seasonal changes. The bin is constructed on a platform elevated 60 cm above the ground, with a ladder on one side to facilitate grain loading. A hole, approximately 60 cm in diameter, is located on the roof for the loading of grains. The walls of the bin are about 23 cm thick, with cement plaster applied on both sides.

The roof is made of reinforced cement concrete (R.C.C.). The bin's base is inclined, and an outlet is included for the unloading of grains. These bins typically have a capacity ranging from 1.5 to 60 tonnes. For cleaning and complete unloading, iron ring steps are installed inside the bin, allowing easy entry and exit for personnel.

Bunker Storage

Bunker storage structures are designed for the long-term storage of large volumes of grains. This system proves to be an effective and cost-efficient method for storing grains securely. By managing insect activity and controlling moisture levels, losses in stored grains can be minimized by up to 0.5%. In this storage setup, the grain is placed on a plastic sheet spread over the ground, and the top is covered with another plastic sheet, as illustrated in Figure: 36.2. Additionally, a drain is included to ensure the proper drainage of rainwater.

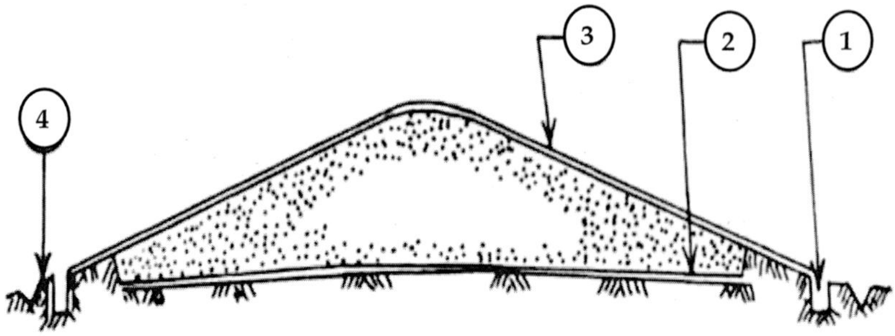

Figure: 6.2 Improved storage structure types

'CAP' STORAGE STRUCTURES

The 'CAP' is a storage system used for both cover and plinth storage. The term "plinth" refers to the foundation or base, while "cover" refers to the protection provided from the top. This type of open storage is considered an intermediate solution and is typically used for short-term storage of food grains in bags. It is a more cost-effective alternative to traditional bag storage godowns. The cover is rectangular, consisting of five sides and is made from 1000 gauge polyethylene film, with the bottom side left open. This cover serves to protect the stacks of bags.

Typically, the stack is placed over an area of 9.11 × 6.1 meters, with a height of 18 bags, offering a storage capacity of around 150 tonnes. The cover, measuring 9.4 m × 6.4 m × 5.5 m, weighs approximately 52 kg. In some cases, smaller covers, known as "Varandah covers," are used to cover stacks in the covered verandahs of conventional godowns. For storage under varandah covers, the stacks are built up to a height of 7 bags, with an average storage capacity of 24 tonnes.

The following steps are typically followed during the construction of a 'CAP' storage system:

- Choose an elevated plot of land and ensure it is leveled.
- Lay wooden sleepers and cover them with one or two layers of bamboo mat as dunnage.
- Install gutters around the area to facilitate easy drainage of rainwater.
- Stack the bags up to a height of 18 on the dunnage and cover the stacks with polyethylene.
- Secure the polyethylene covers by tying them with ropes to prevent them from being blown away by strong winds.

MAINTENANCE OF GRAIN STORAGE

Maintaining grain storage is crucial for preserving the quality of the grain and prolonging the life of a grain silo. Early in the year is the ideal time to inspect your grain silo and its associated conveyor systems. This proactive approach helps avoid unexpected issues during the summer months, providing ample time for any necessary repairs or replacements.

Key maintenance tasks for grain storage include:

- Inspect the silo for signs of wear, leaks, or corrosion.
- Remove any old grain residue, dust, and debris.
- Test and inspect electronic components such as safety systems and the power box.
- Check and test associated conveying and aeration systems, including belt conveyors, conveyor chains, elevators, chutes, augers, and fans.

IMPORTANCE OF MAINTENANCE

Preserving Grain Quality

Maintaining grain storage systems is vital for preserving the quality of the stored grain. Proper upkeep ensures that contamination from pests, rodents, and molds is prevented, which could otherwise degrade the grain's quality and cause considerable losses. By keeping your grain storage in optimal condition, you protect the investment and ensure the grains retain their nutritional content, integrity, and market value.

Reducing Losses and Waste

The global issue of grain loss and waste is substantial, with the Food and Agriculture Organization of the United Nations (FAO) estimating that approximately one-third of the food produced for human consumption is lost or wasted. By performing regular on-farm maintenance, you help minimize post-harvest losses, ensuring that storage facilities and equipment function efficiently. This not only avoids the need for early disposal of spoiled grain but also optimizes the use of limited and valuable resources.

Ensuring Safety and Compliance

Routine maintenance of grain storage facilities is essential for ensuring the safety of farm workers and the surrounding environment. Proper care and attention to maintenance help prevent accidents that may arise due to structural failures, equipment malfunctions, or hazardous spills. Moreover, by prioritizing maintenance, it becomes much easier to adhere to local and international regulations regarding safe grain storage and handling practices.

Prolonging the Lifespan of Storage Structures and Equipment

Regular upkeep not only helps safeguard the quality of the grain but also extends the life of grain storage facilities and associated equipment. Performing timely inspections, repairs, and replacements can drastically reduce the need for expensive upgrades or complete overhauls. This approach makes your grain storage investments more cost-efficient in the long run.

UPKEEP ADVICE FOR GRAIN STORAGE ON FARMS

Regular Inspections

Routine inspections of your grain storage facilities should be a top priority. Look out for any signs of wear, structural damage, or potential pest issues. Pay attention to the condition of roofs, walls, foundations, and ventilation systems, checking for leaks, cracks, or signs of corrosion.

Pest Control

Establish a thorough pest control strategy that includes regular cleaning of the storage facilities and monitoring for pest activity. Use traps and approved pesticides when necessary, always ensuring to follow the manufacturer's instructions for proper and safe application.

Aeration and Temperature Control

Effective aeration and temperature regulation are essential for preserving grain quality. Ensure that your aeration systems are operating properly and frequently monitor the temperature of the grain. Adjust the ventilation systems accordingly to maintain the best possible storage conditions.

Equipment Maintenance

Routine checks and maintenance of grain handling equipment, such as augers, conveyors, and elevators, are essential. Regularly lubricate moving parts, replace any worn-out components, and keep equipment clean to ensure smooth, efficient, and safe operation.

Maintaining on-farm grain storage is key to preserving grain quality, minimizing losses, ensuring safety, and extending the life of storage facilities and equipment. By following a proactive maintenance schedule, farmers can safeguard their investments, support global food security, and retain their competitive edge in the market.

MANAGEMENT OF GRAIN STORAGE OF OPERATIONS

The condition of the products in stock should be evaluated periodically to detect any issues such as infection, tampering, theft, or deterioration, which may arise from pest infestations, aging, unsanitary conditions, or improper temperature and humidity control. Food products must be stored off the floor and away from the walls. Silos should undergo regular maintenance, and wheat storage silos must be kept clean, hygienic, and regularly fumigated.

The interior of grain storage containers should be clean, free from cracks, and devoid of crevices. If the storage tanks are vented, the venting systems must be properly maintained and designed to prevent contamination of the stored contents. Damaged goods should be stored in a designated area to prevent contamination or potential infestation of other products in the storage facility.

RULES FOR HYGINE AND CLEANING IN WAREHOUSE

During storage, agricultural commodities and food grains can deteriorate due to both physical and biological factors. These include moisture, temperature fluctuations, insects, birds, and storage fungi:

- The floor space within godowns or warehouses should be cleaned regularly and thoroughly on a daily basis.
- Grain bags should be brushed weekly and after each fumigation to ensure cleanliness.
- Maintaining cleanliness throughout the entire warehouse complex is essential.
- Measures to prevent bird access to warehouses should be implemented to avoid contamination of the grain and other commodities with excreta or dead birds.
- The roofs within the warehouses should be coated with waterproof materials and must be leak-proof to prevent moisture infiltration.
- Warehouse staff should ensure that all pipes or ducts entering the warehouse are properly sealed with wire mesh to prevent the entry of rats.
- Periodic repairs should be made to address any cracks or structural issues.
- Adequate lighting must be provided inside the warehouse to ensure visibility and safety.
- Proper and timely aeration must be carried out to reduce grain temperature and moisture, while also eliminating pest infestations, including psocids.
- Waste materials and dead inventory, such as used gunny bags, wooden crates, and polythene sheets, should not be stored in the warehouse. A separate room should be designated for such items.

A single bag of infested grain can generate over a million insects in a year, which can travel to other grain storage areas and cause new infestations. Effective grain hygiene practices include removing any grain that could harbor pests, preventing them from breeding. Regular inspections of seed and stockfeed grain should also be conducted to detect and control pest infestations before they spread.

WHERE TO CLEAN?

Grain hygiene, which is essential for preventing pest infestations, revolves around eliminating environments that allow pests to live and reproduce. This includes cleaning all grain handling equipment and storage areas. Pests are attracted to dark, sheltered places and thrive in warm conditions.

Common areas where pests are typically found include:

- Empty silos and grain storages
- Aeration ducts, augers, and conveyors

- Harvesters, field bins, and chaser bins
- Leftover bags of grain
- Trucks used for transporting grain
- Spilled grain around storage areas
- Equipment and rubbish near storage facilities
- Seed grain
- Stockfeed grain

To maintain effective grain hygiene, it's crucial to clean all areas where grain can accumulate in storage and equipment. Grain pests can survive in even small amounts of grain, meaning that any parcel of fresh grain passing through machinery or storage can quickly become infested.

WHEN TO CLEAN?

The optimal time to clean grain handling equipment and storage facilities is immediately after harvest, before pests have a chance to infest them. It's also recommended to discard the first few bags of grain at the start of the new harvest.

HOW TO CLEAN

The effectiveness of pest control largely depends on thorough cleaning, which reduces the opportunity for pests to take shelter. To remove all grain residues, the best methods involve a combination of:

- Sweeping
- Vacuuming
- Compressed air
- Blow/vacuum guns
- Pressure washers
- Fire-fighting hoses

Using a broom or compressed air will eliminate most of the grain residues, while a subsequent wash-down helps remove the dust and grain trapped in crevices or hard-to-reach areas.

It's recommended to wash storage areas and equipment on a warm, dry day to ensure they dry quickly and prevent rusting. While inspecting empty storage spaces, look for ways to improve cleanliness by sealing cracks and crevices, which can otherwise trap grain and foster pest infestations. Leftover grain bags and spilt grain around the storage areas serve as perfect breeding grounds for pests. After cleaning up the spillage, ensure that the residues are disposed of far from any storage areas to prevent further contamination.

7

Integrated Pest Management in Grain Storage System

Storage plays a crucial role between harvesting and the processing or direct consumption of food grains. In developing countries, its significance is amplified, especially since small and medium landholding farmers heavily rely on on-farm storage. In India, however, an annual storage loss of 14 million tons, worth approximately 7,000 crores, occurs due to post-harvest pest damage. The economic loss from storage pests is not only a result of consumption but also due to contamination and spoilage caused by the pests' body parts, excreta, and hoarding. The lack of awareness about storage pests, their damage, and the use of improper storage techniques contribute to these massive losses.

The solution lies in constructing suitable storage structures, which are well-equipped and properly managed, and implementing strict hygiene standards in storage areas, along with efficient pest control measures. These combined efforts are essential to minimize storage losses. This section focuses on identifying major pests in storage and their management strategies.

SIGNIFICANT INSECT PESTS OF GRAINS THAT ARE STORED

The primary insect pests that affect stored grains include:

- Lesser grain borer (*Rhizopertha dominica*)
- Rice weevil (*Sitophilus oryzae*)
- Khapra beetle (*Trogoderma granarium*)
- Rust red flour beetle (T*ribolium castaneum*)
- Long headed flour beetle (*Latheticus oryzae*)
- Saw toothed beetle (*Oryzaephilus surinamensis*)
- Rice moth (*Corcyra cephalonica*)
- Almond moth (*Cadra cautella*)
- Angoumois grain moth (*Sitotroga cerealella*)

- Pulse beetles : *Callosobruchus chinensis, C. maculates, C. analis.*

Non-insect pests encompass rodents, mites, and fungi.

STORAGE OF MANAGEMENT

For efficient management of insect pests in storage, an integrated pest management (IPM) approach should be implemented. This approach includes sanitation of the storage facility, cleaning the grains before storage, monitoring pest activity, controlling temperature and moisture levels both inside and outside the storage area, and using grain protectants as needed.

Sanitation

Sanitation of both the storage facility and surrounding areas is vital for eliminating pest stages and habitats. This helps prevent the accumulation of pest populations and further damage to the stored goods. Whenever new grains or commodities arrive at the facility, it's crucial to remove any old or infested grains. Always use pest-free storage containers such as bins or jute bags. Pay close attention to cracks and crevices in the floors or walls of storage areas (godowns), as these can harbor pests and lead to continued infestation. Prior to storing any commodities for an extended period, it is recommended to apply a preventive spray in the warehouses, godowns, or storage structures. Insecticides such as deltamethrin 2.5 WP (40 gm/l) and malathion 50 EC (1% or 3 liters per 100 m^2) can be used to protect the stored grains.

Sun Drying of Grains

Sun drying is the most widely adopted method before storing food grains. This technique helps reduce storage losses due to mold, discoloration, respiration, and insect damage. The moisture content of grains may vary depending on how long the storage period is. Proper grain cleaning before storage ensures even airflow within the storage structure, which helps minimize fungal growth.

Additionally, cleaning removes unwanted grains from other crops, weeds, and pests that may be present. Most importantly, cleaning the grains boosts the effectiveness of pest management practices such as fumigation.

Grain Protectants

Grain protectants, mainly contact insecticides, are used to eliminate insect pests in storage godowns and other structures. These insecticides can be used for both preventative and curative measures. For example, insecticides like deltamethrin 2.5% WP and malathion 50% EC are applied at recommended doses on the walls, floors, alleyways, and surface of grain bags to target and kill insect stages. Malathion 50% EC is diluted with water in a 1:100 ratio, and a 3-liter emulsion is sprayed over 100 m^2 of surface area every 15 days.

Similarly, 40 grams of deltamethrin 2.5% WP is dissolved in 1 liter of water, and 3 liters of the emulsion are sprayed over 100 m^2 of surface area every 90 days. For curative control, fumigation of grain stacks or godowns with phosphine at the recommended dose is effective. For proper fumigation, storage containers should be airtight or grain stacks should be covered with gas-proof fumigation covers.

Natural alternatives like dried neem or margosa leaves can be mixed with food grains and stored in gunny bags or bins. Additionally, 200 grams of common table salt can be mixed with 1 kg of pulses for storage over a 6-8 month period. Red soil and water can be mixed to form a paste, and seeds are placed in this paste and thoroughly mixed, ensuring that the soil adheres to the seeds. The seeds can then be stored in gunny bags.

Storage Structures

A key element in understanding grain storage structures is ensuring the prevention of air and moisture migration to avoid providing oxygen to living organisms within the storage. Generally, grain storage structures are classified based on factors like material availability, storage capacity, and economic considerations. These structures can be categorized as indoor or outdoor, above-ground or underground, and made from materials like mud, wood, bamboo, metal drums, bins, or containers.

In India, 59-70% of food grains are stored in traditional storage systems, often constructed from materials like paddy or wheat straw, bamboo, wood, bricks, mud, and cow dung. These structures can be found indoors, outdoors, or underground.

Modern storage solutions such as the Pusa bin (developed by ICAR-IARI), domestic Hapur bin (Indian Grain Storage Institute), and PAU bin (Punjab Agricultural University) have been developed for smaller-scale storage needs, ranging from 1 to 3 tonnes.

INTEGRATED CONTROL OF PEST

The challenges associated with stored-grain pest control in tropical regions, particularly in developing countries, are succinctly addressed by Taylor, Golob, and Hodges (1992). They emphasize the critical need for effective pest control for a diverse range of storage operators, including resource-limited farmers, commercial entities, and national marketing organizations, across various storage settings. These storage systems range from simple on-farm techniques to large-scale bag-storage systems. Bulk storage is more common for small quantities at the farm level but is less prevalent in large operations, except in major grain mills or central marketing depots.

Pest control strategies must be integrated into the operational framework, whether small or large scale, to ensure their success. This is a well-established principle that aligns with the modern concept of Integrated Pest Management (IPM). The inclusion of the term 'management' is appropriate, particularly in reference to the necessity of incorporating pest control into broader management systems. However, it is important to recognize that 'management' and 'control' are nearly synonymous, with the key focus being on the term 'integrated.'

Integrated pest control can be defined as the acceptable use of practical measures to cost-effectively minimize pest damage within a specific management system. For these measures to be cost-effective, they must be suitable for and accepted by that system, regardless of whether they are simple or complex. These strategies should align with system objectives and technical capabilities, with cost-effectiveness accounting for all factors, including sociological and environmental considerations.

The term Integrated Pest Management suggests the need for a flexible, well-informed approach. To define IPM, it is often necessary to include scientific, cost-effective pest monitoring systems that allow for informed adjustments in the timing, type, and intensity of control measures. It's also important to note that specific pest control actions should only be included when they are cost-effective and necessary, rather than as a default.

Like preharvest pest management, insect pest management for stored grains has traditionally emphasized good husbandry. Unfortunately, the availability and affordability of synthetic insecticides have led to over-reliance on these products, sometimes at the expense of basic husbandry practices. The current focus on IPM is essentially a reassertion of the importance of good husbandry as the foundation for pest control. In grain storage, as with other long-lasting agricultural goods, effective commodity and store management are crucial prerequisites.

Several more intensive pest control options, outlined in Tables, draw on traditional pest management concepts, such as thermal disinfestation, cooling, and hermetic storage. The latter two methods showcase how storage environments can be managed to prevent insect pest reproduction or, in the case of efficient hermetic storage, eliminate pests entirely. Such methods are far easier to manage in storage than preharvest pest control issues.

Control of the storage environment is a key element in managing grain storage pests. This involves regulating the in-store climate and pest pressure through proper store design and construction. Equally vital is the scientific management of the stored commodity to ensure it is dry and cool when loaded or, in ventilated stores with aeration systems, that drying and cooling occur rapidly. In a fully loaded store, the grain itself largely dictates and stabilizes the temperature and humidity conditions.

Commodity management can also significantly influence the initial level of insect infestation in stored grain. However, in tropical areas where preharvest insect infestation is nearly impossible to fully prevent, achieving the ideal of loading pest-free grain is often unattainable. In such cases, special facilities to entirely disinfest the grain may not be cost-effective. More common alternatives, when early disinfestation is required, include treating the grain with insecticides at intake or fumigating the grain once stored.

Grain quality management before storage, aimed at minimizing the intake of heavily infested or damaged grain, is both feasible and commonly practiced. Even small-scale farmers can segregate crops at harvest, especially maize on the cob or unthreshed sorghum and millet, by selecting relatively undamaged material with good storage potential, and setting aside the more infested or damaged portions for immediate use. This practice helps slow the rate of deterioration due to insect damage in the main stock of stored grain. Many subsistence farmers effectively use this form of commodity management, and it is sometimes possible to observe on-farm grain stocks with minimal insect damage after several months of storage at ambient temperatures conducive to rapid pest population growth.

Scientific approaches to grain storage pest management, which consider grain storage as part of the broader food production and distribution system, have occasionally applied the biological ecosystem concept to better understand the complex interactions involved. Dunkel (1992) used ecosystem principles to provide a comprehensive analysis of the physical and biological dynamics, including socio-economic factors, aiming to improve the understanding of the stored grain ecosystem and identify objectives for future research. Whether or not the term 'ecosystem' is adopted is less significant, and this academic label should not detract from the main issues at hand.

Table 7.1 : Prerequisites and options for on-farm storage pest management

Essential	Optional
Basic IPM	**Additional measures**
Site and store management (protection from birds, rodents and weather plus basic hygiene)	Maintenance of conditions favourable to natural control: - by cooling (where feasible) by insect parasites, pathogens, etc. and/or Thermal disinfestation by solar heat and/or Treatment with traditional additives (if sufficiently available and effective)
Commodity management (cleaning, drying, etc.)	or Treatment with synthetic insecticides (if suitable formulations sufficiently available and effective) or Hermetic storage (pits or metal drums, etc.)

Table 7.2 : Prerequisites and options for storage pest management at main depots

Essential	Optional	
Basic IPM	**Disinfestation** **Prevention of reinfestation**	
Site and store management (protection from birds, rodents and weather plus basic hygiene)	Insecticide admixture * Fumigation! or Thermal *	Provided by the treatment Residual insecticide sprays?! Physical protection! (Sheeted stacks or packaging) or

Essential	**Optional**	
Basic IPM	**Disinfestation** **Prevention of reinfestation**	
Commodity management (cleaning, drying, etc.) - with bulk storage if appropriate	Irradiation * Hermetic! Controlled atmosphere! Grain cooling!	Insecticidal space treatments! Provided by the system Provided by the system Provided by the system
* May entail double handling for in-bag storage. Efficacy doubtful. Extra management skills and/or other inputs required.		

The integration of various pest control techniques within the framework of Integrated Pest Management (IPM) has become a key area of research in the field of stored product pest management. The importance of a multidisciplinary approach in stored grain research has also been emphasized. This is indeed a valid point, but it is worth remembering that much of the research conducted in the past has already followed this approach. As highlighted by McFarlane (1981) at a stored product pest management symposium in 1978, the need for an interdisciplinary approach is widely recognized. Fields such as entomology, mycology, chemistry, engineering, and food science are often involved, but the effective integration of technical solutions remains elusive, possibly because practical disciplines like economics, sociology, and business management are not always sufficiently considered. The interaction between the research team and storage managers—whether individual farmers or large storage organizations—can often be the most significant barrier to progress.

The most important requirement is a clear understanding that solutions must be integrated into the management system, meeting business objectives and fitting within existing management capabilities (Hindmarsh and McFarlane, 1983). In this regard, it is interesting, though not surprising, that a correlation has been observed among Indian farmers between their "grain hoarding capacity" (reflecting their existing business objectives and capabilities) and the adoption of improved storage practices.

Modern pest management theories have introduced the concept of economic control thresholds (ECTs). An ECT is simply the level of pest damage at which the cost of control actions becomes justifiable in terms of cost/benefit analysis. This threshold is always variable because the costs and benefits depend on the specific circumstances. An ECT is therefore context-specific. This variability is particularly significant when comparing small-scale farms in developing countries to more advanced operations. However, it is possible to make generalizations. For insect control in grain storage, the ECT is likely to be very low or close to zero in situations where:

a. Consumer demand requires products to be free from insect damage and any visible sign of infestation.

b. The intention is to store grain for a long period, where substantial insect damage is anticipated, and where the market is sensitive to quality loss.

In these cases, it is assumed that at least one cost-effective pest control package is available, providing for sustained control, including preventing or managing reinfestation. In more sophisticated systems with higher consumer quality standards, these assumptions hold true. If not, the ECT will not be zero, and the required quality would need to be maintained through reconditioning, with the losses, including reconditioning costs, absorbed by the system or consumer. In such situations, a real economic loss may occur, masked by marketing strategies.

When grain is stored for domestic use or for sale in a less demanding market, the ECT may be well above zero, even when all aspects of economic damage are considered. In these cases, the true economic significance of a small percentage of insect-damaged grain is often negligible. The actual loss in food value is likely minimal, and the market value of the associated weight loss, if salvaged, may not justify the full costs of pest control.

The need to minimize pest control costs often discourages the extensive use of environmentally friendly alternatives, which might otherwise be preferred over conventional fumigants and contact insecticides. However, it must also be recognized that chemical pest control methods in grain storage are often the most cost-effective and reliably efficient options available. As long as these treatments are considered safe, an essential aspect of IPM in grain storage is to ensure that chemical methods are only recommended when they can be safely and effectively used and when their economic justification is clear.

The economic justification for control measures, including the use of chemical pesticides where necessary, should consider all associated costs and benefits. Many of these may be subjective, influenced by local attitudes and sensibilities, but measurable losses in quantity and certain quality parameters can be objectively assessed. A manual for evaluating postharvest losses provides useful guidance, though some methods may need modification for specific circumstances. A critical review of this methodology offers further insights, based on fieldwork in developing countries since 1978. When selecting methods—many of which are subject to debate—it is important to consider the specific context and the prevailing objectives. There is no universally "best" method for all situations; in practice, operational ease and repeatability are generally more important than precision. From the storekeeper's perspective, a reduction in loss from 5% to 4%—though statistically significant—may have little practical impact, while a reduction from 10% to 5% (or from 2% to 1% in a more advanced storage system) may be highly meaningful, provided such reductions are achievable in routine operations.

CHEMICAL CONTROL TECHNIQUES

The chemical compounds, including both fumigants and contact insecticides, that are approved by FAO/WHO for use on food grains to manage storage insects are regularly assessed. Their safety for pest control operators and consumers of food grains is thoroughly evaluated before approval is granted, and approval can be revoked if new information suggests that a particular compound should be excluded.

Generally, the contact insecticides approved for use have relatively low mammalian toxicity and are deemed non-hazardous when applied at the recommended dilution rates for their intended purposes. They are also safer to handle than many pesticides commonly approved and used for preharvest pest control. However, the transportation and handling of insecticide concentrates remain hazardous. These risks and the necessary safety precautions will be discussed in more detail later in this section.

Which Fumigants to Use?

Two main types of fumigants are commonly used in grain storage programs for fumigation purposes:

- **Methyl Bromide:** This fumigant works quickly, allowing the grains to be aerated after 12-24 hours of application. However, it is highly toxic, colorless, and odorless, and leaves residual effects in the grain, accumulating in the human body. Due to its harmful nature, methyl bromide is not recommended for use in grain storage.
- **Magnesium or Aluminum Phosphide:** The gas released from this chemical is called Phosphine. Phosphine has a low molecular weight (34.04), giving it excellent penetration ability. Its weight is similar to air, allowing it to easily mix with the air and spread through the stored grains without requiring circulating fans. Phosphine is highly effective against most pests, but does not affect the taste or smell of the grain, and leaves no residues on it, making it safe for food grains. Additionally, it does not impact seed germination, so it can be used for storing seeds as well. However, it is flammable at normal temperatures, requiring careful handling during application. Phosphine has a delayed release, so it requires a longer fumigation period than other fumigants.

Fumigation duration varies depending on the fumigant used methyl bromide requires 24–48 hours, while phosphine typically requires at least five days. Phosphine is more commonly used because its application is simpler; it is distributed in the form of pellets throughout the grain mass. It is crucial to remember that fumigants are highly toxic to humans, so those applying them must be carefully trained. Additionally, safety measures such as masks, gloves, hand washing, and hermetic sealing of phosphine containers must be followed to ensure proper handling and safety during application.

CONDITIONS FOR APPLICATION OF PHOSTOXIN

It is important to note that these treatments are curative and do not have long-lasting effects. As a result, a combination of contact insecticides and fumigation is generally recommended for effective pest control.

- **Location:** Any enclosed space that can be sealed air-tight can be used for fumigating grains.

- **Temperature:** The effectiveness of the fumigation treatment is significantly influenced by the ambient temperature. The higher the temperature, the more effective the treatment will be. Below are some key guidelines to consider:

IPM Strategies Against Pulse Beetle

Table: 7.3 Fumigation treatment is significantly influenced by the ambient temperature

Temperature rangs, °C	Fumigation period
20 and above	4-5 days of exposure
16-20	6 days of exposure
11-15	8 days of exposure
05-10	10 days of exposure
Below 5	Do not fumigate

- **Relative Humidity:** The humidity of the surrounding air directly impacts the rate at which phosphine gas is released. A higher relative humidity (RH) increases the release rate of the gas, while no gas is released below 30% RH. In such conditions, it is advisable to place water containers under the fumigation sheet.
- **Right Concentration:** To effectively control all pest life stages, it is critical to maintain the proper concentration of fumigant in the sealed area for a sufficient duration. The fumigation sheet must be air-tight and properly sealed to the floor using paper tape, and the floor should preferably be concrete to ensure proper sealing.
- **Proper Hygiene:** Since fumigants do not have long-lasting effects, preventing re-infestation is essential. This can be achieved by performing surface treatments of the storage area using Malathion, which is effective against flying insects due to its volatile action.

Some do's and don'ts

- **Post-Fumigation Process:** After completing the fumigation, it is essential to aerate the grain storage and clean it thoroughly. All collected trash should be removed from the area to avoid providing a breeding ground for pests and prevent re-infestation of the grains.
- **Precautions Before Fumigation:** Prior to fumigation, it is important to know how to detect and measure the concentration of the released gas in the air and take appropriate precautions to avoid potential hazards.

Do's:

- Keep fumigants stored securely and out of reach of untrained individuals. Only trained personnel should carry out fumigation.
- Always wear a gas mask with the correct filter.
- Wash thoroughly and take a bath after handling fumigants.
- Display a sign showing the fumigant used, date of application, and the responsible person.

- Use a gas monitoring device to measure gas concentrations during fumigation.
- Ensure proper aeration after uncovering the storage.
- Conduct fumigation away from office or residential areas.
- Dispose of fumigant residues in water and bury the used containers.
- Keep a first aid kit readily available for accidental fumigant exposure.

Don'ts:

- Never perform fumigation alone.
- Do not eat, drink, or smoke during or immediately after fumigation.

LIMITING VALUES OF FUMIGANTS

The threshold limit value (TLV) of a fumigant refers to the safe concentration of gas in the air for human exposure. The TLV indicates the maximum amount of the fumigant that can be present in the air without posing a health risk to humans. The threshold limit values for two commonly used fumigants are as follows:

Table 7.4 : Threshold Values for commonly used fumigants

Properties	Phosphine	Methyl bromide
Threshold limit value	0.3 ppm	5 ppm
Odour thershold value	1 ppm	0 ppm
Skin absorption	Negligible	Slight
Chronic effects	Not known	Affects nervous system

NON-CHEMICAL TECHNIQUES FOR CONTROL

The challenges related to chemical control of insect pests and the growing demand for hygienic food supplies have led to a search for alternative methods of managing storage pests. Among the approaches being researched are temperature, moisture, and atmosphere control, aeration, grain fumigation, cleaning operations, and radiation.

Temperature Control

Temperature plays a key role in the physiological functions of insects such as egg-laying, fertility, lifespan, and development, all of which determine the population growth of insects in stored grain. Most insects thrive in a temperature range of 22°C to 38°C, but optimal temperatures can vary, which is why insect species often have geographic distribution patterns that align with their temperature preferences.

Heat has been used for insect control for at least 75 years, with temperatures between 120°F and 130°F maintained for 10-12 hours being effective in killing most insects. However, insulation and the presence of grain require the temperature to remain constant for several hours to ensure thorough heat penetration. Heating vaults are also used to treat insect-infested products such as bags of flour or feed. With temperatures between 180°F and 200°F, insect life in 100 lb bags can be eradicated in 24 hours.

Low temperatures, on the other hand, are essential for long-term storage and preserving seed viability. Freezing kills many organisms, and low temperatures can prevent damage to seeds. However, when temperatures exceed 115°F, seed viability may be compromised unless the grain is cooled immediately after drying.

Recent heating methods such as fluidized-bed heating use air to transfer heat efficiently, ensuring that each grain receives uniform treatment. In just minutes, this process can disinfect grain at temperatures as high as 65°C. This method has been found to kill all stages of insect pests without affecting the grain's moisture content, germination, or baking quality. Frying small quantities of rice for about 7 minutes is also effective for insect control, although it may not work for certain pests. Conversely, microwave heating was found to achieve complete mortality of certain insect pests in rice after just 10 minutes of exposure.

Grain's Moisture Content

Grains are hygroscopic, meaning they either absorb moisture from the air in humid conditions or lose moisture in dry conditions. The relationship between the moisture content of grain and the relative humidity of the air is governed by equilibrium curves, where moisture transfer continues until both reach a balance. To ensure safe storage, maintaining a low relative humidity is crucial, which can be achieved by:

- Storing grains in areas where the natural relative humidity is low.
- Using refrigeration or dehumidification systems to reduce humidity levels in the storage environment.
- Using impervious sealed containers for storing dry seeds.

In regions with high humidity, grains are often harvested with moisture levels conducive to insect growth but unfavorable for safe storage. Therefore, post-harvest drying using heated air becomes necessary.

Moisture migration is a significant issue in large grain bulks, particularly in subtropical climates, where grain bulk remains warm during the day and cools at night, causing moisture to condense on the surface of the grain. This can lead to mold growth and other losses, exacerbated by heavy insect infestation, which produces heat and moisture. The solution is to control moisture migration by:

- Drying the grain to a low, uniform moisture content.
- Using aeration or ventilation to keep the grain cool and dry.
- Fumigating the grain to remove moisture and control infestation.

Insects cannot survive or reproduce in grain with a moisture content below 9%. Therefore, reducing the moisture below this threshold effectively prevents insect growth and ensures safe storage.

Grain Aeration

Grain aeration, or ventilation, is another effective non-chemical method for insect control. This process involves cooling a bulk of grain by passing air with controlled temperature and humidity through it. As the air moves, temperature and moisture fronts are formed, which interact, thereby reducing both the grain temperature and moisture levels.

Temperatures ranging from 15-18°C prevent the reproduction of pests such as *Rhyzopertha dominica* and *Tribolium* species, and limit the population of other *Sitophilus* species. The drying of grain further reduces *Sitophilus* reproduction. Cooling also helps in suppressing moisture migration, reducing heat from grain respiration, lowering chemical breakdown rates, maintaining freshness, eliminating odors, and optimizing fumigant distribution or removal.

Grain cooling can be accomplished through aeration using either ambient or artificially cooled air. Typically, aeration refers to the controlled movement of air at low flow rates aimed at cooling, although drying may also occur. In tropical climates, storage temperatures typically range from 25-30°C. While some cooling is possible through aeration, reducing grain moisture is often the key to preventing biological activity and managing insect infestations.

An aeration system consists of a fan, ducts to distribute air through the grain bulk, a controller to operate the fan efficiently, and temperature monitoring equipment to optimize cooling. Fans and ducts are essential for delivering air through the grain mass at the right rate and uniformity.

Turning of Grain

Grain turning involves transferring the grain from a full silo to an adjacent empty one. This process helps to break up insect infestations, dissipates some heat, evens out temperature differences, and mixes moist grain with drier parts of the bulk. However, turning does not significantly reduce the overall moisture content of the grain.

Since grain turning requires substantial handling, it is a labor-intensive and time-consuming operation. For example, turning 750 tons of grain in a single silo can take around 40 hours, often hindering other drying and transfer operations at the facility.

Special care must be taken when turning grain that is already infested. This can spread the infestation to previously unaffected areas, potentially worsening the issue. Therefore, surface pests should be eradicated, and any damaged grain should be removed before turning the grain.

Atmosphere Control

As insects are obligate aerobes, the composition of gases in the storage environment significantly affects their populations. In sealed (hermetic) conditions, a reduction in oxygen will eventually eliminate insect pests. Using lethal concentrations of carbon dioxide (CO_2) is a well-established commercial method of pest control in many countries. For this method to be successful, it is critical to ensure the storage is properly sealed to maintain the necessary airtight conditions.

Cleaning Operations

Modern grain storage facilities are typically equipped with elevators and other machinery designed to clean and condition grain before storage. These systems usually employ shifting or aspiration processes to remove most free-living insects.

However, they are not very effective at addressing internal infestations within the grain. Proper disposal of cleaning residues is crucial in preventing cross-contamination and further pest infestations.

Radiation

The application of radiant energy for controlling insects holds great potential, with ongoing research showing promising results. It is expected that the use of radiant energy for insect control will become more widespread. Several types of radiation are being explored for their effectiveness in managing insect pests in stored products.

Insects are particularly attracted to "black light" or ultraviolet light, which is often utilized in insect traps to monitor population levels or the extent of infestation.

- **Infrared Radiation:** generates high temperatures within short exposure times. While electrically powered heat lamps can produce this radiation, gas-fired ceramic panel heaters are more cost-effective for large-scale applications. Irradiation at temperatures around 160°F for 10 to 20 seconds has been found to be effective in both drying grain and controlling insect pests.
- **Ionizing Radiation:** such as X-rays, accelerated electrons, and gamma rays, is a powerful method for sterilizing food products and grain without heat, known as "cold sterilization." These forms of radiation are lethal to insects and are being explored for large-scale commercial applications.

RODENTS AND THEIR CONTROL

RODENTS AND TYPES OF DAMAGE

The second most significant pest in pulse storage is rodents. These pests invade and reproduce in or near storage facilities where food is readily available. They cause extensive damage not only to the stored products but also to the packaging and sometimes to the storage buildings themselves. The main rodents that are most commonly associated with attacking stored products include the following species:

- **Black rat**, also known as roof rat *(Rattus rattus)*
- **Brown or Norway rat**, also referred to as sewer rat *(Rattus norvegicus)*
- **Mouse** *(Mus musculus)*

Rodents not only consume the grains but also contaminate over 20% of what they consume with their feces, urine, and hair. Prolonged infestation by these pests leads to substantial quantitative losses, often reaching 3-4% of the stored products. In addition to these losses, there is a degradation in the quality of the foodstuffs due to the filth—such as excrement and secretions—that rodents leave behind in the stored products. This contamination is crucial not only from a marketing perspective but also in terms of hygiene and public health. Rodents are known to be vectors for several serious diseases, including rabies and leptospirosis.

CONTROL MEASURES

Rodent control is a challenging task and cannot be effectively addressed by simple measures alone. Often, a combination of the following strategies becomes necessary:

- **Sanitation:** Maintaining cleanliness in the storage area and its surroundings
- **Exclusion:** Preventing rodents from entering the storage area
- **Killing:** Eliminating those rodents that manage to get inside

SANITATION

Sanitation, both outside and inside storage facilities and processing plants, plays a crucial role in effective rodent control. The surrounding areas should be kept clean to prevent rodents from finding shelter near the storage location. The following measures should be implemented:

- Keep bushes, weeds, and grass trimmed and mowed.
- Create a 1-2 meter paved area around the building to reduce potential hiding spots, which will also help prevent rats from burrowing under the structure.
- Ensure the area is well-drained and avoid placing garbage bins near the building.
- Avoid discarding equipment, boxes, or garbage around the storage area.

Inside the building, cleanliness is essential to discourage rodents from staying in the space. Recommended measures include:

- Maintain smooth walls and floors to facilitate cleaning. Keep walls and corners free from dust, trash, and spider webs.
- Remove waste products and dust immediately after any operation.
- Stack bags on pallets rather than directly on the floor to reduce potential hiding spots for rats.
- Maintain at least a 75 cm gap between wall and stacks to allow for easy movement of workers and to minimize cover for rodents.
- Paint walls with light-colored paint to eliminate dark corners where rats tend to hide.

EXCLUSION

It is crucial to prevent rats and birds from gaining access to the storage area. While this task is challenging, constructing a rat-proof building and conducting careful operations can significantly help in keeping rats out. The following measures are recommended:

- The outer walls of the building should be made of materials that rats cannot chew, and the surface should be smooth.
- A 25 cm wide rat shield should be installed around the building at a height of 1-1.5 meters to effectively block rat entry.
- The building floor should be constructed at the height of a truck bed to prevent easy access by rodents.

- Doors and window frames should be made of steel and securely fixed to the walls to eliminate any gaps between the frame and the wall.
- Windows should be equipped with metal mesh to keep out flying insects.
- The lower 20 cm of doors should be lined with a metal sheet to provide added protection.
- Doors should be kept closed when not in use.
- For doors that need to remain open for extended periods, transparent plastic panels should be installed to prevent birds from entering.
- Cement plaster slopes should be applied below the windows to prevent birds from nesting.
- Ensure that no boards, bags, or other items are placed outside the building in contact with the walls, as rats can leap over the rat shield and enter the building.

KILLING

Rats that enter the building must be dealt with immediately. Several methods can be used to eliminate them:

- Field rats reside in burrows. To eradicate these rats, one zinc phosphide tablet per burrow is needed, with the burrow mouths sealed with mud after the tablets are placed.
- Rodent control within storage areas can be achieved through physical, chemical, and mechanical methods.
- Various rat traps can be employed to capture rats.
- The chemical method involves using poisoned bait to eliminate rats. Zinc phosphide in food bait or single-dose anticoagulants can be used for poisoning rats. Other chemicals such as barium carbonate and red squill are also effective. Slow-acting poisons or anticoagulants are generally more accepted by rats than fast-acting poisons. To attract rats to the feeding area, offer the baits without poison initially.
- Poisoned water and feeders should be strategically placed inside the building, with no other water sources available.
- Sonic and ultrasonic repellents are also being used to deter rats.

8

Insect Infestation in Food Grains Detection and Diagnosis

The inspection of storage facilities and the food products they contain is crucial for preserving grain intended for human consumption. Stored grain is not simply a passive substance; it is a living, breathing organic entity that undergoes deterioration during storage. This deterioration can occur in terms of quantity, through dry matter loss (DML), or quality, with issues such as discoloration, mold contamination, sprouting, and caking caused by microorganisms, invertebrate pests (insects and arachnids), and vertebrate pests (rodents and birds). Additional weight loss happens during the handling, transportation, and processing of stored grains.

To gather accurate data on all forms of loss, regular and thorough inspection and sampling are essential. These inspections are crucial for making informed management decisions regarding remedial actions against biological deterioration agents or the disposal of grain, taking into account the condition of both the commodity and the storage environment. Regular inspections help maintain a storage environment that supports grain quality by keeping track of any significant pest population increases, grain temperature, moisture migration, spillage, and grain residues.

Such inspections also encourage the general upkeep of the storage structure and its surroundings, which helps to minimize pest access. By addressing cracks and crevices in the storage fabric and removing old, often infested, bags and equipment, the risk of pest infestation is significantly reduced.

The inspection should address several factors:

- The presence of pests, if any
- Identification of species, population densities, and locations
- Damage inflicted prior to inspection
- The growth potential of pest populations or whether they will die out if conditions remain the same

- The duration of safe storage for the commodity
- The need for treatment or disposal (urgency)

Subjective estimates should be avoided. While numerical estimates of pest populations are often impractical, some form of quantitative estimation based on an internationally accepted scale should be pursued.

THE OBJECTIVES OF STORAGE INSECT PESTS

The primary goal of any sampling and inspection program is to provide a foundation for future planning and decision-making. With detailed and accurate records on the history of stock, its current condition, and any pest presence, a practical and cost-effective control program can be initiated. Additionally, these records serve as a critical basis for assessing the commodity's monetary value and whether its quality and condition meet the expectations of potential buyers. Making decisions based on a sample that doesn't accurately represent the entire bulk can lead to incorrect conclusions about the grain's suitability for human consumption.

PROBLEMS IN SYSTEMS ASSESSMENT

It is essential for the inspector to possess a solid understanding of the insect species commonly found in the produce they are inspecting. Recognizing the taxonomic and morphological distinctions of pests is crucial in determining the status of endemic species and identifying any potential introduction of exotic ones. Any species regulated under quarantine laws must be correctly identified by an authorized expert.

Additionally, it is beneficial for inspectors to have knowledge about the biology, ecology, and behavior of various species they may encounter. Understanding the differences between primary, secondary, field, and associated pests, along with the role of beneficial parasites and predators, is also valuable.

Inspection of Storage Facilities and Handling Equipement.

The following categories are used for general inspections of the structural condition of warehouses, silos, or mills, as well as any handling and conveyance equipment that may present potential areas for endemic or residual insect infestations.

The notation used for recording the results of a visual inspection or general inspection without taking samples, as well as for commodity inspection after drawing samples (After Ashman, 1970).

Since the common names for insects can occasionally differ between nations, it becomes necessary to use the scientific generic and specific names when describing the species of insects present. Every attempt should be made to have the specimens in question identified by a specialist taxonomist, but if the inspector is not entirely certain of the species that are discovered, the uncertainty should be noted in the report. The report should also specify the location where the insect species were gathered during the inspection.

Table 8.1 : Inspection of handling equipement

1. Stack inspection	
C = Clear or none	No insects discovered in the course of a prolonged search.
F = Few or light	Small numbers of insects occuring infrequently or irregularly.
MN = Moderate numbers	Insects are visible, frequently seen, and occasionally congregate in small groups.
LN - Large numbers	When a lot of insects are actively crawling across the whole surface of the commodity, such as a stack or bulk, it is immediately apparent.
VLN = Very large numbers	Insects are so active and abundant that their presence can be heard within the bulk or stack. Live insects or exuviae (shed skins) form a continuous layer around the perimeter of the stack or bulk.
2. Storage inspector	
C = Clear or none	No abvious insects or populations signs.
VF = Moderate numbers	Insects occuring regularly and and frequently, often forming populations but not obvious enough to be immediately noticeable.
LN = Large numbers	Insects immediately obvious on commencement of inspection crawling actively on walls and in other situations.
VLN = Very large numbers	Large populations of insects are frequently found on a variety of surfaces, including grain residues on the floor, mill augers, used sacks, abandoned machinery, bins, etc.
3. Sampling inspector	
C = Clear or none	No insects obvious on stacks or sacks or any of the samples. (Require protection from cross-infestation and regular inspection).
VL = Very light	Insects not obvious on sacks, or in sample of produce before sieving. < 20 insects per 90 kg sieved sample (Requires disinfestation in near future)
L = Light numbers	Between 20-300 insects per 90 kg sieve sample.
M = Moderate numbers	Between 50-300 insects per 90 kg sieved sample.
H = Heavy numbers	Between 300-1500 insects per 80 kg sieved sample.
VH = Very heavy numbers	>1500 insects per 90 kg sieved sample

Unless there are extremely severe infestations, they might not have full distribution throughout the warehouse. This information will be crucial to take into account when starting any follow-up control measures. To add to their report, individual inspectors might create their own shorthand notations or utilize drawings of floor plans.

For instance, an inspection's results could be noted as follows:

Table 8.2 : Inspection results

Sitophilus oryzae	VLN (a)
Latheticus oryzae	NM (A,L)
Trogoderma granarium	F (a), MN (L)
Tribolium spp	VF (1), VLN(A,a)

Making the effort to conduct a thorough search, keeping an eye on things, and accurately documenting the findings are the primary tasks involved in a worthwhile inspection program. There is no acceptable substitute for actively participating, whether it be by entering the grain, onto the livestock, or into the area surrounding the handling equipment to physically look for live insects or the telltale signs of their presence. Given how time-consuming an inspection is, the first step should focus on looking for areas where insects, if any, are likely to gather. To make the task a bit easier, some techniques may be used, most of which are designed to encourage insects to approach you rather than the other way around.

Additional aids for visual inspection

For an Effective Visual inspection, a few random bags should be opened, and the folds of sacking and corners of the bags should be examined, as pests like *Trogoderma granarium* larvae and *Tribolium castaneum* adults are often found in such locations. Some bags should be lifted and set aside, and the exposed surfaces of nearby bags should be quickly checked for adult pests and carefully examined for larvae and pupae, such as *Ephestia cautella.*

For detecting light infestations, more detailed methods should be employed, which may include:

- **Agitation of Bags:** This method works well for low-density populations of *Sitophilus granarius, S. oryzae,* and *S. zeamais,* which may emerge from bags after being disturbed. A long stick can be drawn over surfaces of vertical stacks or used to hit bags, activating small numbers of adult moths, making them easier to spot.
- **Feel of Grain in Bulk:** Walking on the surface of bulk grain with bare feet can provide valuable insights into its condition. If the grain feels cool and flows freely, there's likely no immediate concern. However, the presence of hotspots

can be detected, often indicated by solid caked patches caused by high dust content and moisture migration, leading to temperature increases.

- **Traps:** Various traps have been designed to monitor insect activity. Tube traps with smooth inner surfaces and rough outer surfaces (approx. 7.5 cm long × 2.5 cm in diameter) can be placed in bags to capture species like *Tribolium castaneum* that cannot escape from the smooth interior. While effective, these traps do not capture species like *Sitophilus* or *Oryzaepilus surinamensis* and may fail when larvae webs obscure their activity. Additionally, homemade sticky traps and attractant traps using light or pheromones can help monitor insect presence in large warehouses.
- **Artificial Crevices:** Sections of corrugated cardboard (4 cm wide × 20 cm long) placed between bags attract pupating moth larvae. These can be examined after 24 hours or, for lightly infested bulk, checked after 4 to 5 weeks. Plank traps made of wood, hinged together but separated by 3 to 4 mm, are effective for trapping larvae and adults of *Trogoderma granarium* and *Tribolium castaneum*.
- **Dead Insects:** When insecticide treatments are applied and dead insects accumulate, it may indicate the treatment's success or a persistent infestation source. If dead insects are removed and the area marked, any subsequent accumulation would suggest the need for further action.
- **Repellents:** Insecticidal repellents like pyrethrin or synergized pyrethroids can be used to expose hidden insects in cracks and crevices. A light application can stimulate insects to move to exposed surfaces before being killed by the insecticide.
- **Grain Temperature and Moisture Content:** As previously mentioned, it's often more effective to look for signs of insect activity rather than directly searching for the insects. Localized temperature rises or moisture buildup within a bagged stack or bulk are key indicators of insect presence.

QUANTITATIVE SAMPLING INSPECTIONS

The objective of taking random samples of the commodity is to assess the average value and variability of the infestation or contamination level (e.g., percentage of discolored kernels) in a given batch. Ashman (1970) proposed a preliminary "sequel sampling" method, which involves randomly collecting spear samples from the commodity and examining them through sieving (note: this method does not account for latent infestations of immature stages hidden within individual kernels).

The process includes gathering spear samples from various bags, with the number of bags depending on the total quantity in the consignment, but it should not be fewer than the square root of the total number. This continues until a 1 kg sample is accumulated and inspected for insects by sieving. If the findings show low numbers of pests, further resampling is carried out, which may involve three more rounds of sampling, each consisting of 3, 9, or 22 kilograms.

The degree of infestation is assessed, and appropriate action is determined accordingly. Notably, any population of *Trogoderma granarium* Everts requires control measures, regardless of the infestation level.

Spear Sampling

There are several inherent challenges associated with this method, and as a result, it could lead to multiple interpretations:

- Different insect species tend to prefer certain commodities, and this preference can result in varying degrees of damage, meaning pest status is not consistent across all commodities.
- When insect populations are low and unevenly distributed, using spear samples might not accurately reflect the extent of the infestation, leading to either an overestimation or underestimation.
- The sample size required for an accurate assessment using spear sampling can be labor-intensive and time-consuming. For example, with a consignment of 10 bags, a minimum of 10 bags should be sampled at random, while 1000 bags would require 32 bags to be sampled.
- The sample taken is often not truly random due to the challenges in sampling from the central parts of the stack.
- Samples collected from individual bags are rarely random or fully representative of the overall condition of the contents. To obtain a primary sample, at least six additional samples should be collected from each bag, a practice that is often overlooked (usually resulting in around a 1 kg sample).
- The use of sampling spears can cause damage to the sacks, which in turn creates the potential for spillage.

When used with an understanding of their limitations, spears provide an inexpensive, simple, and quick method for collecting grain from bagged produce. To gather more representative samples, a sectional probe should be employed. These probes come in sizes suitable for bags or larger versions for probing deeper piles in bins, sheds, transport vehicles, and more. For bulk grain samples, suction samplers — a hollow spear, extension rods, and end attachments connected to an industrial vacuum cleaner — are effective for drawing samples from up to 10 m deep. A more advanced version features interlocking aluminum extension tubes and flexible hoses connected to an electric vacuum pump.

Samples are drawn into a collecting compartment, reducing grain friction by using suction, and the probe can reach any depth within the grain. However, the main drawback of this method is its higher cost.

Other Direct Sampling Techniques

The other direct sampling techniques include methods such as bag snaking, coning and quartering, and sieving:

- **Bag Snaking:** This method involves emptying a series of bags by pulling the open bag backward across the floor, allowing a steady stream of grain to flow out. Most visible insects will accumulate in the latter part of the flow and can be easily observed along the edges of the bag.
- **Coning and Quartering:** This is an inexpensive and effective technique for obtaining highly representative samples, with an error margin of approximately

10%, making it more accurate than spear sampling. However, it is time-consuming and has capacity limitations. The process involves tipping the contents of bags onto the floor to form a cone. The material is then constantly mixed from the edges to the cone's apex, spread evenly, and divided into quarters, eighths, or sixteenths, depending on the volume needed.

- **Sieving:** "Hand-held sieves" are particularly useful for assessing dust content and detecting live insects in small samples. Different mesh sizes can be used for various particle sizes, or a combination of mesh sizes can be applied for mixed commodities with varying particle sizes. "Sack sieves" are designed to sample an entire sack, with the sieving process taking between 5 and 15 minutes. Insect recovery is influenced by factors such as species, sieving time, the slope of the oscillating mesh, and the mesh size. Tests have shown that insect recovery can exceed 90% and is unaffected by population density.

For improved accuracy and representativeness, larger primary samples are preferable, and subsamples can then be taken to create a suitable working sample. Methods like coning and quartering can be used, or specialized equipment can be employed, such as gravity mechanical types like the Boerner conical divider, the simplified alternate channel box divider, or motorized centrifugal types like the Gamet divider. Simplified dividing trays are also available.

The TSPC developed the Produce Flow Sampler (PFS) for sampling entire bags, originally designed for sampling incoming loads from road transport. The PFS takes about 20 seconds for a 100 kg bag, works with all flowable commodities, and provides completely random samples, making it significantly more accurate than spear sampling.

DETECTING HIDDEN INFESTATIONS

The majority of the damage and weight loss in grain caused by insects is due to the primary grain feeders. These insects are capable of penetrating healthy whole kernels and their life cycle occurs entirely within the kernel where the egg is laid or where the first instar larva enters.

The absence of live adult storage insects in grain samples separated by previous methods does not necessarily indicate that there is no infestation. As a result, various techniques have been developed to identify individual kernels that have become hosts for the immature stages of the primary insect pests.

The effectiveness of detection methods significantly improves when infested material is properly separated from healthy grains, as it reduces the number of grains, dust, and broken kernels that need to be examined. Concentrating the insect-damaged kernels as an initial step is, therefore, essential. To achieve this, flotation in either an air stream or liquid can be used.

- **Flotation Separation in Liquids:** Insect larvae's feeding gradually reduces the density of the grains. By submerging a grain sample in a liquid with an appropriate specific gravity, the infested grains will float while the sound ones will sink. At specific gravities ranging from 1.050 to 1.190, the floating layer contains only the infested kernels, and approximately 50-70% of all infested kernels can be separated. Although absolute separation is not achievable, the method provides a reliable estimate of hidden infestations and a general indication of infestation severity.

- **Flotation Separation Using Air:** By gradually increasing the airflow, it was observed that almost all insect-damaged kernels were eliminated in the first two fractions, from which no emergence had occurred. This method of detecting insect-damaged grain (i.e., grains with exit holes) becomes a faster and more efficient process, potentially accelerating the exit-hole inspection procedure for commercial samples by a factor of ten or more.
- **Projection Separation Using Air:** By projecting the grains of a sample through the air at a consistent velocity, they will separate based on their relative density. The air drag and gravity further divide the grain according to factors like kernel size, shape, and surface texture, which also influence the bulk density or test weight of the grain. Infested kernels tend to fall shorter than sound kernels of the same size and shape.

This separation method has significant practical value. Wheat that is heavily infested can be sorted into different bins, recovering as much as 50% of the grain for food use rather than discarding the entire consignment for feed purposes.

RECORDING OF RESULTS

Maintaining accurate and thorough records is critical, particularly when compiled over time, as they provide essential background information. A standardized inspection record sheet should be used to ensure that the data is recorded in a systematic, comprehensive way for ease of analysis.

When compiling a report, several factors should be considered:

- Weather conditions play a significant role in the development of pest infestations. In tropical climates, where temperature and relative humidity (which are influenced by the equilibrium moisture content, or EMC) are closer to the optimal requirements for many major insect pests, the effects are less variable.
- The type of storage structures used for produce can greatly affect the quality of the stored produce and the subsequent increase in pest populations. It is important to record detailed information about these structures, their condition, and potential sources of cross-infestation.
- Details regarding the type of produce, its variety, grade, and any observed insect damage can provide valuable insights into pest control strategies.
- The origin, destination, and duration of storage for the inspected commodities are crucial factors that influence future control efforts.
- Any previously applied control measures should be documented to assess their effectiveness.
- A layout plan of the storage area, including the arrangement and dimensions of bagged stacks, can also be helpful for understanding potential problem areas.

FUNGI FOR STORAGE

Fungi present in stored food can be categorized into two groups: "field fungi" and "storage fungi." In some instances, it is difficult to clearly differentiate between the two, as fungal growth can begin in the field and continue during storage. However, the initial source of the fungi is always in the field. Storage fungi primarily include species of *Aspergillus, Fusarium,* and *Penicillium.* The growth of fungi during storage is influenced by several factors:

- The composition of nutrients in the grain
- Moisture and temperature conditions
- Biotic factors, such as competition and the presence of stored product insects

Storage fungi are more commonly found in lots that are infested with stored product insects, as insects produce moisture and help distribute fungal spores within the grain.

The following table outlines the minimum moisture contents necessary for the growth of some important storage fungi in grains.

Table 8.3 : Minimum moisture content necessary for the growth of some fungus species

Fungus species	Minimum moisture content in grain
Aspergillus restrictus	13.5%
A. glaucus	14%
A. candidus	15%
A. ochraceus	15%
A. flavus	18%
Fusarium spp.	18-19%
Penicillium spp.	16.5-19%

Fungal development can occur under the following conditions:

- When grain is stored without being adequately dried
- When grain has been damaged during harvest, handling, threshing, or drying
- If the moisture content of the stored produce increases during storage
- Due to moisture absorption from the surrounding air
- As a result of condensation
- In "hot spots"
- Due to water penetration or leakage

Storage fungi can cause the following damage:

- Nutrient loss
- Discoloration of grain
- Decreased germination ability

- Caking of grains
- Rise in temperature of stored goods leading to spontaneous combustion
- Moldy smell and taste
- Production of mycotoxins
- Creation of an environment conducive to the development of specific insect species, serving as indicators of low grain quality

To prevent fungal damage, the following measures should be taken:

- Dry the produce as quickly and evenly as possible after harvesting
- Avoid grain damage during harvest, handling, threshing, or drying
- Keep the storage area cool and dry
- Prevent condensation by maintaining stable temperatures in the storage
- Conduct regular checks
- Prevent moisture absorption due to poor ventilation or water ingress into the storage
- Avoid the development of high insect populations ("hot spots")
- Redry sections of the stack with excessively high moisture content

For instance, an extract from the dried fruits of Xylopia aethiopica (Annonaceae) and dry seeds of the pepper Piper guineense has been shown to completely prevent the growth of Aspergillus flavus. However, for practical fungus control applications, these effects do not appear to be sufficiently reliable.

MYCOTOXINS

Mycotoxins are metabolic by-products produced by various fungi, and these toxins remain in the stored produce as residues. Mycotoxins can appear in the stored produce as early as 24 hours after fungal infestation. The ideal climatic conditions for fungal growth and mycotoxin formation are often not the same and depend on several unidentified factors. As a result, the presence of mycotoxin contamination can only be confirmed through laboratory analysis.

The following table lists some key mycotoxin-producing fungi along with the commodities they affect:

Table 8.4 : Fungus Species Along with the Affected Commodities

Fungus species	Commodities affected
Alternaria alternate	Rice, sorghum, soybeans
A. longissima	Rice, sorghum
A. padwickii	Rice
Aspergillus flavus	Cashews, copra, maize, groundnuts, sorghum, soybeans
Fusarium moniliforme	Maize, sorghum, soybeans

Fungus species	Commodities affected
F. semitectum	Maize
Penicillium citrinum	Sorghum, soybeans

Since the discovery of aflatoxins more than 30 years ago, five mycotoxins have emerged as particularly significant in agriculture:

- Aflatoxin (with aflatoxin B1 being the most toxic of all known fungal metabolites)
- Deoxynivalenol (likely the most widespread mycotoxin found in food)
- Zearalenone (an estrogen-like compound that disrupts female mammalian hormones)
- Fumonisin (a common contaminant in maize-based food and feed)
- Ochratoxin (mainly found in Europe and other temperate regions)

Mycotoxins are extremely toxic to both humans and animals. When consumed, they can lead to mycotoxicoses or even cancer.

The extreme toxicity of mycotoxins is evident in their remarkably low maximum residue limits (MRLs). For comparison, the MRLs for Malathion and Aflatoxin B1 in human food, measured in milligrams per kilogram of grain, are as follows:

- **Malathion:** 5-30 mg/kg
- **Aflatoxin B1:** 0.005 mg/kg

This indicates that the maximum allowable level of Aflatoxin B1 is from 1,000 to 6,000 times lower than that of Malathion, underscoring its severe toxicity.

Mycotoxins are exceptionally stable and cannot be eliminated through common processing methods such as boiling, pressing, or refining. Consequently, once produce is contaminated, it must be destroyed, as it cannot be rendered safe for consumption. The issue cannot be resolved by diluting contaminated grain with untainted produce or by feeding it to livestock, as mycotoxins accumulate in animal tissues and are subsequently ingested by humans through meat and dairy products.

PREVENTIVE MEASURES FOR THE LOSS OF GRAINS IN STORAGE

Heat Treatment

Pests can be effectively eradicated by subjecting them to temperatures of 60°C for more than 10 minutes or 50°C for a duration of 2 hours. This method disrupts their physiological processes, leading to mortality.

Radiation

The use of beta or gamma radiation is a proven method for pest control. These rays induce physical disorders, sterility, and ultimately mortality in pests.

Among the two, gamma rays possess greater penetration power but are also a more expensive technique for large-scale application.

Aeration

Aeration involves the controlled movement of air through processed grain at low flow rates to help preserve and enhance quality. This technique lowers grain temperature, inhibits insect activity, prevents storage odors, reduces moisture buildup, and stabilizes relative humidity (RH). The effectiveness of fumigation is significantly improved when combined with aeration.

Fumigation

Fumigation is a chemical-based pest control process that involves spraying or dusting toxic substances onto stored grains. It works by exposing pests to lethal gas concentrations over a sufficient duration to ensure extermination. The three primary types of fumigants used are:

- **Ethylene Bromide :** A liquid fumigant with a high boiling point, ensuring prolonged effectiveness.
- **Methyl Bromide :** A gaseous fumigant with a lower boiling point, used for rapid pest elimination, but requiring **aeration** post-application.
- **Phosphite Tablets :** Solid fumigants that react with atmospheric moisture to produce hydrogen phosphide gas, which is highly toxic to both pests and microbial contaminants.

PREVENTION IN PREPARATION FOR STORAGE

Grain protection begins even before the grain is stored. The storage area should be completely emptied and thoroughly cleaned. Particular attention should be given to corners, joints, and crevices, as these areas provide hiding spaces for insects. Pests can survive under old grain, in dust, and in cracks and holes, so these potential refuges must be cleaned or removed.

The conveying equipment should also be cleaned and maintained in good working order to prevent damage to the transported grain. For species such as grain beetles, which cannot feed on intact grain, broken grains become an easy source of food. When cleaning the warehouse with pesticides, it must be done in accordance with regulations, and all actions must be carefully documented. Structural measures, such as securing exhaust air vents with meshes or grilles, can help keep birds and rodents away from the grain. Additionally, any purchased grain should be carefully inspected before being transferred to storage.

Fungi Endanger Cereals, Humans and Animals

Field fungi, also known as primary fungi, are introduced into storage along with the harvested grain. Over time, these fungi facilitate the growth of storage fungi (secondary fungi), which thrive under favorable storage conditions. If left unchecked, these molds produce highly toxic mycotoxins, posing serious health risks to both humans and animals.

In livestock, particularly pigs, mycotoxins reduce appetite, slow growth, and cause fertility issues. In cases of severe contamination, highly toxic feed can even lead to the death of farm animals. Due to these risks, the EU has established strict regulatory limits on mycotoxin levels in food and feed.

Factors Promoting Fungal Growth

The presence of heat and moisture significantly accelerates fungal metabolism, promoting mycotoxin production. If harvested crops are not properly cooled, fungi find optimal conditions for growth, increasing the likelihood of contamination and health hazards in stored grain.

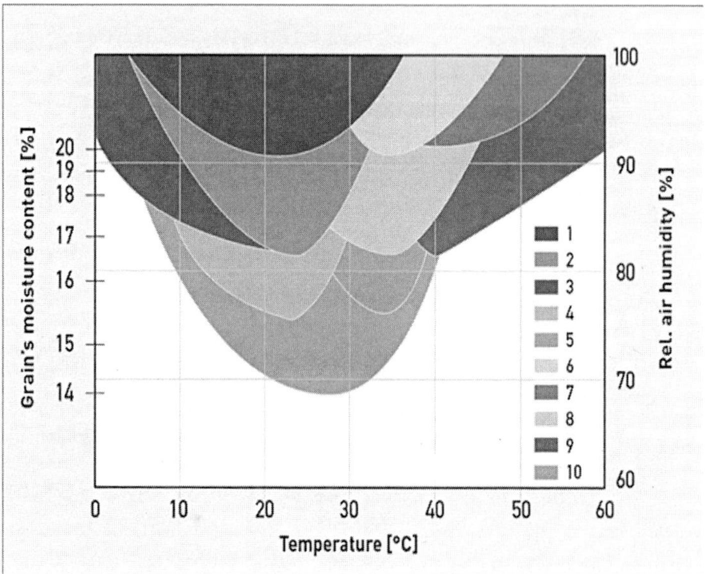

1 Fusarium culmorum	**6 Absidia rhizopus arrihzus**
2 Penicilium rugulosum	**7 Streptomyces altus**
3 Penicilium cyclopidum	**8 Aspergillus candidus**
4 Aspergillus versicolor	**9 Penicilium capsulatum**
5 Aspergillus glaucus	**10 Talaromyces thermophilus**

Figure: 8.1 Growth of various organisms dependent on moisture and temperature

Insect Infestation is Often Discovered Too Late

Insect infestations can cause severe damage to stored grain, leading to substance loss and a decline in quality due to feeding, excretion, and rapid reproduction. Many pests spread silently within loose grain, making early detection difficult.

For instance, grain beetles often go unnoticed until a mass hatching of new insects occurs. Given that these beetles have a short generation cycle of just 25 days under optimal conditions, by the time their presence is detected, significant damage may have already occurred. A single female grain beetle lays one egg per day, meaning that the infestation may include beetles at all stages of development—eggs, larvae, pupae, and adults.

Pesticides are only effective against fully developed beetles, while eggs, larvae, and pupae remain protected within sealed grains, making complete eradication challenging.

The type of insect infestation varies by climate zone, as pests are highly temperature-sensitive. Their activity and reproduction rates fluctuate with the surrounding temperature. When temperatures drop below a certain threshold, insects enter a dormant state, reducing their metabolism and reproductive capabilities.

COOLING SLOWS DOWN PESTS AND FUNGI

Both insects and mold require specific environmental conditions to thrive in stored grain. By controlling temperature and humidity, grain cooling serves as an effective measure to combat both threats simultaneously.

To achieve optimal protection, grain moisture is generally maintained at 14.5%, while the ideal storage temperature varies depending on the type of crop. For instance, rapeseed exhibits relatively high specific heat development, necessitating proper cooling.

When grain is cooled below 15°C, even cold-resistant pests enter a dormant state, significantly reducing their metabolic activity. At this temperature, insect development and reproduction are effectively halted, preventing damage caused by feeding and excretion.

Thus, maintaining a grain temperature of 15°C or lower serves as a highly effective strategy for insect control, ensuring better grain preservation and long-term storage stability.

Ensuring ideal storage conditions is essential for maintaining grain quality and preventing deterioration. Proper regulation of temperature and humidity plays a vital role in minimizing the growth of insects and molds. Utilizing grain cooling methods not only protects against spoilage but also preserves key attributes like germination capacity in grains, rice, corn, seeds, and malting barley for prolonged durations.

9

Acquaintance with Inventory, Logistics, and Collateral Management

Inventory management involves tracking the stock levels of products, ensuring that there is neither overstocking nor understocking, and maintaining an optimal supply to meet demand. Proper inventory management minimizes wastage and helps in cost control.

Logistics management focuses on the movement, storage, and distribution of goods. It ensures that products are delivered to the right place at the right time, maintaining quality while optimizing transportation and storage costs. It includes planning for transportation routes, warehousing, and managing the flow of goods.

Collateral management, particularly in agriculture and finance, involves managing assets (like stored grains) as collateral for loans or credit. It ensures that these assets are properly valued, secured, and monitored throughout the loan term. Efficient collateral management minimizes risks for lenders while ensuring that borrowers can access necessary financing for agricultural operations or business growth.

INVENTORY MANAGEMENT IN GRAIN STORAGE

In grain storage, "inventory management" refers to the methodical process of tracking and controlling both the quantity and quality of grain stored in facilities such as warehouses or silos. This involves ensuring optimal stock levels by overseeing incoming deliveries, coordinating outgoing shipments, and actively preventing losses due to pests, moisture, and spoilage, while upholding quality standards throughout the storage period.

Inventory management encompasses the ordering, storage, use, and sale of a company's inventory, which includes managing raw materials, components, and finished goods, as well as their warehousing and processing. Industries like automotive and healthcare depend on efficient inventory management to streamline production and prevent delays. While inventory management was once a manual task, technological advancements, including Enterprise Resource Planning (ERP) systems and inventory management software, have transformed it into a sophisticated system integrated with supply chain logistics. These tools provide real-time data that enables businesses to forecast, plan, and execute their inventory management more effectively.

So, what does grain inventory management involve? In essence, it's the process of tracking, analyzing, and controlling stored grain to meet both immediate and long-term demands. This is crucial for various reasons. First, grain inventory directly impacts profitability. Overstocking can tie up capital and result in waste, while understocking may cause missed sales opportunities. Furthermore, effective inventory management optimizes operational efficiency, reducing time and resources wasted. By refining grain inventory practices, businesses position themselves for success in the grain processing industry.

Proper inventory and storage management mitigates several operational risks, such as sanitation issues and waste during storage and transportation. As a result, companies achieve higher-quality products at lower costs. For many enterprises, inventory management accounts for nearly half of their assets, including fertilizers, production materials, and assembly components.

However, managing inventory is complex, as it involves factors like climate, soil conditions, seasonality, and labor, all of which vary by crop type. Poor management of these variables can lead to significant waste. A robust warehouse management system helps companies avoid the immediate need to sell products, offering greater flexibility for planning efficient shipping strategies.

THE VALUE OF PRECISE DOCUMENTATION

In grain inventory management, the saying "you can't manage what you don't measure" holds significant importance. Accurate record-keeping forms the foundation of efficient inventory management. By regularly tracking grain stock levels, transactions, and potential waste, you maintain an up-to-date overview of your inventory. This real-time data supports informed decision-making and helps prevent unexpected shortages or excess stock.

On the other hand, neglecting proper record-keeping can lead to serious issues. Inaccurate records may result in financial discrepancies, potentially causing profit losses. They can also disrupt the supply chain, leading to delays or customer dissatisfaction due to unfulfilled orders. Maintaining precise records is key to ensuring that your operations run smoothly and remain profitable.

IMPLEMENTING DIGITAL SOLUTIONS FOR GRAIN INVENTORY

In today's technology-driven environment, relying on manual inventory tracking methods can put your business at a significant disadvantage. Transitioning to digital solutions brings a wide array of advantages. For one, digital systems provide real-time updates, minimizing the errors often associated with manual recording. They also facilitate efficient data analysis, allowing you to forecast demand, identify patterns, and make well-informed purchasing decisions.

LEVERAGING EXPERT CONSULTATION

Managing grain inventory may appear overwhelming, but you don't have to face it alone. By partnering with experts in grain inventory management, you can gain valuable insights and customized solutions that meet your unique needs.

This is where Beyond comes in, offering extensive expertise specifically tailored to the grain processing industry.

FORECASTING AND FUTURE PLANNING

Effective grain inventory management isn't just about managing the present; it also requires anticipating future needs and potential challenges. This is where predictive analytics becomes a game-changer. By harnessing data and advanced analytics, you can forecast future inventory demands, ensuring that you are neither overstocked nor understocked.

The grain industry, like many others, is susceptible to market fluctuations and seasonal variations. Prices can fluctuate, and demand can shift due to factors such as weather patterns or geopolitical events.

Having a strong forecasting system in place enables you to respond proactively to these changes. Instead of being caught off guard by sudden market shifts or unexpected surges in demand, predictive analytics equips you to act swiftly, ensuring your inventory remains aligned with the ever-changing market dynamics.

TRAINING AND SKILL DEVELOPMENT

Even with the most advanced tools and strategies, the success of your inventory management system ultimately depends on the people using it. It's essential that your team, from frontline employees to management, fully understands and follows inventory management best practices.

Training goes beyond simply providing knowledge; it's about fostering a culture of continuous improvement. By investing in skill development, you ensure that your team remains adaptable to industry changes, ready to tackle new challenges, and capable of seizing emerging opportunities.

TAKING THE NEXT STEP TOWARDS GRAIN INVENTORY

Excellence

Effectively managing grain inventory is not merely an administrative duty; it is a key pillar of success in the grain processing industry. With increasing challenges and shifting market conditions, it's more crucial than ever for businesses to adopt modern, reliable solutions that can simplify inventory management and reduce risks.

From integrating digital solutions and training staff to anticipating market changes, each element is essential in ensuring that your business stays resilient and profitable. Expert consultation provides valuable insights, tailored strategies, and ongoing support to meet your unique needs, helping you navigate the complexities of inventory management and position your business for long-term success.

THE BENEFITS OF ACCURATE INVENTORY MANAGEMENT

Accurate record-keeping enables you to make informed decisions that directly influence your profitability. Below are some of the key benefits:

- **Storage Management:** Establish a virtual bin yard to monitor the location and capacity of your bins and bags. By recording the quality attributes of your grain, you can ensure consistency and traceability across the entire supply chain, all the way to the end consumer. If you manage a large network of storage bins and bags, strategic bin management can create efficiencies in haul-ins and haul-outs, optimizing delivery truck operations.
- **Contract Satisfaction:** Inventory tracking solutions provide real-time inventory data, empowering marketers to make informed decisions based on commodity prices and available stock. Knowing the precise location of your product leads to quicker deliveries, improved customer satisfaction, and increased sales revenue.
- **Enhanced Insights:** Real-time access to information reduces inventory management errors and eliminates guesswork regarding your sales position. Accurate reports provide a clear overview of available space, product availability, contract fulfillment, and year-over-year comparisons, offering valuable insights for effective decision-making.

How to Can You Manage your Inventory using Decisive Farming

A comprehensive platform called Decisive Farming was created to assist agricultural companies in streamlining their inventory management, which facilitates tracking and maximizes grain storage. You can effectively manage inventory, cut waste, and increase profitability with Decisive Farming's integration of cutting-edge technology and data-driven insights.

Decisive farming's real-time inventory tracking system is one of its primary features. You can make sure you have the most recent data on stock levels and condition by entering and tracking the quantities and quality characteristics of your grain. By doing this, you can meet market demands without committing too much money or running the risk of spoiling by avoiding overstocking or understocking.

The platform also enables detailed grain tracking from storage to delivery. With decisive farming, you can create a virtual bin yard, tracking the location and available capacity of your storage bins and bags. This feature is especially useful for businesses with large networks of storage facilities, allowing you to optimize haul-in and haul-out logistics, making the process more efficient and reducing transportation costs.

Additionally, decisive farming integrates contract management tools that help you stay on top of contract fulfillment. Real-time data allows you to monitor commodity prices and available stock, making it easier to make informed decisions regarding deliveries and sales. This ensures timely deliveries, improved customer satisfaction, and ultimately, better revenue outcomes.

Using decisive farming to manage your inventory offers a clear, efficient, and data-driven approach to grain storage. By providing real-time tracking, optimizing logistics, and enhancing decision-making, decisive farming can help businesses stay competitive, reduce operational risks, and increase overall profitability.

MANAGEMENT OF LOGISTICS

In the area where the facility is situated, logistics should be at their peak. These include being close to suppliers, customers, and customs facilities for import-export activities. This is a crucial choice that could have benefits if the facility is situated close to the countries that are being targeted for export. This will facilitate exporting and reduce the cost of transportation and other logistical costs.

Logistics management for grain storage encompasses the entire process from procurement and processing to storage and distribution. It plays a vital role in enhancing the profitability and yield for farmers by minimizing waste and ensuring efficient use of resources.

Proper operation is crucial for effective grain logistics. Beyond selecting the right location, equipment, and logistics methods, it is also essential to manage and utilize these resources appropriately.

Key factors to consider include:

- **Optimal Use of Human and Material Resources:** Ensuring that both human labor and materials are utilized efficiently helps streamline operations.
- **Transfer of Knowledge and Skills to the Workforce:** Training and knowledge-sharing are crucial to improving operational efficiency and avoiding mistakes.
- **Productive Use of Time:** Time management is essential for maintaining a high level of productivity and efficiency throughout the operation.

Improving operational practices boosts productivity, enabling facilities to operate more economically, ultimately leading to higher profitability. Implementing an efficient system is just as important as the operation of machinery, as it ensures smooth business functioning and cost-effectiveness.

Grain procurement and logistics start with making investment decisions in the right location, followed by selecting the appropriate equipment and management systems. Once these are in place, the critical steps of product acceptance, processing, and storage ensure that the grain is prepared before reaching the customer. The most important aspect of establishing a successful supply chain is using the right logistical methods and tools to ensure that processed and stored products are delivered to the correct destinations in optimal condition. This approach guarantees that the entire grain storage and distribution system operates efficiently and profitably.

ON-FARM STORAGE AND THE GRAIN SUPPLY CHAIN IN INDIA

On-farm storage plays a crucial role in India's grain supply chain, ensuring food security, reducing post-harvest losses, and providing farmers with the flexibility to manage their harvests. India, being one of the largest producers of grains such as rice, wheat, maize, and pulses, faces a unique set of challenges related to grain storage and distribution. The effective management of on-farm storage is essential not only for the individual farmer but also for the broader agricultural economy. This section discusses the importance of on-farm storage and its role in the grain supply chain in India.

Importance of On-Farm Storage

On-farm storage refers to the practice of storing harvested grains on the farm itself, usually in structures like traditional granaries, silos, or temporary storage bins. The key advantage of on-farm storage is that it allows farmers to store their grain for longer periods, thereby reducing their dependence on immediate market prices.

This is especially important in India, where farmers often face fluctuating market prices for grains, and storage allows them to sell their produce when prices are more favorable. Additionally, on-farm storage helps maintain the quality of grain by protecting it from pests, moisture, and damage, which can lead to significant losses if not properly managed.

The storage facilities used on farms vary widely across India. Small and marginal farmers tend to use traditional methods such as woven bamboo baskets, mud bins, or jute bags, while larger commercial farmers may use more modern storage systems such as steel silos and concrete storage units. However, most of these storage systems are inadequate in terms of pest control, moisture management, and capacity, resulting in significant post-harvest losses, especially in rural and remote areas.

Challenges in On-Farm Storage

One of the major challenges faced by farmers in India is the lack of proper infrastructure for on-farm storage. Many farmers still rely on inadequate and outdated storage methods, which are prone to pests, rodents, and moisture. As a result, a substantial portion of the harvested grain is lost due to improper storage, especially in hot and humid climates that are conducive to pest infestation and mold growth.

Moreover, farmers often lack access to modern technologies and training on best storage practices. They may not be aware of the significance of proper ventilation, moisture control, or pest management in preventing grain spoilage. The lack of financial resources and government support further exacerbates the situation, preventing farmers from investing in better storage facilities or pest control measures.

Grain Supply Chain in India

The grain supply chain in India consists of various stages, including production, storage, processing, and distribution. After harvest, grains are typically stored on farms before being transported to local markets or storage depots. From there, grains are either processed into food products or sent to wholesale markets for distribution. The government also plays a significant role in this supply chain through procurement programs such as the Minimum Support Price (MSP), which guarantees farmers a fixed price for their produce, and Food Corporation of India (FCI) warehouses that store grains for public distribution under the Public Distribution System (PDS).

However, despite the extensive network, inefficiencies and bottlenecks in the supply chain persist, particularly in the storage and transportation phases. Inadequate storage capacity at both the farm and government levels leads to spoilage and wastage, especially during peak harvest seasons when large quantities of grain need to be stored. Additionally, poor road infrastructure and delays in transportation often lead to further losses before the grain even reaches the markets or government warehouses.

Solutions and Way Forward

To improve the efficiency of on-farm storage and the overall grain supply chain, several steps can be taken. One potential solution is to promote the use of modern, low-cost storage technologies, such as metallic silos and hermetic storage bags, which can effectively control pests and moisture levels. Government subsidies and financial support for farmers to invest in these technologies could significantly reduce post-harvest losses.

Furthermore, farmer training programs on proper storage techniques and pest management are essential to help farmers protect their grain. Strengthening rural agricultural extension services to disseminate knowledge about effective grain storage practices would also help improve the quality and quantity of grain stored on farms.

Improving the overall grain supply chain requires investment in infrastructure, such as better roads, transportation networks, and more government-controlled storage facilities. Upgrading the public storage system and enhancing coordination between farmers, traders, and government agencies would ensure a smoother flow of grains from the farm to the market and reduce losses along the way.

On-farm storage plays a vital role in the grain supply chain in India by helping farmers manage their harvests, reduce losses, and secure better prices. Addressing the challenges faced by farmers in storing their grain and improving the broader supply chain infrastructure will help India make significant strides towards food security and reducing post-harvest losses, ultimately benefiting both producers and consumers.

ISSUES CONCERNING LOGISTICS IN THE AGRICULTURE SECTOR

The agricultural sector is essential to many economies, supplying food and raw materials for industries. However, it often faces significant logistical challenges that hinder efficiency. One of the most pressing issues is food waste, which directly impacts hunger and food security. While increasing agricultural output has been a primary focus, minimizing losses along the food supply chain has largely been overlooked until recent years. Poor logistics can lead to higher costs, production delays, and even spoilage of goods, making logistics management critical for the agricultural sector's success.

Several factors affect the efficiency of transporting agricultural products:

- **Transportation Distance:** The distance between the farm and market plays a significant role in logistical efficiency. This is measured in kilometers or miles, depending on whether the transportation is local or long-distance.
- **Time Taken by Land Transport:** The time required for land transport depends on various factors, including weather conditions, vehicle loading capacity, and road availability (the number of hours spent traveling per day).
- **Cost Comparison:** Transport costs per kilogram by land can sometimes be higher than air freight or maritime shipping. Interestingly, air freight can sometimes be more economical than road transport, despite longer transit times.

Despite these challenges, agricultural businesses can improve efficiency by enhancing their logistics systems. This approach can help reduce costs, boost productivity, and better serve customers.

Some of the key logistical hurdles that need to be addressed in India's agriculture sector include:

- **Remote Farm Locations:** Farms located in isolated areas with limited or no road access pose a significant challenge for transporting goods to markets.
- **Food Waste:** Minimizing losses in the food supply chain has historically been neglected, yet it remains a critical issue for reducing hunger and improving food security.
- **Lack of Market Knowledge:** Insufficient awareness of market prices, consumer demand, and supply constraints can result in inefficient logistics management, driving up production costs and reducing market surpluses.
- **Insufficient Resources and Infrastructure:** A lack of proper infrastructure contributes to product wastage and inefficient logistics systems.
- **Fleet Management Inefficiencies:** Farmers and manufacturers often rely on outdated technology or untrained fleet providers, leading to poor fleet management. As a result, fleet operators may be unable to ensure optimal conditions during transportation, further complicating logistics.

Addressing these challenges and improving logistics practices will be essential for increasing efficiency and minimizing losses in the agricultural supply chain.

IMPORTANCE OF LOGISTICS MANAGEMENT IN CROP PRODUCTION

Crop production is a critical component of the agricultural industry, and effective logistics management is key to its success. Logistics involves the strategic planning and coordination of the transportation and storage of goods and materials. In crop production, logistics management encompasses every step from seed selection and procurement to field planning, resource allocation, harvest scheduling, and the distribution of the final product.

- **Quality of Products and Delivery:** For customer satisfaction, both the quality of the crops and the delivery process are crucial. Many agricultural products are bulky, perishable, and consumable, requiring careful handling during transport. Proper packing and transportation methods are essential to protect the crops from damage. The process of gathering a harvest involves several stages—harvesting, threshing, winnowing, bagging, processing, and storage—and each stage demands attention to detail. The quality of transportation is just as important as the accessibility of the product, ensuring the crops remain in optimal condition throughout the logistics process.
- **Optimizing Operations:** An efficient logistics management system helps farmers optimize their operations, enhancing both efficiency and profitability. By reducing waste and making better use of resources, logistics management enables farmers to increase yields and lower costs. In the highly competitive agricultural marketplace, logistics efficiency is vital for farms to maintain a competitive edge. Today, agricultural logistics is evolving, incorporating improved management systems that streamline the collection of raw products from farms, processing, storage, handling, packaging, and distribution.
- **Reliability of Supply:** The reliability of the supply chain has a significant impact on the success of crop production. Issues such as spoilage, delayed deliveries, and production downtime can be addressed by creating traceable, precise, and consistent agricultural supply chains.
- **Technology in Agricultural Logistics:** Software tools for managing agricultural logistics play a crucial role in the delivery of agro-food products. These systems often include sensors to monitor cargo conditions and GPS tracking to ensure timely deliveries. To eliminate the lengthy chain of middlemen, companies and startups must implement web and mobile-based platforms to connect buyers and sellers of agricultural products and services directly. Technologies like Blockchain and AI & ML also have the potential to transform the industry. By providing low-cost, individualized agricultural market information through mobile services, these technologies help resolve information asymmetry, offering solutions to farmers and agricultural producers.

AN EXPLANATION OF LOGISTICS MANAGEMENT'S FUNCTION IN THE AGRICULTURAL INDUSTRY

Logistics management plays a vital role in the agricultural industry of India, ensuring the efficient movement, storage, and distribution of agricultural products from farms to markets. With its large agricultural sector, India faces numerous challenges in managing the flow of produce, maintaining product quality, reducing post-harvest losses, and enhancing overall supply chain efficiency. Effective logistics management helps streamline these processes, thereby supporting farmers, traders, consumers, and the economy as a whole.

Components of Logistics Management in Agriculture

Logistics management in agriculture involves several crucial elements, including transportation, warehousing, inventory management, packaging, and distribution. Each of these components plays a vital role in ensuring that agricultural products are delivered efficiently, in good condition, and at the right time:

- **Transportation:** In India, where agriculture is predominantly rural, the transportation of goods from farms to local and national markets is a significant challenge. Inadequate road infrastructure, poor connectivity, and limited access to modern transport systems often result in delays, high costs, and the deterioration of produce, especially perishables like fruits and vegetables. Efficient logistics management ensures the use of optimal transportation modes, such as trucks, trains, and ships, to move goods quickly and cost-effectively across regions, reducing spoilage and wastage.
- **Warehousing:** Proper storage facilities are essential to maintaining the quality of agricultural products. Warehouses play a crucial role in safeguarding grains, fruits, vegetables, and other products from spoilage, pests, and environmental factors. However, in India, the lack of modern, temperature-controlled storage facilities, particularly in rural areas, leads to significant post-harvest losses. Logistics management is key to ensuring that agricultural products are stored in appropriate conditions and that the movement of goods in and out of warehouses is well-coordinated and timely.
- **Inventory Management:** Managing the supply of agricultural products through efficient inventory control is another important aspect of logistics management. Farmers, traders, and distributors need to keep track of inventory levels to avoid shortages or overstocking. Advanced inventory management systems allow better forecasting of demand, reducing waste and ensuring that consumers have access to fresh produce year-round. By optimizing inventory levels, logistics management contributes to price stability and improved market efficiency.
- **Packaging:** The packaging of agricultural products is essential for protecting the produce during transportation and storage. Poor packaging can lead to damage, contamination, and loss of quality. Effective logistics management ensures that the packaging materials used are appropriate for the product, environmentally sustainable, and cost-effective. Proper packaging also improves the aesthetic appeal of products, boosting their marketability.

Challenges in Agricultural Logistics in India

Despite its importance, logistics management in the Indian agricultural sector faces several challenges. Poor infrastructure, particularly in rural areas, limited cold storage facilities, and inadequate transportation networks contribute to inefficiencies in the supply chain.

Additionally, a fragmented supply chain, with multiple intermediaries between farmers and consumers, increases costs and delays. Poorly coordinated logistics can lead to higher wastage, especially for perishable goods, which significantly impacts farmers' profits and food security.

Solutions and the future

To improve logistics management in India's agricultural sector, several measures need to be taken. Investing in rural infrastructure, including better roads, efficient transport systems, and cold storage facilities, would significantly reduce logistical challenges. The development of integrated logistics platforms, where transportation, warehousing, and distribution are streamlined, can help improve coordination and reduce costs. Additionally, adopting technology-driven solutions, such as digital platforms for inventory management, tracking, and real-time supply chain monitoring, would enhance efficiency and transparency.

Logistics management is essential for the growth and success of India's agricultural industry. By improving transportation, warehousing, inventory management, and packaging, logistics management can help reduce losses, lower costs, and improve the availability of quality products to consumers. Addressing the existing challenges through investment in infrastructure and technology will create a more robust and efficient agricultural supply chain, benefiting farmers, consumers, and the economy as a whole.

THE IMPORTANCE OF EFFECTIVE LOGISTICS MANAGEMENT IN THE INDUSTRY OF AGRICULTURE

Logistics management plays a crucial role in keeping pace with customer expectations and staying ahead of competitors. Here are several reasons why effective logistics management, provided by a reliable transport service, is essential:

- **Improves Efficiency:** Gaining visibility into a company's supply chain can significantly boost production efficiency. With the help of a transportation management system, businesses can analyze data and track the movement of goods in and out of their operations. This process helps prevent potential disruptions by allowing businesses to stay ahead of any logistical challenges, ensuring smoother operations and less downtime.
- **Ensures Seamless Delivery:** Logistics management is the key to ensuring that products are delivered to the right location, at the right time. A well-organized logistics system provided by a professional road haulage company guarantees fast, safe shipping, warehousing, and final delivery to customers. Choosing an experienced team from a reputable transport company ensures a reliable and efficient service, helping businesses meet their delivery commitments.
- **Key to a Successful Supply Chain:** Logistics is a vital component of a successful supply chain. It helps increase sales and profits for businesses involved in production, shipment, warehousing, and delivery. A dependable logistics service can enhance a company's reputation, positively impacting its public image and overall market value. This, in turn, leads to greater customer trust and satisfaction.
- **Provides Quality Customer Satisfaction:** Satisfied customers are the cornerstone of any business, and their satisfaction directly influences a

company's success. Strong logistics management creates reliable strategies that enable businesses to meet customer demands efficiently. When a company consistently delivers products on time and in good condition, it fosters goodwill, leading to repeat orders and long-term customer loyalty. Therefore, it's essential that logistics companies uphold their commitments to maintain customer satisfaction and business success.

COLLATERAL MANAGEMENT

Collateral serves as the bedrock of trust in finance, offering both lenders and borrowers the assurance needed to engage in transactions that shape the financial landscape. It is a tangible guarantee that secures loans, supports mortgages, and facilitates trade finance. The reliability of collateral depends heavily on robust warehousing practices, ensuring its security and value.

Collateral management is the process of overseeing assets that are pledged as security for loans or transactions. Its primary purpose is to reduce the risk of default and ensure protection for all parties involved. It is a vital technique used by banks to quickly identify assets that can be committed as collateral, enabling transactions to move forward.

For example, when a company requires a significant amount of cash, such as to pay a supplier, the bank may ask the business to commit a portion of its equity portfolio as collateral to secure the loan. This provides confidence to the lender, knowing that the loan is backed by valuable assets.

A collateral management system is a sophisticated platform designed to maximize the use of collateral as a risk management tool in lending. These systems dynamically allocate collateral, balancing regulatory requirements with market liquidity needs. They use real-time analytics to assess the creditworthiness and market value of pledged assets, ensuring optimal utilization and minimizing credit risk.

By leveraging automation and advanced algorithms, collateral management systems streamline the collateralization process, improving operational efficiency and enabling proactive risk management. These systems centralize workflow and data storage, reducing manual tasks and minimizing errors throughout the collateral lifecycle. This leads to fewer inconsistencies and ensures that collateral management is accurate and efficient, ultimately reducing risks in financial transactions.

FUNCTIONS OF COLLATERAL MANAGEMENT SYSTEM

A comprehensive and integrated Collateral Management System (CMS) is designed to streamline and optimize the use of collateral in financial transactions. Here are some of the essential functions of such a system:

- **Eligibility and Allocation:** One of the core functions of a CMS is the assessment and allocation of assets. This process involves a thorough evaluation to ensure that each asset meets institutional standards, factoring in elements such as market volatility, legal restrictions, and liquidity. The system does more than just identify eligible assets; it strategically allocates them, balancing risk profiles, loan requirements, and regulatory compliance. This careful and methodical allocation helps mitigate risks and boosts the efficiency of the lending portfolio.

- **Collateral Tracking:** In financial institutions, managing borrowing relationships often requires tracking multiple collateral records for a single loan, as well as monitoring a single piece of collateral pledged to several loans. A robust CMS enables efficient management of both tasks. It allows for tracking of multiple collateral records per loan, including collection, monitoring, querying, and reporting on essential custom data. The system aggregates collateral valuations for comprehensive loan-to-value (LTV) and loan-to-cost (LTC) analyses, ensuring thorough oversight. Additionally, it helps manage collateral pledged to various loans, ensuring clarity and preventing risks like inadvertent collateral release, while also adhering to required documentation and policy guidelines.
- **Valuation Tracking:** An advanced collateral management system offers real-time, integrated tracking of Loan-to-Value (LTV) and Loan-to-Cost (LTC) ratios. This allows your team to manage both standard loan structures and more complex scenarios, such as those involving cross-pledged collateral. Real-time tracking is vital for effective risk management, ensuring that LTV data is always up-to-date and accessible at each loan's interface. The system also supports supervisory oversight through comprehensive reporting tools, giving a clear and detailed view of the loan portfolio and enhancing control over the entire collateral lifecycle.

ADVANTAGES OF COLLATERAL MANAGEMENT SYSTEMS

A well-implemented collateral management system (CMS) offers a variety of significant advantages that enhance operational efficiency and financial security. Here are some of the key Advantages:

- **Improved Risk Mitigation:** CMS helps accurately assess the value and quality of collateral, safeguarding lenders against the risks of default. This protective measure not only secures financial investments but also boosts confidence in lending practices, reducing potential financial losses.
- **Better Compliance:** A CMS ensures real-time monitoring and quick adaptation to changing regulations, helping businesses stay aligned with industry standards. This constant adjustment reduces the risk of non-compliance and ensures smoother regulatory reporting and audits.
- **Ease of Operation:** Traditional collateral management relied heavily on manual processes, which were prone to errors and inefficiencies. A modern CMS automates many of these tasks, streamlining operations and reducing human error, which leads to smoother workflows and more accurate results.
- **Streamlined Liquidity Management:** The system enables the efficient mobilization of collateral assets, making them readily available for liquidation if needed. This capability is crucial for maintaining liquidity balances and

meeting unforeseen financial obligations, ensuring that businesses can react promptly to financial needs.

- **Optimal Asset Utilization:** CMS helps identify the most appropriate assets for specific transactions, maximizing the value and performance of collateral. By strategically utilizing assets, businesses can improve their financial standing and manage resources more effectively, contributing to better overall financial positioning.

WAREHOUSE INFRASTRUCTURE FUND (WIF)

In the Union Budget of 2011-12, a special provision was introduced under the Rural Infrastructure Development Fund (RIDF) through Tranche XVII, with a corpus of Rs. 2000 crore. This initiative aimed to provide dedicated funds for the development of a robust warehousing infrastructure across the country.

This focus continued in the Union Budget of 2012-13, where an allocation of Rs. 5000 crore was made under RIDF - XVIII. To further streamline financial assistance for both public and private stakeholders in the warehousing sector, the Government of India (GoI) established the Warehouse Infrastructure Fund during the 2013-14 fiscal year, with a corpus of Rs. 5000 crore. This allocation was continued in 2014-15 with an additional Rs. 5000 crore.

The corpus remained unchanged after this period. Eligible activities under this fund include the development of various storage infrastructures for agricultural commodities. These include warehouses, silos, agri-logistic parks, storage facilities in market yards and food parks, and cold chain infrastructure. The cold chain infrastructure supported by the fund covers pre-cooling units, cold storage, Controlled Atmosphere (CA) stores, reefer vans, bulk coolers, Individually Quick Frozen (IQF) units, and chilling systems. These initiatives aim to significantly improve the warehousing and cold storage capacities critical to maintaining the quality and shelf-life of agricultural products.

FOOD PROCESSING FUND (FPF)

To promote the food processing industry within the organized sector on a cluster-based approach, the Government of India (GoI) established the Food Processing Fund (FPF) in 2014-15. A corpus of Rs. 2000 crore was allocated to NABARD to provide affordable credit for the establishment of designated food parks. These parks were notified by the Ministry of Food Processing Industries (MOFPI), GoI, with the aim of encouraging the development of food processing units within these clusters. This initiative supports the growth of the food processing industry by ensuring easy access to financial resources for setting up necessary infrastructure and operational facilities in the sector.

The government has outlined several key initiatives to create a robust food processing industry infrastructure and promote its growth:

- **Credit for Infrastructure in Food Parks:** Financial support will be provided for establishing infrastructure in designated food parks and the processing units within these parks. This will facilitate the development of modern food processing facilities, which are essential for boosting the industry.

- **Policy Formulation and Awareness Creation:** Policies and strategies will be formulated to enhance processing infrastructure, raise awareness about the importance of value addition, and develop forward linkages directly to farmers' produce. These efforts aim to improve the value chain and ensure farmers benefit from enhanced market access.
- **Modernization of Existing Processing Units:** Support will be extended to modernize existing processing units within designated food parks. This will involve technology upgradation, automation, increased efficiency, improved product quality, and cost reduction, thereby making the units more competitive and sustainable.
- **Assisting MOFPI with Mega Food Park and Other Schemes:** The government will assist the Ministry of Food Processing Industries (MOFPI) in the effective implementation of various schemes, including the Mega Food Park Scheme, the Scheme for Creation/Expansion of Food Processing and Preservation Capacities (CEFPPC), the Scheme for Creation of Agro Processing Clusters, and the Scheme for Cold Chain, Value Addition, and Preservation Infrastructure. The government will contribute as a member of the respective Inter Ministerial Approval Committees to ensure smooth implementation and coordination of these initiatives.

CORE FUNCTIONS

Warehouse Infrastructure Fund (WIF)

The government has outlined several key initiatives to enhance the storage infrastructure, particularly in rural areas:

- **Creation of Scientific Storage Infrastructure:** Support will be provided for developing scientifically designed storage facilities in rural areas, ensuring optimal preservation of agricultural products.
- **Credit and Non-Credit Support for Greenfield Projects:** Financial and non-financial assistance will be made available for the development of new storage projects, both in the public and private sectors, aimed at enhancing storage capacities.
- **Renovation and Modernization of Existing Warehouses:** Funding will be provided for the renovation, repair, and modernization of current warehouses to improve their functionality and efficiency in storing agricultural commodities.
- **Upgrading Infrastructure of Co-operative Societies:** Support will be extended for upgrading the infrastructure and amenities in existing warehouses managed by Primary Agricultural Co-operative Societies (PACS) and other Co-operative Societies, ensuring that these facilities meet modern storage standards.

- **Formulating Policies and Strategies:** The government will develop policies and strategies to address the storage infrastructure gap in various parts of the country, ensuring balanced regional development.
- **Assessing Storage Capacity Needs:** Efforts will be made to assess the existing storage capacity and accurately estimate the requirements and potential for expanding storage infrastructure across different states and districts. This assessment will guide future investments and infrastructure development initiatives.

Provide Support for Accreditation of Warehouses in Rural Areas

The government has laid out several key initiatives to improve warehouse infrastructure and support small warehouse owners:

- **Collaboration for Upgrading Infrastructure:** The government will collaborate with Collateral Management Companies (CMCs), State Governments, and State-Owned Corporations to upgrade the physical infrastructure of small warehouse owners, including Primary Agricultural Co-operative Societies (PACS) and other cooperatives. This collaboration will focus on improving the efficiency of existing warehouses and leveraging these assets to increase income. Grant assistance will also be provided for the accreditation of PACS warehouses.
- **Training and Accreditation Support:** Efforts will be made to sensitize and train PACS staff, warehousemen, and cold storage owners. This will include encouraging and facilitating the accreditation and registration of their warehouses, helping them meet national storage standards and improve the quality of their operations.
- **Mapping and Identifying Rural Warehouses:** The government will work with NABARD and the Warehouse Development and Regulatory Authority (WDRA) to map and identify existing warehouses and cold storage facilities in rural areas. This will help update the Warehouse Directory, creating a comprehensive database of available storage infrastructure across the country, which will guide further investment and development in the sector.

Provide Post-Harvest Liquidity to Farmers

The government has outlined key initiatives aimed at enhancing storage practices and ensuring better financial outcomes for farmers:

- **Promoting Produce Storage to Prevent Distress Sale:** Efforts will be made to encourage farmers to store their produce rather than resort to distress sales. This will help farmers avoid selling at low prices during harvest seasons and allow them to secure better price realization by selling when market conditions are more favorable.
- **Encouraging the Use of Negotiable Warehousing Receipts (NWR):** The government aims to promote and popularize the issuance of Negotiable Warehousing Receipts (NWR) by accredited warehouses and cold storages. This will provide farmers and other stakeholders with a secure and efficient

way to use stored produce as collateral for loans, enhancing their access to credit and improving liquidity.

Expand Access of Farmers to Wider Markets

The government has laid out strategic initiatives to help farmers engage in commodity trading and improve their market access:

- **Engagement with Commodity Exchanges:** The government will collaborate with both futures and spot commodity exchanges to develop suitable frameworks and contracts. This will enable farmers to trade their produce on National Agriculture Markets (NAM), providing them with better market access and price discovery.
- **Facilitating Produce Aggregation for Exchange Trading:** A mechanism will be developed to ensure the aggregation of farmers' produce, making it easier for them to participate in commodity exchanges. This approach will help streamline the trading process and enhance efficiency.
- **Identifying Aggregators:** The government will identify suitable entities, such as cooperative societies, producers' organizations, NGOs, Collateral Management Companies (CMCs), or any other village-level/community-based organizations, to act as aggregators for farmers. These aggregators will play a key role in consolidating farmers' produce for efficient trading on commodity exchanges.

SUPPORT CAPACITY BUILDING INITIATIVES OF STAKEHOLDERS

The government will organize comprehensive training and sensitization programs for NABARD officers, both at the Head Office and Regional Offices. These programs aim to familiarize officers with various aspects of agricultural storage and marketing, ensuring they are well-equipped with the knowledge to support and implement policies that improve the agricultural storage infrastructure and marketing practices. This initiative will enhance their understanding and effectiveness in dealing with agricultural storage challenges, thereby fostering better outcomes for farmers and the agricultural sector as a whole.

BROAD ACHIEVEMENTS AT NATIONAL LEVEL

Warehouse Infrastructure Fund

The following are the key details of sanctions and disbursements from the fund:

- Total Allocation: Rs. 10,000 crore
- Total Sanctions: Rs. 9,476.23 crore
- Total Number of Projects Sanctioned: 8,172
- Designed Capacity: 13.74 million MT
- Cumulative Disbursement: Rs. 9,094.74 crore

Additionally, a total of 6,243 projects have been completed, resulting in a capacity creation of 9.96 million MT. These projects contribute significantly to the growth of the infrastructure and capacity within the sector.

Food Processing Fund (FPF)

The following are the key details of sanctions made from the fund and the processing infrastructure created:

- Total Allocation: Rs. 2,000 crore
- Total Number of Projects Sanctioned (as of 30th November 2024): 40
- Term Loan Sanctioned (as of 30th November 2024): Rs. 1,179.71 crore
- Loan Disbursed (as of 30th November 2024): Rs. 788.50 crore

The fund has contributed to the development of significant infrastructure across various food processing projects, including:

- **Area Development:** A total of approximately 1,370.03 acres will be developed in 14 Mega Food Parks (MFP), 9 Agro Processing Clusters (APC), 15 Individual Food Processing Units, and 3 Industrial Food Parks projects, all of which will serve as Central Processing Centres (CPCs).
- **CPCs and Associated Centres:** The 14 CPCs in MFP Projects will be supported by 45 Primary Processing Centres (PPCs) and several Collection Centres (CCs), strategically located in the catchment zones of the respective mega food parks. These centres will source agricultural produce directly from farmers, facilitating direct access to the user industry.

Upon completion, these projects will provide essential core and processing infrastructure, including:

- **Dry Warehouse Capacity:** 2,52,200 MT for storing raw materials and finished goods (non-perishable products).
- **Silo Capacity:** 58,500 MT for bulk storage of agricultural raw materials.
- **Cold Storage Capacity:** 97,610 MT for storing perishable finished products.
- **Freezer Capacity:** 11,350 MT for storing products requiring freezing temperatures.
- **Individual Quick Freezing (IQF) Capacity:** 9.50 MT per hour for producing IQF fruit and vegetable products.
- **Sorting and Grading Capacity:** 142.50 MT of fruits and vegetables per hour.
- **Controlled Ripening Capacity:** 1,895.00 MT.
- Pulping and Aseptic Packing Capacity: 39.05 MT of fruit pulp per hour.

These infrastructure developments are designed to enhance the food processing sector and provide much-needed support for both the storage and processing of agricultural produce.

ON-GOING PROJECTS AND SCHEMES

Warehouse Infrastructure Fund

The fund allocated for supporting the creation of infrastructure for the storage of agricultural commodities and the development of marketing infrastructure in Agricultural Produce Market Committees (APMCs) has been fully committed. This initiative aims to strengthen storage and marketing capabilities, ensuring better access to storage facilities and improving the efficiency of agricultural commodity trading within APMCs.

Food Processing Fund

The Special Fund designed to provide affordable credit to agro-processing units, specifically those designated as Food Parks, will remain available during the 2024-25 financial year. This fund aims to support the development and growth of food processing units, facilitating easier access to financial resources for enhancing infrastructure and operations within these designated food parks.

Warehouse Infrastructure Fund (WIF)

- Operational Guidelines - Warehouse Infrastructure Fund.
- List of Projects Sanctioned under Warehouse Infrastructure Fund (as of 30th November 2024).
- Cumulative Sanctions and Disbursements under WIF 2013-14 and WIF 2014-15 (as of 30th November 2024).

These documents provide comprehensive details on the operational aspects, sanctioned projects, and financial disbursements related to the Warehouse Infrastructure Fund.

Food Processing Fund (FPF)

- Operational Guidelines.
- Loan Application Format for Mega Food Park Projects to be implemented by State Agencies.
- Checklist of Documents to be Submitted for Mega Food Park Projects of SPVs.
- Loan Application Format for Mega Food Park Projects to be implemented by SPVs.
- Checklist of Documents to be Submitted for Mega Food Park Projects of State Agencies.
- Loan Application Format for Individual Processing Units in Designated Food Parks.
- Checklist of Documents for Individual Processing Units in Designated Food Parks.
- List of Loan and Security-Related Formats for Mega Food Parks Financed with Grant Assistance from MoFPI.
- List of Loan and Security-Related Formats for Individual Processing Units in Designated Food Parks.
- Consolidated List of 325 Designated Food Parks as of 15th May 2024, Notified by the Ministry of Food Processing Industries.

- Food Processing Fund Sanctioned Projects as of 30th November 2024.
- Application for Term Loan for Establishing an Agro-Processing Cluster.
- Checklist of Documents to be Submitted Along with the Loan Application for Agro-Processing Cluster Projects.

These documents and formats provide detailed guidelines and requirements for stakeholders involved in food park and agro-processing cluster projects, including loan applications and document submissions.

WAREHOUSING'S CRUCIAL FUNCTION

Warehousing serves as the ultimate safeguard, preserving the security and value of collateral assets. Here's how warehousing plays a critical role:

- **Fortress of Protection:** Warehouses act as secure fortresses, protecting collateral assets from theft, damage, or unauthorized access. They provide a safe environment where collateral can remain secure from external threats.
- **Keeper of Inventory:** Collateral assets stored in warehouses benefit from meticulous inventory management. Each asset is carefully documented, preserved, and maintained in a way that ensures it retains its value and remains accessible when needed.
- **Transparency Beacon:** Through advanced technology, warehouses provide real-time tracking and transparency, ensuring that all parties involved in the transaction have clear visibility of the collateral. This fosters trust by ensuring that assets are no longer shrouded in uncertainty.
- **Asset Valuation Hub:** Warehouses regularly assess and evaluate the market value of collateral assets. These valuations are crucial in determining the real-time market worth of the collateral, which is essential for risk management and lending decisions.
- **Swiftness in Need:** In the event of a default, lenders need swift access to collateral assets. Warehouses facilitate this by ensuring controlled and organized access, enabling quick retrieval and response when it's most critical.

10

Guidelines for Procurement and Disposal of Food Grains

In India, the procurement and disposal of food grains are governed by several guidelines to ensure food security and fair market practices. Procurement is typically managed by government agencies like the Food Corporation of India (FCI), which purchases grains directly from farmers at minimum support prices (MSP) to stabilize market prices. Farmers are encouraged to sell their produce through designated government procurement centers, ensuring fair prices.

The quality of food grains is a key consideration in procurement. Grains are tested for moisture content, cleanliness, and pest infestation before being accepted. Once procured, the grains are stored in government warehouses, with regular inspections to prevent spoilage and pest damage. For disposal, food grains are distributed through public distribution systems (PDS) to ensure availability to consumers at subsidized rates. Any surplus grains may be sold in open markets, or occasionally exported, to maintain a balance in supply and demand. Effective management ensures food security and minimizes wastage.

PROCUREMENT POLICY OF WHEAT AND RICE

State Government agencies and the Food Corporation of India (FCI) are responsible for purchasing wheat and paddy within the designated period, ensuring that the products meet the prescribed Fair Average Quality (FAQ) specifications and are procured at the Minimum Support Price (MSP) for the Central Pool. This procurement supports the distribution of food under the National Food Security Act (NFSA) and other welfare schemes (OWS).

The Government of India (GoI), in consultation with State Governments and FCI, finalizes procurement estimates for wheat and paddy before each marketing season. These estimates are based on anticipated production, marketable surplus, and the agricultural crop pattern. The procurement of paddy and wheat is carried out under both the Decentralized Procurement System (DCP) and the Non-DCP system.

CENTRALIZED PROCUREMENT SYSTEM (NON-DCP)

Under the Centralized Procurement System, the procurement of foodgrains for the Central Pool is managed either directly by the Food Corporation of India (FCI) or through State Government agencies. In the latter case, State agencies procure the foodgrains and then hand over the stocks to FCI for storage. These stocks are subsequently issued against Government of India (GoI) allocations within the same state or are moved to other states to manage surplus stocks. This system ensures the efficient distribution and storage of foodgrains across the country.

DECENTRALIZED PROCUREMENT SYSTEM (DCP)

Under this scheme, the State Government is responsible for the direct purchase of paddy/rice and wheat, as well as for storing and distributing these foodgrains under the National Food Security Act (NFSA) and other welfare schemes. In cases where the quantity of rice/wheat procured by the State Government exceeds its allocation under the Targeted Public Distribution System (TPDS) and other welfare programs, the excess stocks are handed over to the Food Corporation of India (FCI) for further management and distribution. This system helps ensure that surplus stocks are effectively utilized across the country.

PROCUREMENT POLICY OF COARSE GRAINS

The Department of Food and Public Distribution (DFPD) has finalized guidelines allowing States to procure coarse grains from farmers at the Minimum Support Price (MSP) for the Central Pool. However, this is subject to prior approval from the Government of India (GoI), based on a detailed procurement plan prepared by State Governments in consultation with the Food Corporation of India (FCI). The entire quantity of procured coarse grains will be distributed under the Targeted Public Distribution System (TPDS) and other welfare schemes (OWS) within the respective State or Union Territories (UTs).

GUIDELINES FOR PROCUREMENT, ALLOCATION, DISTRIBUTION AND DISPOSAL OF COARSE GRAINS AMENDED

- The Government of India has amended the guidelines for the procurement, allocation, distribution, and disposal of coarse grains, as per the updated guidelines dated March 21, 2014. These amendments provide revised protocols to streamline the processes involved in managing coarse grains within the public distribution systems and ensure more efficient allocation and distribution mechanisms.

Prior Provisions

- The procurement of coarse grains was regulated under the 2014 guidelines, which allowed states to procure coarse grains from farmers at the Minimum Support Price (MSP) for the central pool.

- This procurement process was subject to prior approval from the Government of India, based on a detailed procurement plan prepared by the states in consultation with the Food Corporation of India (FCI).
- According to the 2014 guidelines, the entire quantity of procured coarse grains was required to be distributed within 3 months from the end of the procurement period. This timeline ensured efficient distribution and utilization of the procured grains.

Issues

- It was observed that some State Governments faced difficulties with the 3-month distribution period for coarse grains, which was the same for both procurement and distribution activities, regardless of the shelf life of the commodity.
- To address these challenges and improve the procurement and distribution process, discussions were held to find solutions. These discussions aimed to overcome the issues faced by states and enhance the procurement of coarse grains under the central pool.

The Recent Amendment

- The distribution period for Jowar and Ragi has been extended to 6 months and 7 months, respectively, up from the previous distribution period of 3 months. This extension is aimed at addressing challenges related to the shelf life of these commodities and ensuring a smoother distribution process.

Significance

- The extension of the distribution period will boost the procurement and consumption of coarse grains, as states will have more time to distribute these commodities through the Targeted Public Distribution System (TPDS) and other welfare schemes.
- Since these crops are typically grown on marginal and un-irrigated land, increasing their cultivation will promote sustainable agriculture and crop diversification, benefiting the overall agricultural ecosystem.
- With the increased procurement, a larger number of farmers will benefit from the procurement of these crops, improving their income and livelihoods.
- Coarse grains are highly nutritious, non-acid-forming, gluten-free, and possess beneficial dietary properties, making them a valuable addition to the food supply.
- Furthermore, incorporating coarse grains into diets will help strengthen efforts against malnutrition in children and adolescents, fostering better immunity and overall health.

11

Quality Control of Food Grains

Quality control plays a vital role in ensuring food safety and freshness. Inspecting, testing, and grading fruits and vegetables is essential to confirm that food products meet safety standards. In today's globalized food industry, quality control tests are conducted at various stages throughout the supply chain, from cultivation and harvesting to processing, packaging, transportation, and distribution.

In agriculture, the quality of grain is determined by its intended use. In ethanol production, factors such as starch content are crucial, while in food and feed manufacturing, properties like protein, oil, and sugar are of primary importance. In the milling industry, the soundness of grain is the most significant factor in determining its quality. For grain farmers, high germination percentages and seed dormancy are essential characteristics to monitor. For consumers, visual qualities such as color and flavor are key indicators of quality. Quality control ensures that the grain meets the needs of both producers and consumers while maintaining food safety.

RESOURCES FOR QUALITY CONTROL

PRE-HARVEST TESTING

Pre-harvest tests are essential tools that help growers assess the needs of their crops. These tests assist in making informed decisions regarding nutrition or pesticide applications, determining the optimal harvest windows, and supporting various farm management decisions. By conducting pre-harvest testing, farmers can enhance crop health, improve yields, and ensure that their crops are ready for harvesting at the best possible time.

Starch Iodine Test

Starch is a carbohydrate present in various plants, including apples. As apples ripen, the starch gradually converts into sugar. The amount of starch in an apple serves as a key indicator of its ripeness, with higher starch levels indicating that the fruit is less ripe. One of the most important preharvest tests in the apple industry, the starch iodine test, is commonly used to determine the ideal harvest window for apples intended for storage. This test helps growers assess the right time for harvesting to ensure optimal quality and storage conditions.

Harvest Indices

Harvest indices are quality control metrics used to determine a fruit's readiness for harvest and its suitability for long-term storage. These indices help assess various factors, such as ripeness and quality, ensuring that the fruit is harvested at the optimal time for both immediate consumption and future storage. By using harvest indices, growers can enhance the shelf life and quality of the fruit throughout the storage process.

Brix

Brix, or Degrees Brix, is a measurement of the total soluble solids present in fruit. These solids are mainly composed of sugar (typically at least 80%), but may also include soluble acids like citric acid, vitamins such as A and C, or other compounds. When referring to Brix values, it primarily indicates the sugar content in the fruit. Brix testing is conducted at different stages of the fruit's lifecycle; in preharvest testing, it is often used as part of a maturity index to assess ripeness. In post-harvest, Brix testing is mainly used to objectively evaluate the flavor and sweetness of the produce.

Color Assessment

Color is a key indicator of fruit maturity and ripening, and assessing the external color of fruit has long been a traditional method for determining ripeness. However, different crops have varying ripening processes, and the external color may not always be the most reliable metric for all types of fruit. For certain fresh produce that doesn't change color externally, internal color assessments can be used to track maturity and ripeness.

Color also plays a significant role in consumer acceptance, making consistent color metrics essential for quality control. The color of fruit can influence its grade and market price, and in some cases, postharvest color development may need to be induced to meet market standards.

DEGREENING

As citrus fruits ripen, they acquire their signature lemon yellow color through a process known as "degreening," where lemons lose their green chlorophyll during cold nights. In certain climates, the degreening process may not begin until after the fruit has already matured. In such cases, post-harvest treatments are necessary to induce the degreening process and achieve the desired color for market readiness. This controlled process ensures that the fruit meets the expected appearance and quality standards.

Dry Matter

Dry matter measurement represents the total solids present in a piece of fruit, including starches, proteins, sugars, fiber, and carbohydrates. It is essentially the total weight of the fruit minus its water content. Dry matter accumulation varies throughout the fruit growth cycle and is often used as a maturity indicator, particularly in climacteric fruits. This measurement helps assess the ripeness and overall quality of the fruit, ensuring that it meets the desired standards for harvest and consumption.

Titratable Acidity

Titratable acidity measures the total acid content in food and is a key metric for assessing maturity and flavor, particularly in the citrus industry. In less mature fruit, there is a higher acid-to-sugar ratio, which gives the fruit a more tart taste. As the fruit ripens and starch is converted into sugar, the ratio shifts, resulting in a higher sugar-to-acid balance. This shift creates the sweet taste that consumers prefer, making titratable acidity an essential indicator of fruit ripeness and overall flavor quality.

Ethylene Testing

Ethylene (C_2H_4) is a naturally occurring plant hormone, often referred to as the fruit-ripening hormone. To measure ethylene gas concentration, fruits are placed in an airtight container, allowing ethylene to accumulate. After a certain period, the gas inside the container is extracted and measured using a gas chromatograph. Gas chromatography is a technique used in analytical chemistry to separate and analyze gas compounds.

In apples, a gas sample can be collected by inserting a needle directly into the core of the fruit, providing an accurate measurement of ethylene levels and helping determine the fruit's ripening stage.

CLIMACTERIC VS NON-CLIMACTERIC FRUIT

Climacteric fruits, such as apples, have the ability to continue ripening even after being harvested. These fruits will keep ripening while in storage or during transportation post-harvest. Unlike climacteric fruits, non-climacteric fruits, such as strawberries, do not undergo further ripening once they are detached from the plant. Climacteric fruits generate significantly more ethylene compared to non-climacteric varieties, which rely on remaining attached to the plant to reach full maturity.

Figure: 11.1 Climacteric Fruit (Left) and Non-Climacteric Fruit (Right)

Firmness and Pressure

Firmness testing evaluates the internal pulp firmness of a fruit, which directly correlates to the crisp and crunchy texture experienced when consuming fresh produce. The primary technique for measuring firmness involves the use of a penetrometer, a specialized device that determines the amount of pressure and compression required to pierce the fruit's flesh.

DEFECT DETECTION

Imperfections or damage in produce not only influence its grade and market value but can also significantly impact its shelf life and storage durability after harvest. These defects can be classified into several categories:

Growing Defects of Fruits and Vegetables

Growth defects arise due to environmental factors that influence the shape, size, appearance, or texture of fruit. Some of the most common types of growth defects include:

- **Sunburn or Sun Damage:** Often seen in fruit that becomes suddenly exposed due to defoliation, sun damage can lead to visible discoloration and texture deterioration. The affected areas become more vulnerable to rot and fungal infections.
- **Over or Underwatering:** Inconsistent watering can impact fruit shape and uniformity, leading to issues such as splitting or scarring.

Figure: 11.2 Impact of inconsistent watering in vegetable and fruit shape

- **Scarring Damage:** Temperature fluctuations, humidity changes, moisture levels, or the fruit's growing position can cause scarring during development.

- **Limb Rub:** A frequent defect in apples, limb rub occurs when a growing fruit is pressed tightly against a twig or branch, resulting in a distinctive scar.
- **Zippering in Tomatoes:** Characterized by thin, zipper-like scars running from the stem to the bottom of the tomato, zippering is a common defect caused by high humidity during pollination.

These defects not only affect the visual appeal of the fruit but can also influence its market value and storage potential.

Picking Defects of Fruits

Picking defects occur during harvest and are primarily caused by rough handling. While some harvest-related damage may seem minor, any wound or injury to the fruit can make it susceptible to secondary infections or infestations. Common picking defects include:

- **Stem Punctures:** One of the most frequent defects in apples, stem punctures occur when a fruit is wounded by its own stem or the stem of another fruit during harvesting or storage.
- **Clipper Damage:** These wounds happen during harvesting and pruning when improper handling leads to punctures or scratches caused by clippers or other harvesting tools.
- **Bruising:** Likely the most prevalent form of harvest damage, bruising results from rough handling, bin transportation, pressure from other fruit, or impacts along the supply chain. Bruises may appear immediately or take up to a day to become visible. The more a bin of fruit is moved or handled, the higher the likelihood of bruising, leading to potential loss of otherwise marketable produce.

Proper handling techniques during harvesting and transportation are essential to minimize picking defects and preserve fruit quality.

Storage Defects of Fruits and Vegetables

Even after harvesting, transportation, and sorting, stored fruits and vegetables remain vulnerable to storage-related damage. Climate-controlled storage introduces its own risks, as long-term storage can lead to disorders that impact flavor, texture, and overall quality. These issues often include storage rot, fungal growth, and physiological disorders:

- **Gray Mold (Botrytis Blight):** One of the most common fungal diseases affecting stored produce, gray mold spreads through gray fungal spores on the surface of fruits and vegetables, leading to significant spoilage.
- **Bitter Pit:** A disorder found in apples and pears, bitter pit is caused by calcium deficiency and is characterized by browning and the development of small spots. Honeycrisp apples are particularly prone to this condition.
- **Chilling Injuries:** These occur when fruits or vegetables are stored at temperatures that are too low, even if they remain above freezing. Unlike freezer burn, chilling injuries can develop at relatively mild temperatures and typically manifest as discoloration, texture deterioration, and tissue damage.

- **Carbon Dioxide Burns:** A condition affecting apples in controlled-atmosphere storage, where oxygen levels are reduced to prolong shelf life. Excess carbon dioxide exposure can lead to surface burns, affecting fruit quality.

Proper storage techniques and environmental controls are essential to minimizing these disorders and maintaining the freshness and marketability of stored produce.

Grading of Fruits and Vegetables

Produce is evaluated based on multiple quality parameters, including appearance, size, shape, color, firmness, and the absence of defects or imperfections. The grading process involves classifying produce into different categories based on these attributes, ensuring uniformity in quality. Quality control measures follow established standards set by regulatory bodies, industry associations, or market requirements. These standards define acceptable quality levels for various types of produce, ensuring consistency, meeting consumer expectations, and maintaining market credibility.

Sensory Evaluation

Sensory evaluation by human testers is the simplest and most widely used method for assessing the quality of fresh produce. This process relies on the senses of sight, smell, touch, and sometimes taste to determine freshness and overall quality. Sensory evaluation provides valuable insights into qualitative characteristics such as ripeness, texture, and market desirability.

During sensory evaluation, quality control inspectors visually examine produce for external defects, including discoloration, bruises, cuts, or blemishes. They assess key attributes such as color, size, shape, and uniformity, as these factors significantly influence consumer preference and perceived quality.

While sensory evaluation is an essential tool, it is inherently subjective. Individual perceptions of sensory attributes can vary, and personal preferences may influence assessments. To reduce this subjectivity, sensory panelists undergo training to develop a standardized vocabulary and shared understanding of quality parameters. Additionally, standardized evaluation protocols and reference samples are often used to ensure consistency and minimize variability in assessments.

GRAIN QUALITY ANALYSIS: MANUAL VS MACHINE VISION

Traditional manual grain quality analysis is a hands-on, labor-intensive process where workers visually inspect the grains for defects, measure them, and assess quality based on their experience. While this method can provide valuable insights, it is often subjective, prone to human error, and inconsistent.

In contrast, automated machine vision algorithms offer a more efficient and objective solution. These systems use advanced image processing and artificial intelligence to analyze grain quality with high precision, processing large volumes of grain quickly and consistently. This automation is 30 times faster than manual methods, reducing labor costs by the same factor, and it boasts an accuracy rate of 96%, making it an ideal solution for large-scale operations.

QUALITY ASSURANCE IN THE MILL

Hygiene and Safety Rules for Buildings and Equipment

In mills, a major hygiene issue arises from the accumulation of flour or bran dust, which can gather on ledges and floors unless a proper cleaning program is implemented. If allowed to build up, the dust attracts insects, which can multiply and contaminate high-quality flour. Dust accumulating above equipment can become rancid or infested, eventually falling into the product as large lumps, leading to significant contamination.

Furthermore, flour or bran dust attracts rats and birds, which can further contaminate the grain and stored flour with their hairs, feathers, and excrement. To prevent these issues, a daily cleaning schedule should be strictly followed by operators, ensuring that the mill is kept clean and hygienic.

Flour mills and dehullers also pose safety risks, and strict safety procedures must be followed. These include:

- Belts should be equipped with guards to prevent accidents.
- Operators should maintain a safe distance from mills when starting up.
- Loose or torn clothing should not be worn by operators to avoid entanglement with moving belts.
- Operators should be prevented from inserting their hands into feed chutes, and appropriate tools like wooden or cane implements should be provided to clear grain blockages.
- Repairs and maintenance should not be performed until the mill or dehuller is disconnected from the power supply.
- The area around the mill or dehuller should be well-lit to ensure visibility and reduce hazards.
- Electrical equipment should be properly grounded to prevent the risk of sparks and potential dust explosions.

Maintaining cleanliness and enforcing safety measures is essential to ensuring both the quality of the grain and the safety of the operators in milling environments.

Inspection of Raw Material

When grain is delivered to a flour or rice mill, it should be carefully inspected by taking a sample from the batch. In many cases, grain is delivered in sacks to small-scale millers, and a sample should be extracted from these sacks using a "Thief Sampler" The sample must be thoroughly examined for the following quality characteristics:

- Correct type of grain
- Presence/Amount of other seeds
- **Contaminants:** Such as chaff, soil, dust, insects, rat hairs, or excrement
- **Damaged Grains:** Including cracked grains or those affected by insect damage
- Moisture Content
- **Colour:** Any discoloration or abnormal color variations
- **Maturity:** Signs of being overripe or underripe
- Visible Mould
- Presence of Flour Mites

Except for moisture content measurement, these inspections can typically be carried out without specialized quality control equipment. Operators responsible for raw material inspections should receive thorough training. Additionally, implementing an incentive scheme to reward careful and diligent inspection might be a useful approach. All findings from these inspections, including batch details and supplier information, should be recorded in an Incoming Materials Test Book.

PRIMARY PROCESSING

Cleaning

Based on the results of the raw material inspection and the level of contamination detected, it may be necessary to clean the grain before milling. This cleaning process serves two primary purposes: preventing contamination of the finished product and protecting the mill or dehuller from excessive wear or damage caused by sand, stones, or other foreign materials. The cleaning method chosen will depend on the type of contaminants present. Typically, sieving the grain is sufficient to remove dust, sand, insects, small stones, and weed seeds through a fine mesh, while retaining chaff, leaves, and larger stones on a coarser mesh.

The weight of contaminants in each batch should be recorded, and the results must be reported to the supplier. This data may serve as evidence for renegotiating the price in cases of significant contamination, ensuring that both quality standards and fair pricing are maintained.

Conditioning

Conditioning the grain before milling is crucial to ensure the proper separation of its components and to achieve a high yield of flour (or, in the case of rice, effective separation of the hulls). A quality control check on the moisture content should be performed. If the grain is too moist, it should be redried. If it is too dry, a small amount of water should be added, and the grain should be stored for 12-24 hours before being retested for moisture content.

Parboiling rice and the subsequent drying process offer several benefits, including improved dehulling efficiency and better rice quality after storage. Parboiling helps prevent rice grains from cracking and increases their resistance to insect infestations. The key quality control factors in this process are the duration of parboiling and the rate at which the rice is dried, ensuring optimal outcomes in both processing and storage.

Blending

In most cases, the grain supplied to rural millers is milled into a single type of flour that is then sold. However, when millers supply bakers or other secondary processors, there may be a need for flours with specific properties or for composite flours. In such instances, it is necessary to blend different grains before milling.

The quality assurance aspects of blending primarily focus on controlling and identifying stock to ensure the miller knows the storage locations of the different grains. Additionally, accurate weighing and thorough mixing of raw materials are essential to achieve a uniform blend for each batch, ensuring consistent quality and meeting the specifications required by the customer.

Milling

The selection of the most suitable mill for different cereal products depends on several factors, including the type of cereal being milled, the required degree of milling (or fineness) of the flour, power consumption, throughput, available capital, and access to spare parts and maintenance services. Similar considerations apply when choosing a dehuller. While there is a wide variety of milling equipment available, this book cannot cover all options in detail. However, small-scale millers commonly use plate mills, stone mills, and hammer mills for processing all types of cereals. Roller mills for wheat, typically too costly for small-scale processors, are mainly used in large-scale, centralized mills. Rubber roller dehullers are commonly used for rice hulling.

Once a mill or dehuller is set up according to the manufacturer's instructions, it should be regularly checked as part of a routine quality assurance program. This is crucial because grinding surfaces wear over time and need to be adjusted or replaced. For instance, the grinding plates of a plate mill may last 1-3 months before needing replacement, but if the grain is contaminated with sand, this timeframe can be reduced to one or two weeks. Improper plate adjustments can lead to inconsistent flour quality, affecting its fineness. Similarly, the efficiency of dehullers is diminished if the gap between the rollers is not checked and adjusted regularly. Therefore, the miller should inspect the mill or dehuller's adjustment before processing each batch of grain.

Other moving parts should be inspected daily to ensure they are not loose or misaligned. A metal bolt falling into the mill can damage the grinding surfaces, and metal filings from worn parts can contaminate the product. The same checks should be applied to dehullers.

Additionally, a quality control check should involve measuring the particle size distribution in the flour, which provides insights into the degree of milling and the mill's efficiency. While the sieves and shaking machines used for this measurement are relatively expensive, they offer valuable data, especially for millers producing specialized white flours. However, such equipment is generally not recommended for small-scale rural millers.

Sieving

In rural areas, it is common for millers to sell whole-meal flours, where no separation of the grain's components takes place after milling. Typically, whole-meal flours such as maize, sorghum, millet, and wheat are produced by dehulling the grain, milling it into flour, and directly using the flour to produce finished products. However, in some cases, there is demand for whiter flour, where most of the bran and germ are removed, leaving primarily starchy material (as in maize, wheat, and rice flours). This separation is accomplished by sieving freshly milled flour through mesh screens, often equipped with brushes to increase throughput.

A quality control check at this stage involves examining the sieved flour for any bristles that may have fallen from the brushes. The presence of bristles serves as an early indication that the brushes may need replacement. Additionally, checks should be conducted to ensure the flour is free from insect eggs, insect parts, or other contaminants. Larger contaminants can be separated using a sieve test, while small contaminants, such as insect parts, can be identified with a 'filth test'.

Flour mites are a significant concern for two main reasons: their excrement causes the flour to develop a minty smell, rendering it unusable, and their hairs can lead to health issues in operators, causing skin inflammation and lung disorders. If insect parts or mites are found in the flour, the source should be traced back to either the incoming raw materials or an infestation in the flour mill, and corrective measures should be implemented.

Records should be maintained for the amount of raw material milled, batch numbers, and product code numbers assigned to each sack of flour produced. This ensures that any defects in a batch can be traced back to the process and raw materials used, allowing for efficient troubleshooting and quality control.

Packaging

Jute or hessian sacks are traditionally used for packaging flour or dehulled grain, though multi-layer paper and woven polypropylene sacks are becoming more common. Visual quality checks are essential to ensure that the sacks are clean, free from contamination, and free of holes or split seams.

Flour should be carefully filled into the sacks to minimize dust and ensure that the amount of product matches the net weight stated on the label. In many countries, selling an underweight product is a legal offense, while overfilling results in the company giving away product at a loss. For smaller-scale operations, a large capacity scale (e.g., 100 kg) may be used for manual filling. For larger mills, semi-automatic bagging machines, where a weighed amount of product is discharged into an open sack, may be more cost-effective. After filling, sacks are sealed either by tying the neck with rope or by stitching the top using a stitching machine.

These packaging and sealing processes help maintain product quality and ensure compliance with regulatory standards while minimizing waste and losses.

Figure: 11.3 Packaging: An Electric Sack Stitcher

Storage and Distribution

Once cereal or flour has been sealed into sacks, the risks of contamination from insects, dust, and microorganisms are significantly reduced, though not entirely eliminated. Improper storage conditions, such as exposure to sunlight, heat, and moisture, can still lead to spoilage. This is particularly critical because the costs incurred during processing make any losses at this stage financially damaging.

To maintain the quality of flour or dehulled cereals, sacks should be stored on pallets to keep them off the floor. The sacks should be carefully stacked to prevent the formation of poorly stacked blocks that could collapse, potentially causing injury to operators. The storage area should be cool and dark, with good ventilation to ensure a proper airflow. Windows should be screened to keep insects out, and the roof and walls should be secure enough to prevent rats and birds from entering. In addition, cleaning schedules should apply to the storeroom as well, ensuring the environment remains clean and free from contaminants.

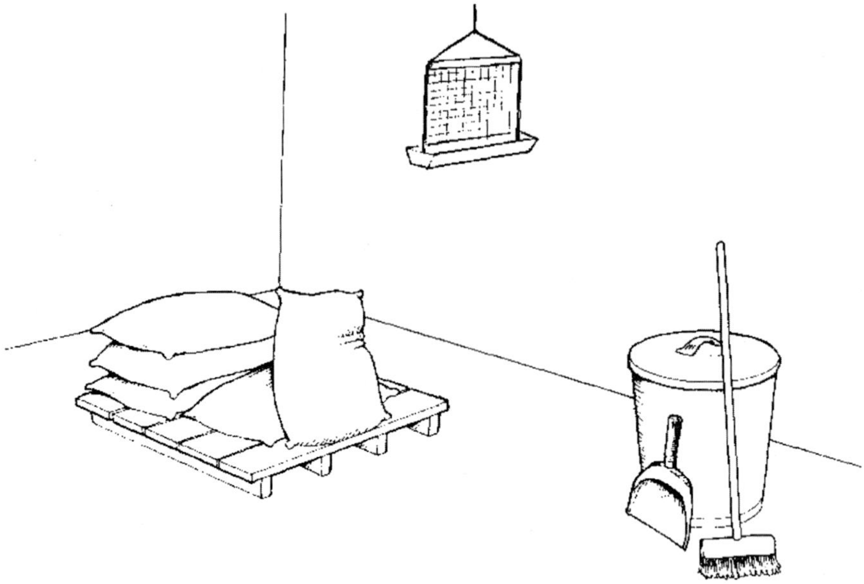

Figure: 11.4 Emamples of Good and Bad Stacking of Flour Sacks

It is essential to implement a management system to monitor products in storage, control stock rotation, and track their destination for delivery. This is especially important when a variety of products are produced, as slower-selling items may be buried at the back of the store and spoil. Simple records should be maintained by storekeepers to track products and materials as they are transferred in and out of the storeroom.

When a miller is responsible for delivering products to other processors, the delivery vehicle should be included in the cleaning schedule to ensure that the products arrive in a clean, uncontaminated condition. In many countries, the risks of dust, rainfall, and contamination from birds and insects necessitate the use of covered delivery vehicles.

QUALITY CONTROL WHILE STORING

CONTROL MEASURES

Proper care must be taken in the storage of both raw materials and finished products to avoid potential issues such as:

- Infestation
- Deterioration in Quality
- Rodent and Bird Infestations
- Weight Losses
- Fire Hazards

Storage areas for raw materials and finished products should be kept separate. Raw materials are often received from various sources, and in some cases, food grains unsuitable for human consumption may be used. In such instances, infestations can spread from one material to another. Regular cleaning, insecticide spraying, and fumigation can help control infestations. Materials should be stacked in a way that minimizes the risk of cross-contamination.

Deterioration in the quality of both raw materials and finished products can occur due to factors like high moisture content, rancidity, mold, and fungal growth. Any damaged materials should be immediately removed from the storage area to prevent further deterioration of the remaining stock. Additionally, raw materials like rice polish fine, rapeseed meal, and grains should not be stored in godowns or silos for more than a month. To manage inventory effectively, a First In, First Out (FIFO) system should be implemented, ensuring that older stock is used or sold first to prevent spoilage.

Figure: 11.5 Finished product

Raw materials with a moisture content exceeding 10 percent may experience significant dryage loss during storage. The longer the storage period, the more moisture will be lost. To compensate for this moisture loss in finished product bags, additional feed should be included in each bag, depending on the season and the duration of storage in the godown.

Several raw materials are flammable, and materials with high moisture content can also ignite due to auto-oxidation. A limit should be set for the acceptable moisture content in materials. To prevent fire hazards, signs such as "no smoking" should be posted and strictly enforced. Additionally, the materials and the godown should be insured against fire. Fire extinguishers should be strategically placed throughout the facility, and staff should receive regular training on fire-fighting procedures.

Fire risks in raw material godowns, silos, or new gunny bag storage areas can also arise from the following factors:

- **Excessive Stacking:** Filled raw material (RM) bags should not be stacked higher than 18 bags.
- **Continuous Stacking:** RM bags should not be stacked continuously for more than 5 meters in length and 3 meters in width. A minimum gap of 600 mm should be maintained between consecutive bags to ensure proper airflow.
- **Lack of Aeration in Silos:** Storing raw materials in silos without an aeration and recirculation system can lead to temperature rise. For grain silos, the aeration system should operate at night for better cooling efficiency. For DORB storage silos, recirculation should be done at least once a day.
- **Improper Housekeeping in New Gunny Bag Sorting Areas:** Waste jute particles, which are fire hazards, often accumulate on the floor during the sorting and printing of new gunny bags. This area must be regularly cleaned and kept safe.

In some cases, raw materials with higher moisture content may be accepted with a rebate. In these situations, the animal nutrition officer should advise the store officer to prioritize using these materials. If the sample contains excessively high moisture or is of poor quality, wet, damaged, or infested, it should be partially rejected, and the stores and purchaser should be informed accordingly.

SORTING OF INFERIOR/DAMAGED CONSIGNMENTS

Receiving wet or damaged consignments of raw materials is not an uncommon occurrence, and sometimes inferior materials can be found inside the bags. These issues should be thoroughly checked during the sampling process.

If the consignment has been transported by road, the vehicle driver should be shown the wet or damaged materials, and their signature should be obtained on the goods receipt slip and in the register. If part of the consignment is inferior, deteriorated, or damaged, the sorting of these materials should be carried out under the supervision of the animal nutrition officer. The inferior materials should be rejected, and the supplier must be informed accordingly. If the supplier does not remove the rejected materials within a specified period, the material should be disposed of at the supplier's expense. Additionally, sorting charges should be charged to the supplier.

Lumps in de-oiled rice bran and rice polishing are commonly found, and adulteration of rice polish fine with rice polish thick is also a frequent issue. The animal nutrition officer can identify these inferior materials at the time of unloading and sampling. Based on the extent of damage, a decision should be made regarding whether to reject the consignment in full or partially.

Inspection of Stores Pertaining to Quality Control

The animal nutrition officer should conduct regular visits to the stores, performing a thorough inspection for signs of contamination, such as weevils, worms, mold, fungal growth, or rancid odors. Any evidence of bag damage caused by rats or birds should be carefully examined. If worms, weevils, or other pests are detected, immediate action must be taken to address the issue. The damaged materials should be sorted out and either used or disposed of without delay to prevent further contamination.

CHANGES IN THE QUALITY OF FOOD GRAINS THAT ARE STORED

In India, food grains are typically stored in bulk. During storage, these grains undergo various physical, chemical, and biological changes due to the presence of natural enzymes and bio-chemicals, as well as enzymes produced by insects, pests, and microbes, or other influencing factors. These changes can lead to the deterioration of grain quality. Such alterations typically occur throughout the processes of harvesting, handling, transportation, and storage, affecting the overall quality of the food grains.

Physical Changes

Healthy and sound grains typically have a shiny appearance with good luster and show firmness. However, during storage, grains may undergo various physical changes. These changes can include a dull color, the presence of bores in the grains, sprouting of seeds, and the occurrence of damaged kernels caused by adverse weather conditions.

Chemical Changes

Cereals are primarily composed of low protein and high carbohydrate content within the kernel. The germ is rich in protein, fat, sugar, and minerals, while the endosperm contains lower levels of protein, fat, and ash. During storage, various chemical changes occur due to increased activity of both endogenous and exogenous enzymes. These enzymes are responsible for quantitative and qualitative alterations in carbohydrates, proteins, and fats, as well as changes in color, flavor, and texture of the cereals.

Carbohydrate

Grain storage in India can result in notable physical and biochemical changes due to the country's fluctuating temperature and relative humidity. Among these alterations are the starch's bursting and gelatinization, which are impacted by the moisture content. During storage, amylases significantly raise the amount of reducing sugars by breaking down the starch into dextrose and maltose. The concentrations of sucrose, glucose, fructose, and raffinose increase when wheat grains are stored at or above 12 percent moisture. Furthermore, because alcohols and acetic acid are formed during the storage of cereals with a high moisture content, a sour odor may develop.

Protein

High temperatures and the use of chemicals during grain storage can lead to the denaturation of proteins, making them less dispersible in water. This process deteriorates the quality of gluten and increases the content of free amino acids. The formation of certain sulfur-containing amino acids can result in undesirable odors. Additionally, these free amino acids may undergo the Maillard reaction, reacting with reducing sugars and causing browning of the grains. Such deterioration is more likely to occur when temperatures exceed 20ºC and relative humidity levels range between 60-70 percent.

Lipid

Oxidation of lipids, particularly unsaturated fatty acids, leads to the development of a typical rancid flavor, odor, and taste in grains. Additionally, the hydrolysis of lipids increases the content of free fatty acids, which serves as a sensitive indicator of grain deterioration.

Contaminants

Food grains typically have a bad appearance due to contamination from foreign objects such as stones, chaffs, toxic weeds, and insect, pest, and rodent excrement. The Government of India (FCI) has established limits for the presence of weeds, uric acid, and insect excrement in food grains that are stored. A thorough assessment of these materials' chemical makeup, toxins, pesticide and insecticide residues, and, lastly, the in vivo feeding value of various livestock categories is necessary before any recommendations are made in this regard.

Colour Plates

Grain storage

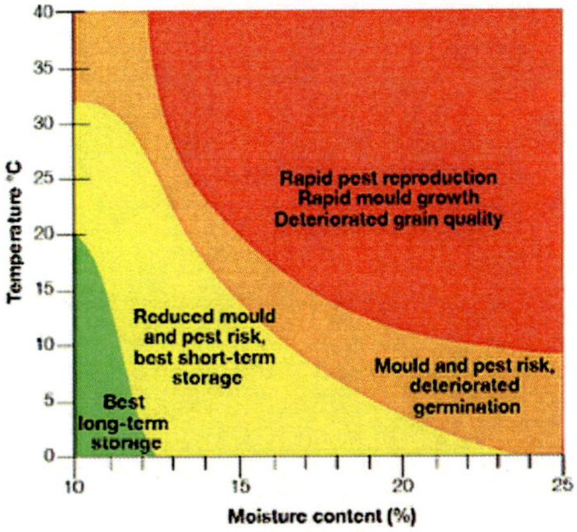

Temperature effects on stored grains

The Insects cause the Damage to Stored Grain

Rust - red flour beetle (Tribolium castaneum)

Rice weevil (Sitophiluso ryzae)

Confused flour beetle (Tribolium confusum)

Pallet jacks

Granary weevil (Sitophilus granarius)

Hand trucks

Platform trucks

Conveyor belts

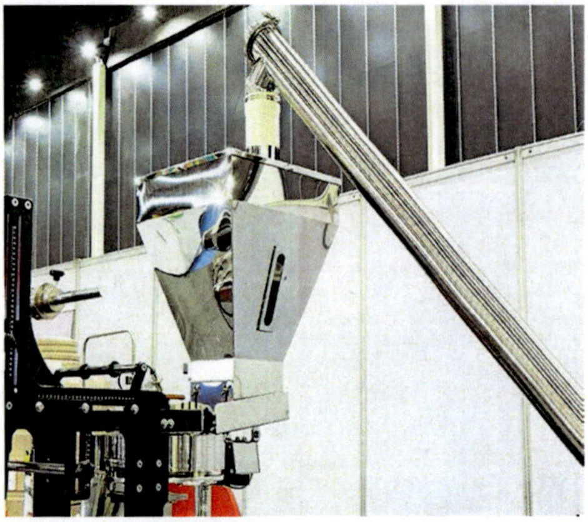

Figure: 3.9 Hoppers

Figure: 3.12 Personal Protective

Figure: 3.13 Industrial and portable stairs

Figure: 3.14 Handrails

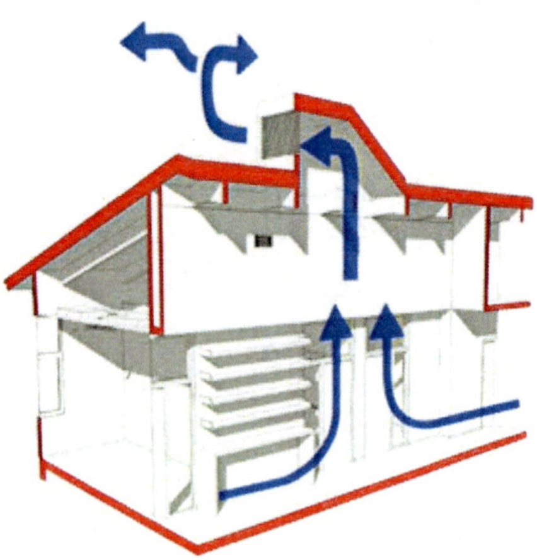

Figure: 4.4 Natural ventilation

Figure: 11.5 Finished product

Bibliography

Adani Agri Logistics Ltd. (2021). Modernizing Warehousing for Food Grains in India: A Private Sector Perspective.

Agarwal, P. (2019). Evaluating the Efficiency of Warehouse Management Systems in Indian Food Grain Storage. Punjab Agricultural University, M.Sc. Thesis.

ASSOCHAM. (2021). Food Grain Storage Infrastructure in India: The Way Forward. Associated Chambers of Commerce and Industry of India.

Banerjee, A. & Das, S. (2019). "Emerging Trends in Scientific Storage and Warehouse Management of Food Grains." Indian Journal of Agricultural Sciences, 52(1), 112-127.

BigBasket. (2021). E-Commerce & Warehouse Management: Enhancing Agri-Supply Chains in India.

Bihar State Warehousing Corporation. (2021). Agri-Warehouse Development in Eastern India: Challenges & Opportunities.

Central Warehousing Corporation (CWC). (2021). Improving Efficiency of Warehouses: A Policy Framework for India.

Chand, R. (2020). Post-Harvest Management & Warehousing of Food Grains in India. ICAR Publications.

Chatterjee, P., & Rani, S. (2018). Sustainable Storage Techniques for Food Grains in Indian Warehouses. Indian Journal of Post-Harvest Technology, 12(6), 227-233.

CII. (2020). Future of Agri-Warehousing in India: Trends & Opportunities.

Confederation of Indian Industry. (2021). The Role of Warehousing in Supply Chain Management. Retrieved from http://www.cii.in/warehouse-supply-chain

CSIR-Central Food Technological Research Institute (CFTRI). (2021). Food Quality & Storage Techniques in Indian Warehouses.

Directorate of Marketing and Inspection, Ministry of Agriculture. (2019). Guidelines for Warehouse Management Systems in India. Government of India.

FICCI. (2020). Agri Warehousing in India: Opportunities and Challenges. Federation of Indian Chambers of Commerce and Industry.

FICCI. (2020). Warehouse Infrastructure for Food Security: Challenges & Solutions. New Delhi: FICCI.

FICCI. (2021). Warehouse & Cold Storage Development: A Strategy for Reducing Food Wastage in India.

Food and Agriculture Organization of the United Nations. (2017). Storage and Preservation of Food Grains: Indian Context and Recommendations. FAO Publication.

Food Corporation of India (FCI). (2021). Annual Report on Food Grain Storage & Distribution in India.

Food Corporation of India. (2020). Warehouse Management and Food Grain Storage Practices in India. FCI Publications.

Government of India. (2016). National Food Security Act. Ministry of Agriculture and Farmers Welfare.

Government of India. (2018). The Warehouse Development and Regulatory Authority Act. Ministry of Consumer Affairs.

Government of India. (2021). Food Security Act, Warehouse Management Section. Ministry of Agriculture and Farmers Welfare.

Government of India. (2022). Food Grain Storage Infrastructure Development Plan. Retrieved from http://www.indianagriculture.gov.in/food-grain-storage

Gupta, S. (2016). Managing Grain Storage Systems: Indian Context. Agro-Tech Press.

Gupta, V., & Sharma, M. (2017). Impact of Warehouse Management Systems on Food Grain Preservation. Indian Journal of Agricultural Engineering Research, 28(5), 162-170.

ICAR-CIPHET. (2020). Innovations in Post-Harvest Engineering & Warehouse Storage Techniques.

Indian Agricultural Research Institute (IARI). (2021). Smart Warehousing Technologies for Food Grains in India.

Indian Council of Agricultural Research. (2019). Food Grain Storage Technologies. Retrieved from http://www.icar.org/storage-techniques

Indian Institute of Management Ahmedabad (IIMA). (2019). Optimization of Food Grain Storage in India: Policy Recommendations.

Indian Institute of Packaging (IIP). (2022). Sustainable Packaging Solutions for Stored Food Grains in Warehouses.

ITC Limited. (2020). Innovative Storage & Warehouse Management for Agri-Produce in India.

Jain, R. (2017). Modern Warehousing for Food Grains in India. Reliance Publishing.

Jain, R., & Patel, H. (2019). Future of Warehousing in Indian Agricultural Supply Chain. International Conference on Agricultural Technologies, Hyderabad, 98-102.

Joshi, A. & Sharma, K. (2020). "Role of Public and Private Warehousing in India's Food Security." Indian Journal of Supply Chain Management, 18(2), 88-104.

Malhotra, T. & Singh, P. (2021). "Impact of Warehouse Management on Food Grain Wastage in India." Journal of Agricultural Economics & Management, 55(3), 212-229.

McKinsey India. (2022). Optimizing Food Grain Supply Chains Through Smart Warehousing Solutions.

Mehta, P. (2020). Technological Advances in Food Grain Storage. Global Conference on Warehouse Management, New Delhi, 45-49.

Mehta, S. (2015). Grain Storage Techniques in India: Innovations and Practices. Agricultural Institute of India Press.

Ministry of Agriculture and Farmers Welfare, Government of India. (2018). Post-Harvest Management of Food Grains. Ministry of Agriculture.

Ministry of Agriculture and Farmers Welfare. (2019). National Policy for Food Storage Infrastructure. Government of India.

Ministry of Consumer Affairs, Food & Public Distribution. (2020). National Food Security Act & Role of Warehousing in India.

MoFPI. (2021). Development of Cold Storage & Warehousing in India. New Delhi: Government of India.

Mother Dairy. (2019). Warehouse Infrastructure for Dairy Products & Grains in India: Lessons & Strategies.

NABARD. (2020). Warehouse Infrastructure and Food Grain Storage in India. Retrieved from http://www.nabard.org/food-security

NABARD. (2021). Financing of Warehouses and Storage Infrastructure in India. Mumbai: NABARD Reports.

NASSCOM. (2021). Technology-Driven Solutions for Agri-Warehousing & Storage in India.

National Agricultural Research Institute. (2021). Best Practices for Warehouse Management in India. Retrieved from http://www.nari.gov.in/warehouse-management

National Institute of Agricultural Extension Management. (2021). Food Security and Grain Storage Infrastructure in India. NIAM Report.

National Institute of Food Technology Entrepreneurship and Management (NIFTEM). (2019). Digital Warehouse Management: Smart Solutions for the Indian Agricultural Sector.

NITI Aayog. (2020). Warehouse Infrastructure Development Strategy for Food Grains in India.

Patel, M. (2016). Post-Harvest Management of Food Grains in India. Agricultural Press.

Pathak, D., & Mehta, S. (2019). Effective Use of Modern Warehousing Technologies in Indian Food Grain Storage. Agricultural Systems Journal, 44(2), 65-74.

PwC India. (2021). Warehouse Management & Post-Harvest Storage Solutions for Indian Agriculture.

Rajasthan Agricultural Marketing Board. (2021). Cold Chain & Warehouse Development in Rajasthan: A Study on Impact & Growth.

Rathi, A. (2018). Food Storage and Logistics: Key Issues in India. Distribution Solutions Press.

Reliance Retail. (2021). Cold Storage Logistics & Warehousing: A Case Study on Indian Food Distribution Network.

Saxena, R. (2021). Food Grain Storage & Warehouse Management in India. New Delhi: Oxford University Press.

Sharma, P., & Yadav, R. (2019). Food Storage Infrastructure and Warehouse Operations in India. Prakashan Publishers.

Singh, R. & Iyer, A. (2021). "Digitalization in Warehouse Management: Transforming India's Food Grain Supply Chain." International Journal of Logistics & Inventory Management, 9(4), 33-47.

Singh, S. (2018). The Role of Warehousing in Reducing Post-Harvest Losses in Indian Agriculture. IIT Delhi, Ph.D. Dissertation.

Singh, V., & Gupta, P. (2020). Warehouse Management Practices in India: Challenges and Solutions. XYZ Publishers.

Soni, N. (2014). Technologies in Food Grain Preservation and Storage. Research & Education Publications.

Uttar Pradesh State Warehousing Corporation. (2021). Development of Rural Warehouses & Their Impact on Food Security in Uttar Pradesh.

Verma, M. (2017). Innovations in Food Grain Storage Systems. Proceedings of the International Conference on Food Security, New Delhi, 234-239.

Verma, P. (2022). Food Security and Warehouse Infrastructure in India. McGraw Hill.

Verma, S., & Joshi, D. (2020). Post-Harvest Loss Reduction and Warehouse Management in India. Journal of Food Science and Technology, 55(12), 4578-4591.

Warehousing Development and Regulatory Authority (WDRA). (2021). Regulatory Framework for Warehouse Management in India.

West Bengal Food Processing & Horticulture Department. (2020). Warehouse Infrastructure for Perishable & Non-Perishable Commodities in West Bengal.

Index